Art Rule

Art Rules

Pierre Bourdieu and the Visual Arts

Michael Grenfell and Cheryl Hardy

BERG

Oxford • New York

English edition
First published in 2007 by
Berg
Editorial offices:
First Floor, Angel Court, 81 St Clements Street, Oxford OX4 1AW, UK
175 Fifth Avenue, New York, NY 10010, USA

Berg is the imprint of Oxford International Publishers Ltd.

Library of Congress Cataloging in Publication Data
Grenfell, Michael, 1953-
Art rules : Pierre Bourdieu and the visual arts / Michael Grenfell and Cheryl Hardy. — English ed.
p. cm.
Includes bibliographical references and index.
ISBN-13: 978-1-84520-233-0 (cloth)
ISBN-10: 1-84520-233-3 (cloth)
ISBN-13: 978-1-84520-234-7 (pbk.)
ISBN-10: 1-84520-234-1 (pbk.)
1. Aesthetics. 2. Art—Philosophy. 3. Bourdieu, Pierre, 1930-2002. 4. Culture—Philosophy. 5. Civilization, Modern—21st century—Philosophy. I. Hardy, Cheryl. II. Title.

BH39.G677 2007
306.4'7092—dc22 2006032270

British Library Cataloguing-in-Publication Data
A catalogue record for this book is available from the British Library.

ISBN 978 1 84520 233 0 (Cloth)
978 1 84520 234 7 (Paper)

Typeset by Avocet Typeset, Chilton, Aylesbury, Bucks
Printed in the United Kingdom by Biddles Ltd, King's Lynn.

www.bergpublishers.com

For P B

Contents

Acknowledgements

We wish to acknowledge the patience and support of our editor, Tristan Palmer. We also thank him for pushing us to go further.

List of Tables and Figures

The majority of the paintings and photographs which are discussed in the text are available on line through the websites of major galleries. Recommended sites include:

www.Tate.org.uk
www.MoMA.org.uk
www.NationalGallery.org.uk
www.musee-orsay.fr
www.guggenheim.org

Tables

Figures

–1–

Introduction

In 1992 the French social theorist Pierre Bourdieu published *Les Règles de l'art* – later translated as *The Rules of Art* (1996a). It is from this book that we have borrowed the title of our own book – *Art Rules*. In it, we take Bourdieu's ideas and theories, both derived from studies of art and culture, and from other social topics such as education, economics, philosophy and politics, and apply them to a range of art fields. It is comparatively rare to have topics such as painting, photography and museums discussed almost entirely in terms of the ideas of one person. So why do it?

First, the work of Bourdieu is now attracting considerable attention in a range of disciplines in the social sciences and cultural studies. This interest can be seen as the culmination of more than forty years' work as a researcher since his first publications in the 1950s. His death in 2002 seems to have done nothing to lessen the enthusiasm of researchers and scholars in diverse academic fields to understand and apply his thinking to their own work. There is clearly a sense that approaching various topics and problems from a Bourdieusian perspective offers insights which are not readily available through conventional approaches. Such areas as language, media studies, sport, fashion, poetry, painting and literature, as well as culture and art, have all drawn on Bourdieu's work (directly and indirectly) in developing and elucidating a number of strands hitherto underrepresented by established methods.

The Rules of Art was published rather late in Bourdieu's career, for much of which he was best known internationally as a 'sociologist'. His major topics of study were Algeria, where he undertook military service in the 1950s, and education. Indeed, it is probably still as a sociologist of education that he is most well known, and he was a seminal figure in the renaissance of that discipline from the early 1970s. Works such as *Les Héritiers* (1964) and *La Reproduction* (1970) offered an entirely new perspective on the principles and outcomes of contemporary education for those who passed through it. These works culminated with major publications on Bourdieu's own academic world – *Homo Academicus* (1984) – and the elite training school in France, *La Noblesse d'état* (1989). It was not by chance that Bourdieu targeted education for his studies. In a climate of post-war renewal, education was seen as a principal means by which the new world would be built, and so it proved in many respects. In these works, Bourdieu offers a kind of social anthropology of the French education system, employing a range of statistics and ethnographic data to elucidate its underlying generating structures. Education is not content-free, however, and we see that Bourdieu takes a particular interest in culture from the earliest works. In 1965 he published *Un Art moyen*, which examined photography and photographic practice in society; and then, in 1966, *L'Amour de l'art* (revised and expanded in 1969), which dealt with the museum and gallery visiting habits of the French. This latter work very much grew out of his education studies, especially the cultural practice of students – their tastes in music, art and literature, for example. Education and culture should be seen here as two sides of the same coin. The cultural strand of his research continued to develop over a number of years and finally culminated in the publication of *La Distinction* (1979). In this book, Bourdieu offers a sociological analysis of taste and, by implication, aesthetics. It shows that cultural practice and consumption must be understood in terms of social differentiation across the class structure. Briefly, that we behave culturally according to socially formed dispositions which are acted out whenever we engage in diverse areas of culture. This book quickly became a best-seller and entered the canon of both sociology and cultural studies. It is now cited frequently in discussions on culture, and the way it operates and is accessed.

In the years which followed the publication of the English translation (1984) of *La Distinction*, it was often assumed that Bourdieu was mainly interested in cultural consumption per se rather than its production. However, as far back as 1968, we see Bourdieu questioning the nature of aesthetics itself (for example, 'Outline of a sociological theory of art perception' (1993b)), and then, in 1987, how it was that individuals acted in the way that they did ('Manet and the Institutionalization of Anomie', 1993d/1987). In these publications we see a much wider discussion of artistic practice: the nature of aesthetics, artistic groups, the formation of the avant-garde, technique and the social role of artists. *The Rules of Art* is very much a summative statement of this work. The chapter headings indicate the direction in which Bourdieu would lead us: Flaubert, Analysis of Flaubert: A Reading of *Sentimental Education*; Three States of the Field; The Emergence of a Dualistic Structure; The Market for Symbolic Goods; Foundations of a Science of Works of Art; Questions of Method; The Author's Point of View – Some General Properties of the Fields of Cultural Production; To Understand Understanding; The Historical Genesis of the Pure Aesthetic; The Social Genesis of the Eye; A Theory of Reading in Practice; Illusion and *Illusio*; For a Corporatism of the Universal. In fact, what Bourdieu does is to take us on a journey. It begins with a tour of the literary fields in France in the second half of the nineteenth century. It targets Flaubert as a sort of ideal type of artist in the way he operated in his milieu and how this characterized the artworks he produced. However, it is clear that Bourdieu is not interested simply in the topic of Flaubert in itself, but rather what his case illuminates and illustrates about artists and artistic practice in general. Thus, we are offered proposals for an account of how the artistic market operates – the book is subtitled *Genesis and Structure of the Literary Field*. This involves elucidation of methodological tools and the general character of artistic fields. The discussion is illustrated with copious examples from a wide range of cultural practice, including journalism. What emerges is a field analysis of the way artists, writers, curators and gallery owners are mutually engaged in a symbiotic practice, the totality of which is 'art'. The state – politicians, ministers, museums and national galleries – is never far away. Bourdieu shows how their individual and combined practice needs to be understood in terms of the 'rules' which govern them. What we need to comprehend as part of this engagement is what we understand by the term 'rules'. Hence, there is much to say about the theory of practice which is brought to bear on the topic of 'art' and the philosophy which underpins it. We shall see how Bourdieu argues that the social philosophical approach to studying art implies that we apply the same method to both researcher and the researched as part of what he calls an 'invitation to reflexive sociology'.

Despite this very developed and sophisticated 'theory of the history of the science of art', Bourdieu did not take his empirical investigation very much further than this study of Flaubert, with one exception: in 2000, he devoted the entire ten-week *leçon* at the Collège de France to the pre-Impressionist painter, Edouard Manet. This work itself was developed from an earlier study; however, it remained unpublished at the time of Bourdieu's death. In a way, this book is predicated on accepting an implicit challenge thrown down by Bourdieu, namely, to offer further exemplification of the 'rules of art' in various areas of the art field.

The book is divided into three sections. After this Introduction, Part I: Theory begins. Chapter 2 offers a background to both Bourdieu and his theory of practice. Here we are aiming to establish some biographical details about Bourdieu as a way of showing what he thought and why. We discuss some of the major philosophical antecedents to his epistemological theory of practice before presenting the theory of practice itself. His main thinking tools – habitus, field, capital, and so on – are presented and explained in general terms, with examples from a range of Bourdieu's own empirical studies.

In chapter 3 we discuss specifically Bourdieu's work on cultural consumption and production. Our *point de départ* is *La Distinction*. We show how this book should be understood in terms of a sociological critique of aesthetics and taste. We begin by considering the contemporary tradition in aesthetics in the Western world as established by the German philosopher Immanuel Kant, and the implications of his position. We then show how Bourdieu challenged this tradition and in what terms. We consider the implications his analysis has for both the consumers of art and artists themselves (producers). Finally, we offer the 'three-stage' methodology developed by Bourdieu for the analysis of 'fields'. We show how various concepts are involved in such an approach and how it might be put into practice. This 'method' is presented as a framing structure for the next part of the book.

Part II is entitled Practice. Here we use a Bourdieusian approach to three practical case examples; in others words, we offer our own analysis of three parts of the artistic field: museums, painting and photography.

Chapter 4 begins with a discussion of Bourdieu's own analyses of consumption in the visual arts. Mostly, this involves public trends in museum and art gallery attendance (*L'Amour de l'art* and *La Distinction*). This work is contrasted with analysis of other field examples: the Museum of Modern Art (MOMA, New York), the Musée d'Orsay (Paris) and the Tate (London). In each case, the founding of the establishment is discussed and details provided of the socio-historic field and the place of the gallery within this structured space. The development and influence of each museum is considered in terms of its associated agents and institutions, audience attendance patterns and exhibition policy. The aim is to extend Bourdieu's work on museums to other examples.

As we have noted, Bourdieu's main coverage of artistic production was presented in his own analysis of Manet. Chapter 5 presents the main tenets of his study in terms of the art field of the nineteenth century, the roles of patrons, the state and critics in establishing an autonomous field of painting. The way this field developed includes consideration of the Impressionists. The structure and morphology of this French case is contrasted with the examples of mid-century American expressionism and the young British artists of the 1990s. The intention is to show how field conditions determine what is produced, and how, and the way in which this leads to the social construction of artistic movements.

Bourdieu was an avid photographer. Chapter 6 discusses the development of photography in terms of technical equipment, photographic technique and the socio-historic field. The evolution of photography from a low- to mid-brow art form is illustrated with examples from pop culture, journalism and recognized 'artist-photographers'. Among others, Lichfield, Brassaï, Mapplethorpe and Serrano are used by way of illustration. Bourdieu's own uses of photography are covered, including the numerous photos he took in the Béarn and Algeria. We draw attention to the 'social constructivism' of photography.

Part III includes just one chapter. It aims to offer a series of concluding remarks concerning the visual arts in terms of the theory and practice examined in the rest of the book. We reconsider Bourdieu's theoretical approach to aesthetics compared to other philosophical and sociological treatments. We refer to various treatments of aesthetics. The 'problem' of aesthetics is considered in the light of Bourdieu's theory of practice. Bourdieu denies economism most strongly. We make clear that his approach to aesthetics is based on an economy of 'symbolic' goods and action, which also often have real financial implications. Modernist and postmodernist perspectives are addressed by highlighting questions of method and approach in the light of the practical applications discussed in chapters 4–6. Issues of 'reflexivity' and 'reflection' feature in this chapter as a way of making explicit a sociocultural theory of aesthetics and criticism in the visual arts. The aim of this chapter is to provide some preliminary remarks for a new approach to the visual arts in the twenty-first century. Is Bourdieu offering anything more than a sociological deconstruction in place of a postmodernist philosophical one? His position is termed by us a 'post-postmodernist' account of aesthetics. This approach involves an exploration of his 'reflexive methodology' and concepts such as the *illusio*.

Different readers may want to approach the book in different ways. Those interested primarily in any or all of the practical case example topics – museums, photography and painting – might begin with Part II and then refer to chapter 3 for the main theoretical rationale to the approach employed. Those interested in philosophy and theory will wish to examine chapters 3 and 7 in detail. Those looking for an introduction to Bourdieu may begin with chapter 2 and then proceed to Part II before considering the main theoretical chapters.

Bourdieu begins *The Rules of Art* with a quotation from Sallenave: 'Shall we allow the social sciences to reduce literary experience – the most exalted that man may have, along with love – to surveys about leisure activities, when it concerns the very meaning of life?' – a statement which we might apply to any artistic or aesthetic experience. Bourdieu himself anticipated objections when art came under the sociologist's scalpel. The following is what happens when we do exactly that…

For MUCVIC use 'method' for History of Galleries.
As 'corrective' to weeks 1-3
Use 'Saatchi' in week 3 + → Tate Modern as
direct response to Saatchi'

Also use for Special Studies.

Part I

Theory

–2–

A Brief History of Theory

In this chapter we set out Bourdieu's theory of practice. We do this first by discussing the background to his work and then by addressing the theory itself. The intention here is to establish a theoretical base for Bourdieu's approach so that we can consider art and aesthetics in depth in the next chapter.

Introduction

Any one individual's body of work must be shaped by that individual's biography; that is to say, the impetus for any work, both physical and mental, is always a response to external and internal exigencies. At one point in his writing (Bourdieu 2000a/1997: 130), Bourdieu evokes Pascal's description of the universe 'swallowing' up the individual 'like an atom'. There is the sense of an overwhelming world into which each individual is thrown. Despite the enormity of what confronts us, individual responses are particular to each man and woman. The power of an individual's work is the extent to which such responses go beyond the personal and idiosyncratic to express something of the universal condition of human beings. In undertaking this discussion of art in terms derived from a single individual's theory, we are suggesting that Bourdieu's ideas do indeed touch what we might call the 'universal'. The ultimate source of those ideas is not personal, but a product of the social and cultural period in which Bourdieu lived and his own experiences of it. This chapter addresses Bourdieu's individual biography and the world – both physical and intellectual – that surrounded him. It sets Bourdieu within the intellectual current of his day. It considers the intellectual climate in which he trained and how this shaped his thinking. However, it does not do this simply by presenting the various intellectual strands which were available to him, but by placing these in their socio-historic context. This initial discussion leads to a presentation of Bourdieu's main theoretical concepts. The intention is to set out his main 'thinking tools' and show their derivation. These key conceptual terms will form a background to the rest of the book. They will be central to both the theoretical coverage and the case examples on museums, photography and painting in Part II.

Bourdieu's Biography

In this section we set out details of Bourdieu's biography. However, we intersperse this with discussion of the intellectual ideas of the time in order to show how his own intellectual trajectory was shaped by the ideas and events which surrounded him.

Bourdieu eschewed personal biographies and, for most of his professional life, worked to establish his ideas as separate from his own trajectory. He was keen to argue for the scientific objectivity of his work and the broader applicability of his methods and ideas. Ironically, however, among his very last works, he performed something of an epistemological volte-face (for example, 2004a) in presenting his entire corpus as a kind of attempt to understand the social forces which acted on him. We will return to this idea much later in the book, as it goes to the heart of Bourdieu's philosophy and method. Here, we begin with a sketch of his life trajectory.

It is now well known that Bourdieu came from a relatively humble background. He was born and spent his early boyhood in the small village of Denguin in the south-west corner of France in the heart of the Béarn region. His father was an itinerant farm worker turned local functionary in the post office. Pierre Bourdieu was born in 1930, a pivotal point in the twentieth century. This was an age before mass communication. At this time France was still predominantly agricultural. The south-west of the country was a world away from Paris and its cosmopolitan metropolis. Even those cities which were relatively close to Denguin were essentially provincial and inward-looking, for example, Montpelier, Toulouse and Pau. To be born into a rural community meant adopting the local dialect – in Bourdieu's case, Gascon – along with the habits, traditions and ideas of the area.

Allegedly, Bourdieu's father did not complete his own schooling, although his mother did so in the nearby town of Pau. His parents must have understood the power that education had in social advancement because Bourdieu was eventually also sent to a *lycée* in Pau as a boarder. This would not have been an unusual move at the time; either in France or other Western countries. Before mass schooling and education beyond the basics of reading and writing, anyone looking for higher educational experience could expect to have to leave home and spend a substantial part of their childhood and adolescent years in an educational institution. Bourdieu himself subsequently completed his secondary education at the *lycée* Louis Le Grand in Paris. Unsurprisingly, such a move was not without consequences. First, and perhaps most personally, he was removed from the family milieu, with all its comforts and support. The world of the school boarder scarcely matched these, offering instead a closed community where he would be expected to fend for himself. Bourdieu himself described the systemic bullying, the fights and detentions (2002a). The need to conform was acute. Second, such conformity was far from straightforward. The *lycée* itself was not homogeneous. Boarders from the country, such as Bourdieu, mixed with the sons of local urbanites, who came from a totally different cultural background. For the latter, lessons in schools simply represented confirmation of a way of thinking which was already theirs, coming as they did from the local professional classes. The same was not true for those who originated from rural farming communities. The sense of 'us and them' was therefore accented. These groups even dressed differently. While the local pupils were already dressed in a middle-class manner, the boarders wore grey smocks. A third consequence was manifested in the relationships established with scholastic knowledge and the realm of sensual experience. In contrast to the immediate experience of home life, education inducted pupils into the world of ideas, of the imagination and of individual thinking. Scholarly activity was not without ambiguity, however. For those pupils already brought up in families where intellectual pursuits were a natural occupation, schooling at this level represented only a small difference from their customary way of thinking and acting. For those not from such a social milieu, it offered a world which was both strange and enchanting. Bourdieu himself writes of this, together with the feelings of discomfort – if not betrayal – he experienced when embracing such a way of being that so obviously meant turning his back on the culture of his home and family. Liberation and advancement were therefore mixed with rejection and estrangement.

It is probably easy to make too much of Bourdieu's move into *lycée* education in Pau. As mentioned above, such a move was hardly unusual. Many hundreds of pupils must have had (and up to a point continue to have) these experiences, and with them a mixture of resentment and excitement of a new world now available to them. It would certainly be wrong to see any heroic intent in Bourdieu's own mixed emotions about stepping on to the academic ladder to success. Nevertheless, in his case, it seems to have been a dilemma from which he never fully recovered. Once he had completed his secondary education in Paris, he gained a place in the *Ecole normale supérieure* (ENS) in 1951. The ENS was, and still is, one of the most prestigious training schools in France. In fact, to call the ENS a training school is somewhat of a misnomer. The word 'training' in English has connotations of vocational and manual work. However, in the French case, the training referred to is for the highest positions in the country. If other training schools prepared their students for the most prestigious jobs in government, the army and industry, the ENS can be understood as the incubator of the French intellectual class. Most of France's highly reputed intellectuals and philosophers have at one time been students of the ENS. It is less a school than a 'super-university' or academic hothouse.

Bourdieu seems to have taken his sense of being an outsider with him to the ENS. Entry to the school is by competitive examination. This exam is so difficult that the only chance of passing it is to enter into a long and arduous preparation phase. Here, Bourdieu's resentment came to the fore. He writes of being 'forced' to take the ENS preparation exam while the offspring of the Parisian elite classes seemed to develop 'effortlessly'. There is, then, in Bourdieu's own education a series of disjunctures: between town and country; between Paris and province;

between bourgeois and peasant working classes; between intellectual and physical endeavour; between effort and ease. And it is as if Bourdieu played out the resultant tensions in these dichotomies for the rest of his life.

Contemporary France

What was the background to Bourdieu's academic trajectory? It is now probably impossible for us to imagine what it was like to grow up in rural France in the 1930s. What we do know is that this decade was pivotal in the development of the modern nation state of France. The previous 150 years had been marked by revolution and war. French territory had twice been occupied by German invaders. The devastation and catastrophe of the First World War was mainly played out in the fields of north-eastern France. Throughout this period, war resulted in political instability. The struggle between Empire and Republic had seemingly been resolved, but there remained deep-seated tensions at the heart of French society about how they saw themselves. In an important respect, France had enormous influence on the international stage through its substantial colonies in North Africa and the Far East. The belle époque had made the country a world leader of culture and style. The World Fair of 1889 had attracted visitors from around the globe, establishing Paris as the centre of Europe. Parisian life was the modern world made manifest.

However, by the 1930s war and economic crisis had undermined the confidence of the French ruling classes. It is arguable that by the 1930s France had not fully industrialized. Certainly, there was enormous activity to the north in its iron and coal industries, and pockets of industry elsewhere, but essentially, outside Paris, France remained locked in its old ways. There had been a rural exodus of sorts, but even here, the local towns and cities to which French men and women moved were provincial in character, inward-looking and attached to their regional ways of life. Many of those working in the towns and cities went home at weekends, and family ties in the country remained strong. There was ambiguity about the extent to which modern ways should be embraced. Economic crises and incidents of corruption at an international level only fuelled the fires of suspicion about the modern capitalist world. The Second World War brought these tensions to a head.

War and Liberation

Now, with knowledge of the Nazi Holocaust and the Soviet Gulag, it is easy to overlook the fact that in the 1930s, faced with an economic crisis, with all that implied in terms of wages and unemployment, National Socialism and Communism represented credible alternatives to American-styled liberal capitalism. The latter was seen to represent all that was bad about the modern world, with its secularity, rampant consumerism and corruption. For a while, National Socialism might have been misunderstood as a version of Communism, with its anticapitalist doctrine. In France, on the other hand, sufficient Republican zeal remained to keep alive the commitment to a philosophy of 'all for one and one for all'. In the late 1930s, the French Popular Front attempted to introduce a series of sweeping social reforms, aimed at improving the lot of the mass of the French population. There was also support for resistance to the Fascist threat in Spain. However, for a large proportion of the French population, the problems lay in the way traditional values had been abandoned in an increasingly materialist, money-led world. If the growing industrial working class was mostly de-Christianized, those remaining on the land still lived in the shadow of the Church. For these people, family and tradition were all. It is perhaps unsurprising, therefore, if the French response to invasion by Germany in 1940 was ambivalent. Certainly few actually welcomed occupation by their old enemy from the north. However, when Pétain sued for peace and set up a semi-independent government based around traditional principles of 'work, family, and country', many Frenchmen rallied around this call as a return to the 'old ways'. Arguably, de Gaulle, that very personification of French resistance, fought more for independence than a return to the socio-political systems which had been swept away by war. Despite the violence that replaced it, it seems few regretted the loss of the Third Republic, with its political impasses and lack of direction.

Bourdieu's Early Career

These were the years in which Bourdieu passed his boyhood and attended secondary school. Of course, he was too young to be directly involved in these events and we know little about his own encounters with war, collaboration and resistance. He was not of the generation of Sartre, Camus and de Beauvoir, whose philosophical and political thinking was deeply marked and shaped by war. It is perhaps unsurprising that in a climate of occupation, where death and reprisals were a daily event, existentialism – that philosophy of personal choice, responsibility and action – should become the dominant force among the French intellectual class. However, this did not yet include Bourdieu.

In 1951 Pierre Bourdieu went to the ENS, some six years after the conclusion of the Second World War hostilities. Not for him the concerns of military combat and fighting for freedom. During his adolescent and early adult years, France was more concerned with rebuilding and renewal. The war had offered the French the possibility of reaction and reform. For a while, collaborationists, and those who supported them, flirted with the idea of a return to the past. Defeat of the Germans by Allied Forces quashed belief in the old ways and offered a clear victory for those who sought to create a modern France, genuinely placed in the forefront of the twentieth century. Bourdieu's generation was part of this group who sought to put the past behind them and build a new modern society and state. Nevertheless, the past was not dispensed with so easily. France still had her colonies and, among these, the most problematic was Algeria.

Bourdieu and Algeria

Arguably, Algeria was the jewel in the crown of French colonialism. Invaded in 1830 in order to add strength to the restored monarchy, it had provided large numbers of Frenchmen with a place to seek a new life and work in order to get away from the social and economic upheavals of the homeland. Often arriving dirty and with no shoes, these French colonizers were referred to as *pieds noirs*. Nevertheless, once settled, they procured for themselves the best land, jobs and social positions – so much so that by the end of the Second World War virtually all the most prestigious territory and positions of power were held by Frenchmen or their representatives. This state of affairs could not continue. Algerians themselves were looking for change; in fact, they had sought independence from their French rulers. This search for independence was a long-standing and unsuccessful one. However, in line with the mood of the times, which saw anticolonial victories elsewhere in the world, the Algerian case became more pressing. Much was at stake. Algeria had been held up by the French as a celebration of French culture and the French way of life. Still smarting from military defeat in the Second World War, the French army was reluctant to 'give in', this time to an apparently much less formidable foe. Many Frenchmen living in Algeria were now second- or third-generation *pieds noirs* and considered themselves as Algerian as those they had colonized. For them, the case for independence was not evident. The fact that the French political establishment itself was unstable – as Fourth Republic systems set up in the aftermath of war proved to be unworkable – meant that French political rulers were reluctant to cede to demands, which could be interpreted as a further sign of weakness. All these factors combined as the background to the Algerian war of independence, which broke out in 1954 and went on for some eight years – eight years of bloody and often cruel combat that shook French society and its politics to the core.

Bourdieu himself went to Algeria in order to do his military service in 1955. It was an experience which shaped his thinking for the rest of his life. In Algeria, Bourdieu was not only faced with military conflict, but with completely different ways of life. On the one hand, traditional Algerian society represented the pre-industrial world, with its traditional values, beliefs and practices. Although many elements of this traditional way of life had been displaced by colonialism and imported Western capitalism, much remained. On the other hand, modern urban life flourished, a version of the cosmopolitan world from which Bourdieu had come. What sense could he make of these two worlds and the suffering they caused for the people caught between them? The answer to this question takes us to the dominant intellectual ideas of the day and the way they had shaped Bourdieu's interpretation of what surrounded him.

Bourdieu's Intellectual Influences

Background and Climate

Any intellectual must necessarily be shaped by the tradition which precedes and surrounds him. The intellectual tradition of France, of course, is as a major European presence. It would not be surprising, therefore, to identify many of its salient strands in Bourdieu's own thinking. What might these be?

Bourdieu, Comte and Durkheim. Even before the secular revolution of 1789, which saw the overthrow of both aristocracy and Church and their separation from the state, France gave the world a major intellectual movement in the form of the Age of Enlightenment. Through the works of such writers as Voltaire, Montesquieu, Tocqueville and Rousseau, progressive ideas were expressed, for example, in the *Encyclopédie* (1751–65). These ideas shared a common spirit: one of scepticism for religious and traditional beliefs. In their place, they celebrated nature and rational ideas, and proposed alternative political systems, which, they argued, better represented the interests of society as a whole. Of course, it was this spirit that fanned the flames of revolution which saw the separation of Church and state and the final banishment of the French monarchy from political power. In the wake of this revolution, the intellectual current which would shape future and contemporary France was set. The French philosopher Auguste Comte (1798–1857) is attributed with inventing the word 'sociology'. He studied at the *Ecole polytechnique* (the other principal Parisian state training school) and founded modern positivism, namely, the identification of natural scientific laws. However, for Comte, such laws did not apply to the natural sciences alone; they could also be identified in socio-political systems. The logical conclusion was that society and politics could be informed and organized by the 'laws' which had been discovered about the way men behaved. Comte saw positivism as a possible replacement for the Church as a new 'secular religion' for the modern age; at one point, he even set himself up as 'Pope of Positivism'!

In passing, we might connect this rather absurd idea with Bourdieu's own references to religion, aristocracy and the place of sociology with respect to them. He likens his own elite training and trajectory to being prepared for the priesthood. The fact that he gave the title *La Noblesse d'état* (1996b/1989) to his major study of the French training schools indicates the ways in which he was attempting to draw analogies between the *Ancien Régime* and the modern world. The fact that this book was published in the year which saw the 200th anniversary of the French Revolution is not without significance. In a later book – *Méditations pascaliennes* (2000a/1997) – Bourdieu concludes with a quote from Durkheim: 'society is god' (p. 245). What is important to note here is that there was a strong moral strand running through the French intellectual tradition. It began before the Revolution, when the excesses of the French Church and the monarchy partly encouraged the emergence of the Enlightenment philosophers. However, the destruction of or separation from Church and monarchy clearly left the question of what were the principles around which society could be organized and to which its people could offer alliance. Contenders were 'virtue' (Montesquieu), the 'general will' (Rousseau), 'democracy' (Tocqueville) and 'positivism/sociology' (Comte). All or any of these might have done the job. The point was that something had to replace the force of religion and aristocracy once these had been overcome. Bourdieu, some century and a half later, seemed to sympathize with Comte's view that sociology could take on the role.

Another 'founding father' of sociology, Emile Durkheim (1858–1917), was also preoccupied with this moral issue. He too questioned what might constitute 'organic solidarity' in the hearts of men and society at large. Durkheim addressed head-on the issue of the moral *faiblesse* of French society. His analyses highlighted the ambiguities of the modern age. In traditional society, a state of what Durkheim referred to as 'mechanical solidarity' reigned. Here, men and women were held tightly in the bosom of the community which they inhabited. They had their place in the world: they were what they did and what they contributed to the community, and there was no space to question this role. There is a hint of nostalgia here for a past age when such questions about the health of social patterning were not posed. There is an implicit connection with Rousseau's noble savage, who enjoyed a natural freedom before civilization seduced him to modern wants and needs. Yet, no one could possibly regret a system which imposed community's exigencies on the individuals who made it up. In *The Division of Labour in Society* (1964/1933) Durkheim catalogues the characteristics of the society of the new world: its organic, functional nature, its secularization, its changes guided by ruling principles. Indeed, 'man' is more free in the modern industrial world: free to choose where to live and work; free to divide his time between work and rest; free to be who he wants to be. Yet such freedom is bought at a cost; most notably the anomie which results from the loss of norms when traditional values have been removed and established practices overturned. At its extreme, chronic and acute anomie results in the breakdown of social structures, which causes direct harm to the individuals concerned. Such is the message in *Suicide* (1952/1897). Here, Durkheim set out to explain the rising instance of suicide in contemporary society.

As discussed earlier, the distinction between traditional and modern society is at the heart of Bourdieu's own response to Algeria: on the one hand, the traditional ethnic groupings, each with their own beliefs, practices and laws; on the other, modern life, with its urban habitat, open lifestyle and systems of communications. The crux of Bourdieu's own analyses of Algeria was that the latter was destroying, or had destroyed, the former and that this destruction was not without consequences. As well as the abandonment of the land, whole sections of traditional Algerian society were rendered obsolete. The colour of traditional customs was being replaced by the anonymity and greyness of modern living. Bourdieu goes into some ethnographic, statistical and theoretical detail to catalogue these changes (see 1958, 1963, 1964a). A similar distinction between the old world and the new can be found in his account of the bachelor farmers of his own home village in the Béarn (see 2002b, but based on work and publications in the 1950s and 1960s). He set out the consequences of changes in agricultural practices for the traditional marriage strategies within the farming communities. These changes, along with the growth of nearby towns at the expense of rural populations, led to large numbers of men and women simply being left on the shelf. Here, in a mirror of what he found in Algeria, is the picture of a group within society being brushed aside in terms of its social trajectory, as the world literally passes its members by. Of course, such changes must occur. Nevertheless, Bourdieu seems to be saying that we should not ignore the social cost and personal suffering they impose on the individuals concerned. This concern with the consequences of change can also be found in Bourdieu's work on social suffering in the 1990s – *La Misère du monde* (1999/1993). Among the many anecdotes, vignettes and case studies of poverty in France, the underlying theme is the personal cost of social change; for example, the effects of educational reform on teachers, the problems caused by new industrial practices, the need for modern housing and the price individuals are prepared to pay in order to 'invest in their future'.

In response to a question concerning his apparent lack of attention to a phenomenon such as anomie, Bourdieu stated to Michael Grenfell that he never invented a concept simply in order to complete his repertoire of theories (Bourdieu (with Grenfell) 1995b). Nevertheless, in his later work (for example, 1996a/1992) he calls this state hysteresis, namely, where the individual and the social context which he inhabits are 'out of line' with each other. Here, personal expectations and collective expectations do not balance and lead to contradictory messages – double binds. In these cases, individuals are confused and do not know how to act. Another word for this might be alienation.

Bourdieu and Marxism. It is impossible to discuss Bourdieu without mentioning that other nineteenth-century socio-political thinker – indeed, probably the greatest of them all – Karl Marx. For many, Bourdieu was a Marxist, although he always eschewed this description, while acknowledging the importance and influence of the Marxist tradition on his thinking. Of course, there are different 'Marxes': there is Marx the historian, who gave us a careful historical account of the French 'revolutions' of 1789, 1848 and 1871; Marx the economic philosopher, who presented in *Das Kapital* a highly developed analysis of the capitalist economy and society; and Marx the polemicist, who drew up the *Communist Manifesto* as a political rallying cry for the masses to rise up against their bourgeois bosses in anticipation of the revolution that his analysis predicted as inevitable. Similar strands can indeed be found in Bourdieu's own work. For example, many of his major books – *La Noblesse d'état* (1996b/1989), *La Distinction* (1984/1979), *Le Sens pratique* (1990b/1980), *Homo Academicus*

(1988/1984) – are devoted to careful socio-historical analyses of French society. What they share with Marx is an attention to the structures within society and the way different factions play off against each other in the processes of social evolution. He argues that the development of contemporary French society can be understood in terms of the displacement of the old ruling classes, who based their claim to power and privilege on their economic capital, by a new managerial class, who held relatively little financial wealth, but who, through education and training, had amassed large quantities of cultural capital in the form of qualification, education and lifestyle. Bourdieu, in a similar way to Marx, brought philosophy to his discipline. Indeed, his ideas amount to a kind of 'philosophical sociology' in the way that he attempts to found a 'theory of practice' which is both philosophically robust and informed by a certain epistemological stance, and of practical use. This approach has been referred to as a 'science of existential structure and social meaning' (Dreyfus and Rabinow 1993). This is discussed in more detail in the latter part of this chapter. For the moment, we can say that Bourdieu's approach is characterized by a concern to connect the social realm of ideas with the structured patterning of society – what Marx would call the superstructure and infrastructure – in a relationship which is best called dialectics.

Dialectics are central to the Marxist view of history and society. The term is in fact a Greek word, meaning to converse, and the discursive method ascribed to Socrates is close to this conversational approach to argument, involving question and answer. The term 'dialectics' can be found in the work of both Aristotle and Kant, but it was the German idealist, Hegel, who probably set the parameters of its contemporary usage. For Hegel, thought was reality, and developed through a pattern of contradiction and reconciliation of contradiction – thesis, antithesis, synthesis. By analogy, Marx's historical materialism applied a similar patterning to the development of human history; namely, that history advances through the interpenetration of contradictory forces, which result in reconciliation giving rise to new contradictions. Allied to this view are the main tenets of dialectical materialism: the primacy of material conditions over ideas in forming these contradicting forces, indeed of materiality itself being shaped by ideas in the processes of contradiction and reconciliation. In brief, material forces are often expressed and played out in the realm of ideas which themselves can subsequently impact on material conditions.

We shall see later that Bourdieu's own theory can best be understood as dialectical in the way it attempts to link what we think and how we act with our material surroundings, in particular, in the ways we are organized into social groupings, for example, artistic avant-gardes. Besides the issues surrounding this particular philosophical approach to society, history, economics and, indeed, politics, there is the further issue of an alternative world view. In other words, what Marx and Bourdieu share is a sense of an alternative take on the contemporary world. A positive understanding of the succession of capitalism and technological society might express it in terms of liberalization – liberty, progress, improvement in living conditions, meritocracies and democratic politics. However, both Marx and Bourdieu argued for a different, more negative version, of alienation and hysteresis, exploitation, partisan politics and human misery in the face of the capitalist machine. For Bourdieu, it is an issue of misrecognition, in that oppression can best proceed by being occluded or hidden from view, so that the true reality of things is not immediately acknowledged or available. For Bourdieu, as for Marx before him, it was the task of sociology to say what others cannot, will not or do not want to say as tools for liberation.

In the last decade of Bourdieu's life, he moved increasingly to address a popular audience in terms of what he referred to as 'acts of resistance' (1998a). He attempted to make available to a wider public the findings of his life's work – both practical and theoretical. What pushed him towards this was partly a growing concern with the intensification of the capitalist system to be found in neoliberal economics, and with all the effects this had on increasing human misery (1999/1993). This was Bourdieu the polemicist, who was active in his support for striking miners in the name of those who fought against 'the destruction of a civilisation' (1998a: 24).

French Intellectuals in the Twentieth Century

So far, we have seen how the French intellectuals rooted in the Age of Enlightenment had bequeathed a heritage which highlighted the nature and structure of society; how its structures were organized; and the tensions between the individual, the community and the state. This was a question of social cohesion and representation in a capitalist democracy which had separated itself from those traditional unifying institutions: the Church and the Crown. This question was particularly acute in France, where it was formulated as a question in moral philosophy. However, Marxism went beyond moral concerns with the order and functioning of society and offered a much more radical critique of its very socio-economic mechanisms; a critique which saw innate contradictions leading to the intensification of human suffering through further exploitation and alienation, the outcome of which was inevitably revolution. But how did these developments influence Bourdieu's ideas?

The way in which French intellectuals had become enmeshed in political ideas was exemplified in a single action on the cusp of the twentieth century. In 1898, the French writer Emile Zola published an open letter to the French president – *J'accuse* – in which he accused the military of misleading in the way it had used Captain Dreyfus as a scapegoat to cover up its own corruption when faced with evidence of a traitor in the camp. A petition followed to which many of the leading writers of the day lent support. A consequence of the case of Dreyfus was that these acts precipitated the public recognition of a separate intellectual class which was able to operate outside mainstream politics. By separating from the dominant political culture, they were able to articulate a freer, more independent voice.

Moreover, they gave themselves licence to comment on the ills of the society of the day. Certainly, they had much material on which to express themselves.

As suggested earlier, the turn of the century saw the dying years of the belle époque and the gathering clouds of global war, which would be fought mainly on French ground. The consequences of which would be devastating for France. Following the armistice, France could take solace in being on the side of the victors and regaining previously lost territory in Alsace-Lorraine. However, the world political situation, the Communist Revolution in Russia and its own social frailty left France with a strong sense of vulnerability. The Maginot line was built, apparently to protect it from its traditional aggressors in the north. Later, in the 1920 and 1930s, came economic crisis and further political corruption. French intellectuals were divided in their particular perspectives, but united in their joint disgust for a socio-political culture which it saw as being 'rotten' and for the capitalist economic system which it supported.

The contemporary diagnoses of these ills and the suggested remedies spanned the political spectrum. The Paris Commune of 1871, the Communist Revolution in Russia in 1917, together with the strength of the *Internationale* in France, combined to give many on the left of French politics a tried and tested method to offer as an alternative to the capitalist way of doing things, which had proven not to work. At the other end of the spectrum were those who had never forgiven the Republic for separating Church and Crown from the state, and who were nostalgic for traditional ways of doing things. Despite the growing de-Christianization in industrial and urban environments, France was far from secular in mood. Indeed, a large portion of the population still lived on the land or went back there every weekend. There were, then, conflicting views of what French society could and should become.

Bourdieu and Catholic Intellectuals. At this stage, and up until the Second World War, intellectual dynamism was largely Catholic, with common godfathers such as Jacques Maritain and Charles Péguy. The latter famously declared that 'tout commence en mystique et finit en politique'. This phrase sums up the recognition that religion needed to be involved with the realities of the world which surrounded it. That involvement amounted to political activism of an intellectual kind. Numerous reviews were founded, pamphlets were written, Catholic pressure groups were formed. Allegiances were inevitably divided: some sympathized with the right (nationalism and more traditional forms of Catholicism), others with the left (the Marxist language of freedom from oppression and the end to alienation struck a resonant chord with a theology of personal salvation). The common spirit of 'revolt', where liberal democracy was itself seen as an imposition on the part of America, is probably best summed up in the 'Ni droite, ni gauche' slogan around which so many French intellectuals rallied in their search for a third way which would combine the best of the old with the new, the right with the left. But such consensus was short-lived. Events on the world stage divided them: Munich,

Spain, the Popular Front. By the time of the outbreak of the Second World War, and the subsequent collapse of France in the face of its German invaders, some intellectuals aligned themselves in relation to their sympathies or opposition to Fascism and Communism, and, by definition, collaboration or resistance. Others fought to maintain a more autonomous voice.

Bourdieu can have had little directly to do with these nonconformist, Catholic intellectuals of the 1920s and 1930s. He was only a boy when they were at their most active. Also, Bourdieu was always avowedly non-religious in the conventional sense of the word. And yet, there is beneath their individual concerns a common belief in human potential. For personalists such as Emmanuel Mounier, this is summed up in the expression 'l'épanouissement de la personne' – literally, the flowering or blossoming of the human spirit, or at least the potential for this. All this is expressed in terms of a liberation from societal forces which deform men and women. Bourdieu would share this idea that society as we know it oppresses individuals, but for him the source of liberation would be his own brand of sociology. In this liberation there is a common acceptance of belief in the transformative potential that individuals hold; namely, that another self is possible if the right conditions – both material and ideational – are set. As we shall see, this aspect of the intellectual project led Bourdieu to look at education and culture in the 1950s and 1960s, with the implicit objective of examining the extent to which transformative potential could be realized through society and its institutions.

Bourdieu's own associations with the nonconformists of the 1930s did not remain entirely distant. An early article was published in the *Esprit* (1961) review, which was founded by Mounier and remains a major vehicle for the voice of the 'enlightened Catholic' in France. He also published a major historical analysis of these movements from the 1930s and 1940s, and argued that their rhetoric should be seen as both right-wing and forming the major guiding principles of post-war political culture. This argument came to a head in 1995, when Bourdieu and the *Esprit* group occupied opposing positions over social welfare reform in France. For Bourdieu, their sympathy to the reform amounted to a betrayal of the most needy in society, while for them, Bourdieu was not sufficiently pragmatic and could be accused of currying political favour with the popular classes.

Bourdieu and Existentialism. Existentialism, the heir to Catholic intellectual movements in France, did have a direct influence on Bourdieu's thinking. It can be linked to German idealism and Kantian metaphysics, but its direct roots extend from the Danish philosopher Søren Kierkegaard (1813–55). What we find in this philosophy is in many ways the familiar nineteenth-century preoccupation with the status of man in a harsh new world and the role that religious belief holds for him. What is stressed is man as the 'existing individual'; in other words, the primary condition of life as it is lived. Kierkegaard's philosophy was particularly influential in Germany, especially with Jaspers, Husserl and Heidegger, who were considered the modern godfathers of existentialism. Many of the nonconformists of the 1930s were heavily influenced by these writers, so that there was a Catholic brand of existentialism. Mounier referred to philosophers such as Kierkegaard and Jaspers extensively. Here, existentialism is translated into a semi-gnomic belief in a transcendent human spirit which is ultimately an expression of God: an idea at the core of personalism. However, twentieth-century existentialism is probably best remembered as an avowedly secular, if not atheistic, philosophy. Existentialism in France was personified by the philosopher-cum-novelist-cum-playwright Jean-Paul Sartre (1905–80). Sartre preceded Bourdieu at the ENS and was of an altogether different generation, having won a scholarship to the French Institute in Berlin, where he studied under Husserl, who had been Heidegger's teacher at Freiberg; indeed, Sartre's magnum opus, *Being and Nothingness* (1969/1943), can be read as a reinterpretation and reaffirmation, albeit through a Gallic lens, of Heidegger's *Being and Time* (1962/1927). At his intellectual height at the outbreak of the Second World War, Sartre espoused a version of existentialism which was radical and atheistic. He professed to be a Marxist long after leaving the Communist party, a doctrine which he saw as sharing his own preoccupation with the freedom inherent in human nature. Man is nothing at birth and carries with him no incarnate spirit – humanist or otherwise. Rather, he is *condemned* to be free, to be the sum total of his individual choices. For Sartre, there is a distinction between 'normal' behaviour, which might be described as 'going along with situations' without being aware of one's freedom to choose – which for Sartre was characterized by philosophical bad faith (*mauvaise-foi*) – and 'authentic' living, where man is alive to his situation and the responsibility to choose how to act. This focus on freedom of/and choice is perhaps unsurprising in an intellectual who came from a culture which was constantly confronted by the requirement to choose; in particular, choices about whose side to be on – most recently, with the Dreyfus affair, Spain, Munich, the Popular Front and then collaboration or resistance. Indeed, in war the consequences of choice are brought into sharp relief when its outcomes can literally result in life or death for those involved.

The spirit at least, if not the philosophical content, of existentialism extended well into the 1960s, when its apparent support for throwing off such metaphysical institutions as religion, state and even family resonated with the beat generation and its desire for free individual expression in the face of an old system, which was seen as acting as a straitjacket on youth and the forces of progress. This was the spirit of 1968; although by this time Sartre was in decline.

Nonetheless, for Bourdieu, Sartre was a significant figure. In many ways, he represented the older generation, the war generation. Certainly, by the 1950s, when Bourdieu was completing his higher education, Sartre was from an age which the younger generation now wished to put behind them. Later, Bourdieu criticized Sartre for his blinkered Marxist views over the events in Algeria, which, he argued, blinded him to a real appreciation of what was at stake and the perils involved in the course that the war had taken there. It was not a revolution leading to liberation, but a breakdown of societal structures that would leave a vacuum which would have to be filled, most probably by the forces of reaction – a suspicion which eventually proved to be true. Bourdieu also attacked Sartre's presumption in setting himself up as the 'total intellectual', as the voice of the people. There is, of course, an irony here, since Bourdieu himself eventually seemed to assume this mantle. But this is not the only way in which Sartre and Bourdieu can be linked. In a way, Bourdieu's own theory seems to offer the same sort of insights and choices between authenticity and bad faith, the latter now translated into 'misrecognition' in sociology. His sociological vision offers at least a certain kind of freedom in the knowledge it provides for those caught in the clutches of social forces. There is, then, much ambiguity in Bourdieu's relationship with Sartre; it is almost that of the spurned lover, forced to denounce all while remaining fascinated by the object of desire. Nevertheless, Bourdieu is explicit in his rejection of existentialism, which he refers to as 'insipid humanism'. Neither did he have time for the study of classical philosophy 'for its own sake'.

If Sartre represented a 'subjectivist' philosophy of the individual, there was a countervailing 'objectivist' strand. Marxism can be seen as a grand theory of society and its structures. Durkheim also was concerned with the overall structures of society: how these characterized themselves, the systems and consequences of change and the general integrability of social institutions. These seemingly different writers therefore shared a concern with the character and operation of structures in society. 'Structuralism' was another direct influence on Bourdieu, but 'structures' interpreted in vastly different ways.

Bourdieu, Structuralism and Phenomenology. Both prior to and following the Second World War, American sociology was heavily represented by a search to find an alternative to the conflictual, revolutionary theories of Marxism. The most obvious case is that of Talcot Parsons (1949, 1951), who sought a theory to prescribe the healthy, 'functional' state of 'normal' society, basically expressed in terms of individual and collective cohesion and complementarity. His approach considered society in terms of a set of interconnecting and mutually supporting structures. But there was also an earlier, more overt form of structuralism, one which was more grounded in continental Europe. The father of this structural tradition in Europe was Ferdinand de Saussure, the twentieth-century founder of linguistics. Saussure posited a distinction between *langue* and *parole*, namely, language in its totality and individual speech acts. This difference was also taken up by Noam Chomsky in the 1950s, when he distinguished between competence and performance, following lines similar to Saussure. Chomsky also argued for a 'universal grammar': the deep linguistic structures of the human brain which were the base of the world's languages, despite the plurality of surface differences.

The idea that there are comparable generating structures behind diversity lies at the heart of continental structuralist philosophy. The main leader of this approach in the 1950s was Claude Lévi-Strauss. Lévi-Strauss arose from a strong anthropological tradition in France with a preoccupation to study and comprehend foreign cultures, especially tribal ones (see also the place that photography played in this tradition). Lévi-Strauss was particularly interested in the universal generating rules of society, for example, the distinction between the raw and the cooked (nature and culture) and the incest taboo. For Lévi-Strauss, many different myths and practices shared 'deep structures' which were homologous. In other words, while individual component parts were varied, indeed almost incidental, the actual structural relations set up were the same. This notion of the near arbitrariness of content also echoes Saussure's own discovery that the signifier of anything signified was arbitrary; any word can be chosen to represent a particular meaning, as long as there is social consensus. This discovery of symbolic arbitrariness also lies at the basis of postmodernism.

Lévi-Strauss was the chief rival to Sartre in France in the 1950s. For Bourdieu, because of his interest and training in anthropology, he could not have avoided being influenced by him. Early work in Algeria (1958) was carried out from a 'structuralist' perspective and published in honour of Lévi-Strauss, who subsequently supported Bourdieu's nomination to the Ecole des Hautes Etudes en Sciences Sociales in 1964. There even developed a Marxist brand of structuralism which saw the deep structures in terms of the reproduction and representation of class divisions. Bourdieu took on board parts of both Marxist and non-Marxist accounts of structuralism. However, he saw much to dispute in both perspectives. The work he carried out in his native Béarn region of France in the 1950s was also essentially 'structuralist'. Bourdieu had studied the marriage patterns in the local communities in order to explain the way in which traditional matrimonial practices were changing. He was able to identify the 'rules' which dictated who married whom. However, he also showed that a whole analysis – both statistical and ethnographic – was needed in order to grasp the reality of what was happening. Central to his conclusion, and in direct opposition to Lévi-Straussian structuralism, which he saw as being too static, Bourdieu argued that any notion of 'rule' must be discarded in favour of 'strategy'; namely, the general disposition to maximize opportunity and profit when marrying, which might mean the direct manipulation and even avoidance of established ways of doing things (Bourdieu 2002b). This conclusion therefore distanced him from the traditional structuralist approach. Bourdieu does credit Lévi-Strauss (along with other structuralists such as Cassirer, Elias, Tynianov, Lewin and Sapir) with establishing the necessity of a relational approach to studying social contexts, as opposed to an idealist, substantialist mode:

> I could twist Hegel's famous formula and say that the real is relational: what exist in the social world are relations – not interactions between agents or intersubjective ties between individuals, but objective relations which exist 'independently of individual consciousness and will', as Marx said. (Bourdieu (with Wacquant) 1992a: 97)

Such objective relations are expressed and identifiable as 'structures' since they pertain to the topography of social space. On the one hand, they are present in both the material and ideational content of civil society. On the other hand, they are experienced, grasped and articulated through the particular sensual and intellectual functions of individuals. This latter point returns us to the subjective world, but this time not through an existentialist view but to the philosophy of phenomenology. This 'science of phenomena' was established through a return to 'things in themselves'; in other words, once the everyday world was 'bracketed off', phenomenological study proceeded through the in-depth enquiry of individual consciousnesses. This method was developed by Husserl, who, as we know, in turn influenced Heidegger. Its most well-known exponent in France was Merleau-Ponty (1908–61), whom Bourdieu acknowledged as an early influence. What the phenomenological approach gave Bourdieu was a theory of the social world grasped as and in a 'sense activity'. Thinking about the social world itself sets up intensional structures (the 's' in 'intensional' standing for relational structures) which can be identified as the generating product of thought. Moreover, they have an underlying principle or constituting logic which can be grasped as such. Husserl called his method 'transcendent subjectivism'. For Husserl, there was a distinction to be made between *noema* and *noesis*; in other words, everything that is known about an object of thought, and an individual act of perception based on this thinking. There is here a kind of dialectic between what is known and an act of knowing. More than this, such a process was for Merleau-Ponty, and later for Bourdieu, incorporated into the body, literally embodied – a kind of social incarnation in the individual of the pre-given, now part of their generating thinking schemes.

This point is central to Bourdieu's theory. He begins his summative statement about method with a quote from Marx:

> The principle defect of all materialism up to now – including that of Feuerbach – is that the external object, reality, the sensible world, is grasped in the form of *an object or an intuition*; not as *concrete human activity*, as *practice*, in a subjective way. This is why the active aspect was developed by idealism, in opposition to materialism – but only in an abstract way, since idealism naturally does not know real concrete activity as such. (Marx in Bourdieu 1977b: vi)

There were, then, a variety of influences on Bourdieu: the founding fathers of sociology – Comte, Marx, Weber, Durkheim – as well as more contemporary writers – Lévi-Strauss, Merleau-Ponty, Sartre. To this list we could add philosophers of the history of science (see below), such as Bachelard and Canguilhem, and, eventually, the American sociologist of the micro-instance, the dramaturgicalist Ervin Goffman. These were intellectuals, but were formed and shaped by the socio-historical conditions from which they emerged. It is time to consider Bourdieu's theory directly.

Bourdieu: A Theory of Practice

For Bourdieu, any adequate methodological approach must begin with concrete human activity, not idealized, predetermined views of it. The way to proceed is through structural analysis, but not structure in the traditional (Lévi-Straussian), reified sense, but structure as both sense activity and objective surroundings – a kind of dialectic between the individual (including all that they share in common with other individuals, as well as their particular idiosyncrasies) and what confronts them in culture and the material world. Bourdieu's own approach proceeded through what might be considered to be a series of breaks. First, he wished to break with the naive, unreflected view of the world which is the everyday lot of men and women. Second, he wished to break with the substantialist mode of thinking which 'is inclined to treat activities and preferences specific to certain individuals or groups at a certain moment as if they were substantial properties, inscribed once and for all in a sort of biological or cultural essence…' (see 1998c: 4). He looks to replace this mode of thinking with a relational view which 'is nothing other than difference, a gap, a distinctive feature, in short, a relational property existing only in and through its relation with other properties' (p. 6). The third and fourth breaks follow on from this situational praxis. In the third, he sought to break with what he sees as the overt subjectivism of existentialism and phenomenology, since it gives insufficient account of material and social surroundings (although he is more sympathetic with the latter than the former). Fourth, he saw the need to break with materialism, as found in both Marxism and structuralism, since these give insufficient attention to the way reality is individually perceived, grasped and responded to as a process of sense apprehension. Structure is the linking phenomenon in Bourdieu's work, but it is structure as subjective and objective, as both *structured* (and thus identifiable) and *structuring* (and thus dynamic and responsive with individual contexts) (see Bourdieu 1968). The world is somehow a product of this dynamic interplay and is probably best summed up in Bourdieu's own description of his approach as structural constructivism or constructive structuralism (see 1989a). In each case there is a dynamic process of constructivism in terms of the interplay between the objective and the subjective structures. It is therefore an epistemological approach which is bound to the here and now.

Earlier, we traced the antecedents to Bourdieu's approach from the Age of the Enlightenment through to preoccupations with the structural make-up of society, the moral force of institutions, the status of the individual and how all these could be mixed from different philosophical and political perspectives – some emphasizing the health of society, others concerned with religion and spirituality, and still others offering a revolutionary slant. It is clear that writers such as Marx, Durkheim, Lévi-Strauss, Merleau-Ponty and Sartre did indeed influence Bourdieu's thinking, since the academic climate of his formative years was saturated by their ideas. What he eventually distilled from these forebears was a kind of structural phenomenology, or phenomenological structuralism, rooted in an anthropological approach. Structure is indeed the key unifying concept, since it could be used in both an objectivist and a subjectivist mode: the structural relation arising in individuals' sense activities with their surroundings and in the organizing structures of society – both material and ideological. Indeed, for Bourdieu, social phenomena were accountable in terms of the homologies resonant in the logics of practice between these 'levels of reality'. One does not precede the other, but there is a kind of dialectic between the two in a continuously dynamic process of externalization and internalization.

Bourdieu and the French Marginals

We have noted that Bourdieu was not always in agreement with the leading academic figures of his day. Often, he cites other (at the time less well-known) intellectuals who, although he describes them as 'marginals', were central to his thinking. One such figure was Gaston Bachelard (1884–1962). Bachelard worked at the Sorbonne, where Bourdieu could seek him out. He is known as a philosopher of science, but he made a crucial break from previous approaches to this academic area by stressing the importance of the epistemology of science. His main argument was that scientific observation did not take place in an empirical space where contact could be made with reality. Rather, the space one sees is a representation according to one's individual perspective and thus not a real space. It followed that scientific advancement did not occur through a linear line of progress, where there was continuity between past and present scientific theories, but through contradiction and discontinuity. In other words, the progress of ideas often occurred by a radical break from all preceding ways of thinking. For Bachelard, such a break was present in the development of physics from Newtonian theories to Einstein's. For this to occur, a process of objectification takes place, where the meaning of concepts is fundamentally redefined. This redefinition comes about through seeing phenomena relationally rather than as objects possessing essential immutable natures – an echo of the distinction between substantialist and relational thinking we noted above. In fact, thought is always an objectification, which means it is contingent on space and time, the thinker and the space which he occupies.

Bourdieu also cited Georges Canguilhem, who succeeded Bachelard in the chair of philosophy at the Sorbonne. Canguilhem was a major influence on Michel Foucault and, in fact, was on the jury when the latter defended his doctoral thesis in 1961. The major strands of Canguilhem's work again argued that the history of science should not be understood as evolutionism – closure and continuity – but as contradiction and conflict – openness and discontinuity. His search was less for 'truth' than for how truth was constituted on the basis of a particular point of view.

In a sense, writers such as Bachelard and Canguilhem can be seen as preparing the ground for postmodernism. How postmodernism features in alternative approaches to artistic production and understanding the processes of art will be discussed later in this book (chapter 7). What is significant to note at this stage is that the philosophies of Bachelard and Canguilhem implicitly undermine the certainties of modernism born out of the Age of Enlightenment, with its confidence in reason, progress and the ability of man to know and consequently shape his world. From their view, such a knowledge of the world could only ever be contingent on a particular perspective within a certain social space and time. Thus knowledge would be contested and fought over as different versions of reality struggled for ascendance. Such a philosophy was both radical and critical compared to a normative, blindly humanist view of philosophy. Coincidentally, this philosophy chimed with one of the main tenets of Saussurian linguistics mentioned earlier – that language itself was relative to whatever signifier you applied to the signified: an idea which opened the door to radical doubt about our ability to stabilize meaning sufficiently in order to know ultimately what we were all talking about.

Bourdieu's Thinking Tools

Bourdieu's conceptual tools for thinking can be seen as a distillation of disparate strands within this plethora of theoretical ideas. The two most basic are habitus and field. We can understand these as constituting respectively the subjective and objective dimensions of the epistemology referred to above. Both occupied Bourdieu for most of his academic career. His understanding and use of them developed throughout his various works and in the light of applications of them in a wide range of studies of practical contexts. Here, I shall look at each theoretical tool briefly.

Bourdieu used habitus in his very earliest studies. For example, in his analysis of the bachelor farmers in the Béarn he used it to describe aspects of their physical appearance as well as their speech characteristics. More formally he defined it as follows:

> Habitus is both a system of schemata of production of practices and a system of perception and appreciation of practices. (1990b: 131)

Bourdieu admits that habitus is hardly an original concept; it had been used by such diverse writers and philosophers as Aristotle, Hegel, Weber, Aquinas, Durkheim and Mauss. Husserl also used the term *habitualität* to refer to the environmental 'pre-given' in a phenomenological apprehension of life-world experience. For Bourdieu, however, it is more explicitly 'socialized subjectivity'. It therefore attempts to go beyond what might be termed philosophies of consciousness – for example, existentialism and personalism – and to connect with and mediate through objective structures and practices:

> Its operation expresses the social position in which it was elaborated. Consequently, habitus produces practices and representations which are available for classification, which are objectively differentiated; however, they are immediately perceived as such only by those agents who possess the code, the classificatory schemes necessary to understand their social meaning. Habitus thus implied knowing one's place but also a 'sense of the place of others'. (ibid.)

The structural mapping of this social positioning, and the underlining logic which orders it, is accomplished through the second of Bourdieu's major analytical concepts: field. Bourdieu defines fields:

> ...synchronically as structured spaces of positions (or posts) whose properties depend on their position within these spaces and which can be analysed independently of the characteristics of their occupants... a state of the power relations among the agents or institutions. (1993a: 72f.)

Fields are therefore networks of positions objectively held. They are constituted by the logic of the field, which also positions who and what is to be found within it. Clearly, Bourdieu saw field and habitus as mutually constituting; in fact, he spoke of the 'ontological complicity' (1982: 47) between the two, meaning that both are involved in the making of what we take to be existence. On the one side, there is the cognitive construction of reality (habitus) by those whose total actions make up the field; on the other, there is a structured world of sense and meaning, which presents itself to that cognitive construction, and which is already representing the 'immanent logic', indeed necessity, of that field.

In one sense, what Bourdieu is offering is a radical historicization of how we interpret the world, or at least a theory of knowledge similar to that developed by Bachelard and Canguilhem in their history of science. It certainly focuses on social praxis at the interface between the objective world and individual subjectivities, mediated through structure in its dual phenomenological-Marxist sense. In this case, sociology becomes a philosophy of human praxis and all that constitutes it.

Several other theoretical concepts follow from this approach. If, in a sense, everything that constitutes social reality within a designated field has meaning and can be interpreted in terms of the nature of the field itself, there must be a defining logic, a kind of ultimate currency exchange rate which values social products differentially.

For Bourdieu, this valuing occurs in terms of what is held up as the ruling ideal (logically expressed) and legitimated as such. Indeed, the whole *raison d'être* of fields is to constitute such a logic and consecrate it so that everything else in it can be valued in its terms. It is worth emphasizing the point: Bourdieu is not arguing that various areas of social life exhibit shared values and characteristics – this would be an anthropological truism; rather he is claiming that a whole epistemology is involved in the way social reality is constructed. Such construction occurs as a result of the interplay between habitus and field. Although, in one sense, the logic involved in particular manifestations of these is quite arbitrary (and to an extent it is), there is a logic no less. For Bourdieu, the presence of a specific logic of practice behind a field was a universal fact. One of the aims of sociology is consequently to identify that logic: the principle of differentiation operating within a particular field in its relationship to other fields. For Bourdieu, because what occurs in a field is essentially arbitrary, it needs to be understood symbolically: it does not have value in itself, but accrues value because it is attributed meaning according to the logic of the field.

Bourdieu uses the term 'symbolic capital' to designate such valuing of the constituents of the field. Of course, 'capital' is a term resonant with Marxist undertones, referring as it does to the basic features of the capitalist economy, namely, the possession of materials and human resources. Bourdieu does not explicitly connect with the Marxist notion of capital. Rather, for him, capital is the medium through which the processes of the field operate. A conceptual term such as capital has a lot of theoretical work to do. In effect, it has to express everything that passes for social reality within fields. For Bourdieu, there are three basic forms of capital: cultural, social and economic (1990c/1987: 127). Cultural capital refers to the possession of symbolically valued cultural accoutrements and attitudes. These may be material in nature – books, painting, clothes – or symbolically prestigious – for example, a 'good' accent, educational qualifications, refined manners. In this way, capital can be expressed materially, corporally or gesturally, but in each case it is symbolic because it attracts acknowledgement of value from those sharing positions within the given field. Economic capital is perhaps the most material form of capital; it refers to financial wealth or possessions, such as income, land and buildings. In a way, it is a capital which speaks for itself – it does not have to be symbolic. Finally, social capital refers to the network of personal relations that an individual builds up. Such networks are symbolic – you are valued by who you know – but these networks do 'buy' advantage in an way analogous to money capital – it is not what you know, it is who you know. Social capital acts to amplify the efficiency of both economic and cultural capital.

For Bourdieu, the way that capital works is through processes of acknowledgement and recognition. Capital can only have value, especially in its most symbolic form, if it is recognized as such. The likelihood of this occurring is ensured by the social reproduction of the symbolic manifestations of the logic of particular fields, as described above; in other words, because the generating logic of any individual habitus is saturated by a consequent symbolic valuing, it is unlikely that the logic and value will not be recognized in others. Bourdieu draws attention to both the 'volume' and 'configuration' of capital available in a field at any one time.

A characteristic of capital is that it is, by definition, a scarce commodity; if it were available to all, like air, it would lose one of its main functions – to act as an arbitrator of social differentiation. Possessing capital is only useful because some possess more than others. Therefore, although everyone implicitly recognizes the value of capital, not everyone possesses it. Yet Bourdieu is not arguing that fields and capital operate through an open and explicit struggle for what is of value and available in the field. Rather, he argues that much of this process goes on in a misrecognized form: although this competitive struggle is indeed what is occurring, most of those involved are not consciously aware of the fact – indeed many would deny it as such. For Bourdieu, such a denial, a kind of sociological bad faith, is an essential constituent of the mechanisms of legitimation which lead to the preservation of the field and its operations.

Moreover, since capital exists in this multivariant form, different individuals hold distinct configurations of its three forms; indeed, whole sections or groups of people may be identified in terms of the separate configurations (patterns of possession) of capital they hold. But these patternings are not simply a measure of individual effort and activity, which by chance it has been possible for one individual to accrue, but are determined primarily by their position in the field they already occupy. Capital is symptomatic of field positioning according to a hierarchy logically defined by the field. In this way, it is ultimately power relations which exist. Of course, to speak of the constituents of capital, field positions, patternings and symbolic phenomena is again to return to the notion of structure at the heart of Bourdieu's theory of practice. In all these aspects – field and habitus, their defining logic, configurations of capital, and processes of recognition and misrecognition – Bourdieu is seeking to construct a dynamic epistemology based around objective structures and their realization through individuals' practical and sense activities. Therefore, in theory at least, Bourdieu sees structural homologies everywhere. Vastly different social phenomena are at base generated from and characterized by the same defining structural logic of differentiation existent in the field, including its links with other fields.

It is probably worth pausing for breath here! Setting out Bourdieu theory in this way can lead to a sense of abstract obtuseness. It seems as if what we have is a highly conceptualized grand theory. Two things warrant emphasis. First, Bourdieu developed this theory over many years – it did not appear *ex nihilo*. He was constantly returning to concepts and reworking them. It is arguable that the notion of habitus receded somewhat in his thinking towards the end of his career, and was overtaken by field – or at least 'field theory' – as his main analytic tool. Second, Bourdieu argued on several occasions that he did not theorize for its own sake; rather he did so in order to understand practical situations. This pragmatism was most certainly the case for his encounters with the farmers in the Béarn. Here, there is the image of Bourdieu as the observer noticing a particular social phenomenon and then setting out to understand it. The same intent can be found in his early work in Algeria. He claims that despite the enormous impact the events in Algeria had on the French nation, very few Frenchmen understood it as a phenomenon. Similarly, his first major empirical study, after taking up directorship of the Centre de Sociologie Européenne, was on education; again, he claims to have sought a practical understanding of the student population and what they were about.

Briefly, Bourdieu had imbibed the main intellectual currents of his day. He reacted against both existentialism and structuralism. He was suspicious of personalism and Marxism, while acknowledging the validity of some of their aspirations. He located himself in a history of science which emphasized the need to see any investigation as involving both an individual perspective and a social context. And he sought to link all these strands together in a single epistemological vision, which had structure at its heart as the medium for the dialectical relations between individuals and the material/ideational conditions that surrounded them.

Bourdieu's Biography: The 1960s and Beyond

The 1960s were auspicious times. Post-war euphoria gave way to the pressing need to reconstruct whole nations and, in so doing, make judgements about the sort of society that was needed. Education was seen as a prime motor in this process of social transformation. Student numbers in France expanded enormously as the nation sought to train a workforce for the twentieth century. In postcolonial countries like Algeria, education was again seen as a key factor in redefining a national character, liberated from the colonialists, as well as producing the necessary skills for a modern economy. In one sense, Bourdieu himself was swept along in this dynamism. Higher student numbers in France led to expanding opportunities for teaching and research.

Bourdieu took over the directorship of the Centre de Sociologie Européenne in 1964, and thereafter it provided him with an important institutional base for his work. The theory we write of above was developed through his empirical work on education, photography and museums, undertaken in the 1960s. In 1968, France experienced enormous, near-revolutionary upheaval when the country was gripped by national worker and student strikes. It is important here to recall the spirit of these times. In a sense, Sartrean existentialism had finally come of age as part of the beat generation, who, with the vitality of youth, were ready to turn their backs on what were considered outmoded ways, not only of doing things but even of 'being'. These sentiments chimed with grievances about working practices, salaries and the impositional powers of the government in France. In a sense, France had been all too successful in putting in place the mechanisms to drive its reconstruction and modernization.

Bourdieu maintained an ambiguous relationship to the events of 1968, sympathizing with its spirit, while fearing for its outcomes and being suspicious of the motives of those leading it. But these were significant years for Bourdieu, both at the Centre de Sociologie Européenne and at the ENS, where he gave a series of influential seminars, through which he built a reputation for originality and innovation. His main theoretical statement – *An Outline of a Theory of Practice* – was published in 1972 in French and appeared in English in 1977. Here he set out in detail the epistemology we have outlined above. However, by then he had already collected almost all the data that would keep him occupied for the remainder of his academic life: Algeria (*Le Sens pratique* 1990b/1980), culture (*La Distinction* 1984/1979), higher education (*Homo Academicus* 1988/1984) and *La Noblesse d'état* (1996b/1989). *La Distinction* further extended his work on culture, museums and photography published in the 1960s: *L'Amour de l'art* (1991d/1969/1966), *Un Art moyen* (1990a/1965). He also published extensively on education itself: *Les Etudiants et leurs études* (1964b), *Les Héritiers* (1979/1964) and *La Reproduction* (1977a/1970).

In these works, Bourdieu set about explaining the social dynamics of these areas of French life in terms of his epistemology of practice. His analyses are therefore a kind of personification of his conceptual tools, the value of which he argued was only assessable in terms of the resultant insights they provided. In effect, they give us a sociological anthropology of twentieth-century France. But they are more than that. They also suggest that the same processes he had identified are in fact universal. In other words, although the surface phenomena were different, the underlying generating mechanisms were the same from topic to topic and from country to country. To this extent, these works offer a kind of challenge to us: is this the same elsewhere?

Direct Political Engagement

As the decades rolled on and the twentieth century moved to a close, Bourdieu's intellectual stature grew. After the deaths of major figures such as Sartre, de Beauvoir and Foucault, Bourdieu succeeded them as the leading intellectual in France. For a brief period in the 1980s, when the socialists finally came to power after years in opposition, he became actively involved in shaping education policy. In 1981 he was elected as chair in sociology at the Collège de France, that august institution which provides a home for France's leading intellectuals. In the 1990s, and somewhat against his earlier pronouncements, he became much more actively involved politically, entering public debates on the economy, immigration policy, education and foreign affairs. The detail of this political engagement need not detain us now (see Grenfell 2004). However, it is worth noting that Bourdieu increasingly saw his theoretical approach as applicable to a wide range of social contexts, and these included the personal and private as well as the refined world of academia. *La Misère du monde* was published in 1993 as a kind of sociological state of the nation analysis of French society and culture. In this book we see the consequences of neoliberal economic reform on the lives of everyman, literally, their everyday poverty of experience. It immediately became a best-seller.

In 1996 he took on the media with *Sur la Télévision* (1998b/1996), in which he castigates the communications industry for the way it constructs and presents a version of reality which favours few (basically the company owners and their representatives) at the expense of the many (the public). These direct interventions were followed by publications which included shorter polemical statements – *Contre-feux* (1998a) and *Contre-feux 2* (2001b) – aimed at a more general readership. Bourdieu was active in a number of social pressure groups and movements representing unions, immigrants, students and pupils, journalists and gay rights. In 1995 he stood alongside striking miners, declaring himself in support of those who 'fought against the destruction of a civilisation' (1998a: 24). These activities do need to be understood as acts of resistance to what Bourdieu believed to be the totalizing pressure from central governments, which he saw, in turn, as being controlled increasingly by international financiers and global companies, especially in the telecommunications industries.

However, Bourdieu did not abandon his interest in art and culture. In 1992 he published *Les Règles de l'art*, which was his most comprehensive statement to date on how to understand the working of artistic fields. This book used the French novelist Flaubert as a case example to show how the field he occupied needed to be analysed in order to understand why and how he wrote what he did. Many of the ideas in this book will be considered in detail in the chapters which follow. Every year, Bourdieu gave a ten-week *leçon* at the Collège de France. In 2000, the subject of this series of public seminars was the pre-Impressionist painter, Manet. In these lectures he further exemplified the workings of art fields. We shall see how his approach to art and culture offered a radical critique of aesthetics and the place they hold in the processes of art and culture.

Bourdieu died of cancer in January 2002, just a few months after delivering his retirement speech at the Collège de France (see Weill 2001). He spoke of his work in terms of a personal journey of self-analysis. By this he did not mean a kind of personal introspection of problems, strengths and weaknesses. Rather, he argued that his theoretical approach needed to be understood in terms of apprehending the social forces which acted on him and, eventually, on us all. In this chapter we have looked at the events which surrounded Bourdieu's life and thus shaped his thinking. It is necessary to understand Bourdieu's work in terms of the social forces of the age which produced him. However, we should not overlook the intellectual daring and verve of Bourdieu. Like Sartre and Simone de Beauvoir before him, Bourdieu, as a philosophy student, was preparing to become a *lycée* teacher and then a university professor. However, his experience in Algeria, together with his reflections on his home culture in the Béarn, led to him abandoning his doctoral research into neo-Kantianism to pursue sociological fieldwork. Sociology was a discipline which had very little status at the time, since it was not taught in schools and had low prestige in universities. Similarly, Bourdieu's direction at the Centre de Sociologie Européenne needs to be seen in terms of him setting a path which was intellectually distinct from the official university system embodied in such institutions as the Sorbonne. The whole thrust of his academic career, from the direction of a research seminar series at the Ecole des Hautes Etudes, to his lectures at the Collège de France, and his launching of journals such as *Actes de la Recherche* and *Liber*, was a persistent and coherent enterprise to create an academic space which was not ruled by the traditional university system – and this from a man who had neither a doctorate nor a tenured teaching post.

In a similar way, art and creativity are often seen as the very means for individuals to escape the impositions of society or the groups which surround them. It therefore threatens to be a corrosive project to 'put', as Bourdieu would have it, 'the love of art under the scalpel' (1996a/1992: xvi). The rest of this book shows what constitutes this sociological surgery and what are the outcomes of such an undertaking, asking, finally, why do we do it? However, before doing so, in the next chapter we address the 'problem' of aesthetics and Bourdieu's response to it.

–3–

Aesthetics and the Visual Arts

When anyone stands in front of a painting, or any other visual art work, what do they see? Maybe they are taken by a range of sensual experiences: they like that shape, those colours, or they do not like them – they are offended. Visual art has the power to provoke personal reactions, to involve emotions and feelings. This aspect of art is perhaps the most fundamental, the most naive. It is also the most personal; something is touched which evokes the individual and is unique. Art can also touch some timeless realm; there can be a feeling of transcendence, or a communication with a higher sense of being. Indeed, art can take on an almost religious significance; it can provoke us to spiritual experience as we enter into some sublime realm of hyper-reality which offers a way out of the mundane world of everyday life. However, this is clearly not the only possible response to the visual arts.

When someone stands in front of Leonardo da Vinci's *Mona Lisa*, they react not only to the composition, the colours and the forms of what is before them, but also to the history of this painting. There is an understanding of it as a famous painting with its own provenance and biography. They interpret technique, shape and colour as a sort of iconic deciphering. They 'read' the painting in order to understand what it means, what it is representing or suggesting, what the artist had in mind. On the one hand, they have an affective response; on the other, there is an intellectual one. This perspective on viewing art raises a question about where to locate the sources of such reactions. This question goes to the core of what we commonly term aesthetics, or aesthetics sense, and it is the main focus of this chapter. It considers the tradition of philosophical aesthetics and how issues to be found there link with these considerations of how we apprehend visual culture. The chapter then sets out Bourdieu's own interpretation of aesthetics, and the implications this has for both the consumption and production of art. Finally, it provides a methodological framework which will be used in forthcoming chapters when considering empirical examples of institutional and visual art fields (museums, photography and painting).

Kant and the 'Problem' of Aesthetics

Aesthetics can be defined briefly as a branch of philosophy which addresses questions of beauty and taste. By implication, aesthetics is therefore concerned with art itself in the broadest sense of the term, denoting the process and product of creative endeavour. Aesthetic concerns can be traced back to the Greek origins of contemporary philosophy; both Plato and Aristotle were concerned with art and whether and how it might act as a carrier of 'truth' and 'knowledge'. For Plato, at least, art could not be a vehicle for truth. The modern tradition of aesthetics stems from the seventeenth and eighteenth centuries, when attention was directed towards beauty in art and nature. The founding father of this approach to aesthetics was the German philosopher Immanuel Kant (1724–1804).

In the last chapter, we referred to the Age of Enlightenment as a time when traditional religious and aristocratic structures were challenged and partly, in France at least, overthrown. Kant lived at this time. This period gave us not only the Age of Enlightenment, but also romanticism, and its preoccupations with individual emotional and intellectual experience. Both movements can be understood as essentially humanist, as asserting human rationality and/or human emotions in the face of colossal social change. Behind such movements, we can also find philosophical issues similar to those implied in the opening paragraph of this chapter, namely, the distinction between rational thinking and affective responses. But beyond this dichotomy there is a deeper question about the status of knowledge and, by implication, how we know. Such epistemological issues were central to both the Age of Enlightenment and romanticism. Clearly, we can perceive the objects around us, but that is not the limit of all that we know. Other things seem to be 'god-given', or concern matters of value, belief and tradition. Do we imagine these or are they real? How can we know?

For the Scottish philosopher David Hume (1711–76), an immediate precursor to Kant, the external world cannot be apprehended directly through our sense perceptions, only our beliefs about that world. These 'perceptions of the mind' – impressions and ideas – were merely the products of our own minds, not the things themselves. In the eighteenth century, a spirit of mentalism was thus evidently in the air. For Kant too, the enquiring mind was the means to progress beyond man's hitherto immaturity of thought and action. Like many philosophers, before and since, Kant wanted to provide a foundation for 'objective knowledge'; in other words, that which we can know to be universally true, irrespective of individual subjective interpretation. But there was a paradox in how he formulated his views. In the Middle Ages and earlier, man was indeed the centre of the universe and everything was understood to revolve around him and the earth. The Copernican revolution had displaced man's pivotal position and established that in fact it was man who revolved around the sun. What Kant did, as Hume before him, is to argue that we can only know what human minds can know. This view, however limiting, must also establish objective knowledge, albeit in a way which, in a collective sense, is profoundly and humanly subjective.

The ideas of our mind were the only basis of knowledge. Even scientific discoveries and certainties were essentially ideas. Such idealism formed a link with Plato's 'ideal forms', which exist in a realm beyond materiality. For Kant, this ideal world was based on a distinction between unknowable things (noumena), as 'things-in-themselves', and the knowable world of material things (phenomena), as 'things-as-they-appear' to our senses. He then provided a complete philosophical (ideal) taxonomy of how man apprehends them. In Kantian metaphysics – literally, beyond the physical – there are faculties of the mind (the soul) which do not so much represent objects of perceptions, but animate them through the innate conditions of the human psyche. Such faculties are knowledge, desire, feeling, and man's cognitive faculties – imagination, understanding and reason. In this sense, cognition becomes an active process beyond the dichotomies of subject and object. The process involves imagination – representing through intuition an object that is not itself present – and understanding – classifying and ordering of data presented to it by the imagination. Reason then becomes an attempt to organize and make sense of information in terms of three a priori ideas: the soul, the cosmos and god. These ideas are 'unconditioned', that is, they are unrepresentable both in and to themselves. However, they are actualized in the realization of imagination and understanding. The ideas of reason consequently exist in and through understanding and imagination.

It is possible to see how this philosophical approach acted as a foundation for twentieth-century phenomenology, which was itself a strong influence on Bourdieu (see chapter 2). Phenomenology defined itself as the return to 'things in themselves', and as a product of the cognitive process of the human mind. In effect, what Kant did was to define what could be categorized as 'objective' in relation to the a priori faculties and ideas of the mind. It is in this way that Kant can be seen to be the founding father of all subsequent humanist metaphysics. It is an approach to which Bourdieu took exception. However, before considering Bourdieu's disagreement with Kant, we need to say a little more about how the Kantian approach extended to aesthetics.

The first part of the *Critique of Pure Reason* (1961/1781) has the title 'The Transcendental Aesthetic'. For Kant, aesthetics is not the preserve of art, but actually relates to the Greek work meaning 'sensation' (the opposite being 'anaesthetic' – without sensation). By 'transcendental', he means a priori, or needed for experience. It is sensation which provides the data for the faculty of imagination. For Kant, it is the form which this data takes that is most important. What the data actually is or what it represents is less important. What is necessary to experience objects as such is a priori knowledge; in this case, space and time shapes form. As indicated above, the a priori element in this argument points to what lies beyond sensation, and thus gives rise to experience itself rather than being an element of existence. In other words, space and time are a priori conditions of existence. Kant contrasted such faculties of imagination with understanding. Understanding is a power to form concepts; it is through concepts that understanding 'knows'. Kant gives ten concepts: Substance, Quantity, Quality, Relation, Place, Time, Position, Possession, Action, Passivity. Here, Kant investigates the process and constituents of how judgements of knowledge are therefore made. However, in *The Critique of*

Judgement (1987/1790) he examines the power of judgement itself. It is this book that forms the core of Kant's exploration of aesthetics as we know it.

Kant's objective is to locate a higher form of feeling which can be said, a priori, to determine experiences of pleasure and pain. Such questions of taste cannot be based on concepts, since if they were they would not be able to 'lay claim to other people's assent'. Kant subsequently makes a distinction between what is beautiful and what is agreeable and pleasurable. The latter is associative and comparative, and connected with simple sensual enjoyment. However, in order for judgements of the beautiful to arise, imagination must present data (in time and space) to understanding. This data is not now converted via concepts, because a 'non-cognitive' feeling accompanies the intuition by which the data of imagination is presented to understanding. At this point, we connect with a perception of pleasure or displeasure, which serves to define the non-cognitive feeling itself and replaces concepts. Since there are no concepts to provide form, what is presented is the power to form in itself – a consciousness without anything to be conscious of. In this sense, what arises is a 'disinterestedness', a contemplative judgement as opposed to a cognitive (conceptual or theoretical) judgement.

For Kant, as for Hume before him, the 'problem' with aesthetics can be reduced to this simple question: how can judgements which are essentially subjective, in that they provoke feelings for individuals, also relate to a commonality of assent over value? Kant argued that a judgement can only be considered to be aesthetic when it is disinterested, that is, free from any desires, needs or interest in the actual existence of the objects apprehended which might distort that 'pure' appreciation. At this point, there is nothing to differentiate one person's aesthetic response from another's – it is shared sensibility (*sensus communis*). Some objects, by nature of their form and appearance, encourage a 'free play' between the faculties of imagination and understanding. Understanding is prompted to speculate when faced by the beautiful, giving rise to both pure feeling and the pleasure of thought. Thinking has sensuality which separates understanding from imagination in such a way that understanding no longer dominates imagination. It creates feeling rather than transforming it. In Kant's four 'moments' of his analysis of the beautiful, he sets out the nature of aesthetic pleasure in judgements of taste: namely, that it should be disinterested and give an impression of finality, and that it should demand and comply to a universal assent, which distinguishes it from judgements of mere 'agreeableness'. This appreciation of beauty is tied to a recognition of form and design which is independent of content. In determining beauty, for Kant, much hangs on achieving universal assent, on reaching shared aesthetic agreements. How does this philosophical discussion connect with Bourdieu's sociological approach to aesthetics?

Bourdieu and Aesthetics

As discussed in chapter 2, Bourdieu's interest in art and culture goes back to his earliest empirical work in the 1950s and 1960s. The climate we described in that chapter was one of post-war rebuilding and rejuvenation, both at home and abroad. The spirit of social renewal flourished. Education was seen as a principal motor of such reconstruction. It is therefore probably not surprising that one of his earliest pieces of research was conducted on the student population in France (*Les Héritiers* 1979/1964), in order to 'to find out better what it was to be a student' (see Bourdieu (with Grenfell) 1995b: 22). A central theme to his Algerian studies (1958, 1963, 1964a) was similarly the foundation of a 'rational pedagogy', in order to neutralize the sociocultural effects of colonialism on scholastic achievement. In short, Bourdieu saw that in education lay the key to building the 'emancipated' structures needed in the new world. The degree to which this was possible, and indeed to which Bourdieu concluded it was likely, is another matter. However, we have noted that education also formed part of the central core of the personalist philosophy of the 1930s and 1940s, with its preoccupation with developing the human potential of individuals. This idea animated a number of projects in the post-war situation; for example, the Maisons de la Culture, instigated by the first minister of culture, André Malraux, whose aim it was to bring culture to the people. Such movements as Peuple et Culture also set about organizing a number of adult education courses and workshops in the name of *l'éducation populaire*.

Central to all these projects was culture and the place it held in defining the content of education. If education was important in training the workforce for the modern jobs needed in French and colonial reconstruction, it was also important in the way people developed personally in an intellectual and aesthetic sense. Bourdieu turned his attention to culture at more or less the same time as he was working on education; in other words, the two – education and culture – should almost be regarded as two sides of the same coin. In 1965 Bourdieu published a book on photography (1990a/1965). The reasons for this were simultaneously practical, theoretical and economic. As the young, newly appointed director of the Centre de la Sociologie Européenne, he needed to procure financial backing for research, and for this project the film company Kodak provided some funds. Bourdieu himself was also a keen photographer (he took literally thousands of photos in Algeria – see Bourdieu 2003). However, he was also interested in considering the content of culture. By taking a popular art form, photography, Bourdieu was implicitly setting it against the 'high art' to be found in museums, art galleries and classical music concert halls. No surprise, therefore, to find a second book on culture, *L'Amour de l'art* (1991d/1969/1966) – this time on art museums – published in 1966. Further articles and papers followed. However, the summation of this work, in its first phase at least, came in 1979, with the publication of *La Distinction* (1979), in which Bourdieu set out his most developed thesis yet on the nature (both in terms of product and process) of aesthetics and taste. The subtitle of the book itself reveals the allusions to and intended critique of Kantian aesthetics: *A Social Critique of the Judgement of Taste*. What Bourdieu had to say about museums and photography will be discussed in the individual chapters dedicated to these topics later in the book (chapters 4 and 6). The present chapter will consider why *La Distinction* is so important (it has become a sociological best-seller, entering the canon of required reading for cultural theorists). First, however, we wish to consider the nature of Bourdieu's critique of Kantian aesthetics, as addressed in the last section.

At the beginning of this chapter, we asked what it was to look at a painting or a work of art. We then described the sensual engagement with which one is presented, and contrasted it with a more intellectualist response. We have seen that for Kant, and many philosophers following in his wake, aesthetic appreciation was defined in terms of a separation from immediate sensations and reactions. Indeed, for Kant, the aesthetic response is rather characterized by a degree of 'separateness', the pure gaze of the disinterested in some sublime realm beyond the everyday. In the introduction to *La Distinction*, Bourdieu announced his project as offering a sociological critique of Kantian aesthetics. In effect, his approach is to attack the very 'separation' on which it is founded:

> [to abolish] the opposition, which has been the basis of high aesthetics since Kant, between 'taste of sense' and the 'taste of reflection', and between facile pleasure, pleasure reduced to pleasure of the senses, and pure pleasure, pleasure reduced, which is predisposed to become a symbol of moral excellence and a measure of the capacity for sublimation which defines the truly human man. (1984/1979: 6)

What Bourdieu argued for is a much more socio-historical reading of aesthetics. For him, an aesthetic response presupposes the possibility of a non-aesthetic response, and, necessarily, such responses are by nature socially differential and differentiated – some have it and some do not. In this, aesthetics is returned to the world and the social structure of societies rather than being definable in terms of a necessary philosophical logic. Bourdieu argued that the pure gaze itself implies a break with the ordinary attitude to the world, an ethic, 'or rather, an ethos of elective distance from the necessities of the natural and social world' (Bourdieu 1984/1979: 5). This break is, by definition, a mark of distinction, a claim and legitimation in the name of rarity by a certain faction of society in its assertion of justified dominance. In many ways, the aesthetic disposition is more or less defined in terms of distance from the social world. The aesthete personified is therefore nothing other than an extreme form of bourgeois denial of the social world when this is pushed to its limit. This is why Kant 'strove to distinguish that which pleases from that which gratifies and, more generally, to distinguish disinterestedness, the sole guarantor of the specifically aesthetic in contemplation, from the interest in reason which defines the good' (ibid.).

Bourdieu's own position argues for a fundamental dichotomy in aesthetic response between the bourgeois and the working class. It is important to understand at this point that Bourdieu was not arguing that social class structure can be expressed simply in terms of a bipolar dichotomy, or even a slightly more differentiated form of the split, which included factions of both these social groups, together with the aristocratic and underclasses. He understood that class was in fact a multifaceted and dynamically evolving structure. Nevertheless, he did argue that much of the complexity inherent in such a structure – which, by being obscured, allowed it to operate – was conducted in terms of a common value currency which was indeed defined in terms of opposing social classificatory forms. In this case, what is at stake is the opposition between the refined, or tasteful, and the vulgar. There is a kind of double play, where not only is rarefied taste opposed to everyday taste (for example, in the way that luxury foods are the prerogative of those who presumably can afford them, in contrast to everyday eating), but those common everyday objects and actions of taste are also appropriated and aestheticized. The world is then turned upside down, so to speak. It is not enough for the bourgeois aesthete to possess what others cannot. They also take possession of common objects and actions as a sign of their complete mastery over both the vulgar and the refined, therefore twice legitimating their social elevation.

At base, what we have here is a phenomenology of representation. The popular aesthetic (of the working class) is based on an aesthetic 'in itself' rather than 'for itself'. It allows for a naive stance; the passions, feeling and emotions that ordinary people invest in life. Pure taste, on the other hand, is the opposite: it suspends naive involvement because it provides no place for the necessities of life themselves. Bourdieu sums up: 'Intellectuals could be said to believe in the representation – literature, theatre, painting – more than the things represented, whereas the people chiefly expect representations and the conventions which govern them to allow them to believe "naively" in the things represented' (1984/1979). Bourdieu further argued that when it comes to art, the popular aesthetic sees it as an extension of life. Nothing should get in the way of a personal identification with it and finding unity in the emotions demanded and given. Form is here subordinated to function; the purpose art has is in affirming the naive, sensual view, including morality and agreeableness. In contrast, the detachment and disinterestedness of the pure aesthetic gaze asserts, as Kant does, form over function, and with it, an often moral ambiguity where art can only be taken for art's sake.

Bourdieu began his 1987 paper – 'The Historical Genesis of a Pure Aesthetic' (Bourdieu 1993b: 254–66) – by raising the issue of what distinguishes works of art from everyday things. He had already argued in *La Distinction* that the popular aesthetic needed to reduce the 'things of art to the things of life', allowing, as argued above, for no distance between form and function. He concluded that for something to be considered a 'work of art', it needs to have a place in the art world (for example, museum, gallery, public space, publication, performance). He stated that this is a common definition of 'art'. However, he then asked what distinguishes a philosophical discourse from an ordinary one? Only in this issue can we understand the underlying valuing of the two spheres. He goes on to suggest that if the foundation of the aesthetic disposition and of a work of art is to be found in the history of an artistic institution, then the foundation of the philosophical disposition should be found in the history of the philosophical institution. This argument leads to a critique of the very philosophical discourse which produced Kant and his aesthetic vision.

For Bourdieu, philosophers' responses to aesthetics have almost uniformly been to define a 'transhistoric' essence. Essentially, the 'pure thinker' establishes a singular relation with the art by taking as the subject of reflection their own experience, without 'focusing on the historicity of that reflection and the historicity of the object to which it is applied' (Bourdieu 1993b: 255). The resultant sense of singularity (the feeling of uniqueness this gives makes it very attractive) is the transhistorical norm of aesthetic appreciation. It is a form of phenomenological narcissism. However, Bourdieu argues that this understanding of aesthetics is itself an institution, 'an historical invention', which can only be understood by historical analysis. This approach connects with the phenomenological approach discussed in chapter 2. Indeed, it is a kind of 'historical phenomenology', in which the *noema* (the basis of knowledge) against which individual acts of perception – *noesis* – need to be understood is the result of history; in other words, the historical development of the field of classical philosophy. In a similar manner, Kant's a priori definition is in effect history itself. Bourdieu subsequently argues that the pure gaze needs to be understood historically – in terms of the historical development of the art field – and is therefore inseparable from 'the emergence of an autonomous artistic field capable of imposing its own ends against external demands' (p. 256).

The inherent detachment implied by Kant's 'disinterestedness' and the consequent reasoning concerning a priori transcendent categories of aesthetic experience needed to be understood for Bourdieu as a by-product of structural changes in society and the emergence of a 'free' bourgeois class, liberated from the feudal caste systems. What follows from this historical understanding of aesthetics is to see that the pure gaze is a historical product, produced as a result of specific conditions of society and the art world at a particular point in time – in the case of Kant, the eighteenth century. Simultaneously, by continuing to claim aesthetics as a universal, philosophers are in effect enshrining it as a universal constituted by particular social practices and conditions of privilege which are occulted. The exceptional, in terms of life experience, becomes universalized by ignoring the socio-historic conditions from which it is produced. In effect, what philosophers are doing by continuing to focus on transhistoric essence is perpetuating the misrecognition of power and privilege implied, indeed embedded, in this definition of aesthetics. Bourdieu concludes that the institution represented by such a philosophical amnesia 'enjoys a twofold existence, in things and in minds':

> In things, it exists in the form of an artistic field, a relatively autonomous social universe which is the product of a slow process of constitution. In minds, it exists in the form of dispositions which were invented by the same movement through which the field, to which they immediately adjusted themselves, was invented. When things and minds (or consciousness) are immediately in accord – in other words, when the eye is

> the product of the field to which it is related – then the field, with all the products that it offers, appears to the eye as immediately endowed with meaning and worth. (Bourdieu 1993b: 257)

There is, then, a kind of ontological complicity between the way people think and the state of the social field.

Consuming Art

In *La Distinction*, Bourdieu brings his theory of practice to bear on aesthetic practice. True to the approach outlined in chapter 2, his method is to apply the terms habitus, field and capital in order to illuminate empirical data. For example, he has (1984/1979: 17) data on individual preferences for three musical works: the 'Well-tempered Clavier' (Bach), 'Rhapsody in Blue' (Gershwin) and the 'Blue Danube' (Strauss). These preferences are set against measures between some sixteen social 'classes', from manual workers through to higher professionals and education lecturers (categories which also include technicians, doctors, public sector workers, shopkeepers, and so on). He demonstrates oppositions which show that Bach is least preferred by manual workers. Preference for Bach increases as one 'ascends' the social class structure. The opposite is true for Strauss and the 'Blue Danube'. Bourdieu argues that taste carries with it social labelling; indeed, taste is a means of social distinction, not simply a naive preference. In this case, the 'Blue Danube' has become so popular, it cannot mark distinction and is therefore abandoned by middle and upper classes, who instead turn to the Bach, a less-known piece which therefore has sufficient rarity value to confer 'superior' taste. The case of the Gershwin piece is less clear-cut, since there is an even distribution across classes. Behind aesthetic judgement, therefore, there is what Bourdieu terms 'an aristocracy of culture'. This is not a separate realm removed from everyday life, but is part and parcel of an entire social condition. As we have stated previously, aesthetic response is based on developing an apparent level of disinterestedness, a pure gaze removed from the economic necessities of life. To possess it, and, perhaps more importantly, to demonstrate that one possesses it, is to be able to define oneself in terms of a certain distance from the practical exigencies of life. The urgency, real or not, to occupy a place of ease in the social space, itself betrays an underlying impulse to rise above the struggling masses and assert one's autonomy and uniqueness, which is the autologous condition of legitimizing privilege. However, such positioning is not merely a gesture. Rather, aesthetic practice – attendance at museums, theatres, art galleries, concerts, reading, listening to music, lectures, and so on – is bound up with a whole universe of material objects – furniture, clothes, painting, books – making up a certain 'cultural capital', which has symbolic value in the way it 'buys' social distinction. Capital, it will be recalled, only has value initially because it is scarce, and because it is recognized by others (whether they possess it or not). Indeed, part of the power of cultural capital to perform this symbolically defining function is that it is relative and multifaceted. In other words, almost everyone possesses a certain amount of it. Also, because it covers such a wide range of objects and practice, its social defining role is misrecognized, even though the underlying aesthetic logic of practice is consistent.

> The dialectics of conditions and habitus is the basis of an alchemy which transforms the distribution of capital, the balance-sheet of a power relation, into a system of perceived differences, distinctive properties, that is, a distribution of symbolic capital, whose objective truth is misrecognised. (Bourdieu 1984/1979: 172)

As we saw in chapter 2, Bourdieu also demonstrates that such configurations of capital change over time and, indeed, conform to particular changes in the social structure. Therefore, for example, in the Middle Ages, painting performed a different function to that of today. At one time, it was little more than a social function of decoration, a demonstration of wealth and privilege, and a celebration of the aristocracy and, most particularly, religion. Now it has a much more exclusive role in defining a particular, often critical, relationship to society, a stance which itself is part of the modern aesthetic. Moreover, the form and content of cultural capital changes over time. So, at a time when money wealth dominated society, it was sufficient to display the trappings of economic capital. However, Bourdieu argues that, increasingly in the contemporary world, a new, educated middle class has arisen, relatively poor financially, but high in academic capital. In this case, one form of capital is contested by another as a base currency in legitimating privilege. The uneducated 'rich' will be disdainful of everything 'scholastic', condemning by implication what they do not possess – formal education – while the educated 'poor' assert their right to privilege in terms of personal effort in achieving academic status, rather than access to economic means.

The main message of *La Distinction* is that this aesthetic extends to all aspects of life: what we eat, how we talk, our opinions, what we wear, how we use our knife and fork, how we blow our nose. In short, a certain habitus implies a certain lifestyle. And habitus is a kind of incarnation of social history, actualized at a certain point in time, and within the field in which it finds itself, realized as a particular instance within a specific field.

> As structured products (*opus operatum*) which a structuring structure (*modus operandi*) produces through retranslations according to the specific logic of the different fields, all practices and products of a given agent are objectively harmonized among themselves, without any deliberate pursuit of coherence, and objectively orchestrated, without any conscious concentration, with those of all members of the same class. The habitus continuously generates practical metaphors, that is to say, transfers…or, more precisely, systematic transpositions required by the particular conditions in which the habitus is 'put into practice'. (Bourdieu 1984/1979: 173)

In other words, the content of habitus is formed in the processes of socialization: not simply as specific points of knowledge and practice (declarative and procedural), but as generating structures which, both mentally and physically, generate specific responses in the light of what is presented in a particular field at a particular time; and the consequent (for practice) homologies which are or are not set up there. In terms of aesthetics, this process means that judgements of taste, as well as the strong and weak versions of cultural capital, are manifest in everything we do, and are therefore observable and explainable in terms of a particular state of the field, albeit in microcosmic contexts. Bourdieu gives the formula: (<Habitus> <capital>) + field = practice. This equation shows how habitus and capital within fields constitute practice. Consumption of art is therefore not simply a naive or discrete event, but an actualization of an entire aesthetic dynamic: 'every appropriation of a work of art which is the embodiment of a relation of distinction is itself a social relation and, contrary to the illusion of cultural communism, is a relation of distinction' (p. 227). There is a struggle for such distinction, played out in terms of capital definition and configuration, both between and within fields in the dynamic of development as they change and, as various fields – or those within them – ascend or descend in relation to each other. The endless changes in fashion are perhaps the most overt form of this struggle, the sense of logic which is obscured by the fact that it often converges around social groups who are themselves evolving at such a pace that the cultural content of their practices is outstripped by the necessity to move on to new practices. Bourdieu uses the term 'elective affinities' to designate the empathetic connections which are established, both consciously and unconsciously, between individuals (habitus) and the contexts (fields) in which they find themselves. The degree to which this occurs depends on the degree to which they match. They are therefore structurally, and generatively, homologous. These sites are contested, however, and there is a symbolic struggle for what is valued and therefore confers and exerts power in defining social distinction. This struggle, and the resultant winners and losers, should not obscure the fact that all those involved, and that which is involved, only exist 'in relation' to each other:

> The opposition between the 'authentic' and the 'imitation', 'true culture and popularization', which maintains the game by maintaining belief in the absolute value of the stake, conceals a collusion that is no less indispensable to the production and reproduction of the illusion, the fundamental recognition of the cultural game and its stakes. Distinction and pretension, high culture and middle-brow culture – like, elsewhere, high fashion and fashion, haute coiffure and coiffure, and so on – only exist through each other, and it is the relation, or rather, the objective collaboration of their respective production apparatuses and clients which produces the value of culture and the need to possess it. (p. 250)

Thus, a Kantian view of an idealized pure gaze becomes an effective tool for the privileged to hide their struggle for cultural dominance.

Making Art

For Bourdieu, art is akin to religion; it is, for believers, a 'collective act of magic' (see Bourdieu 2001d: 52), an illusion (*illusio*). However, if society needs art to form part of its necessity of distinction in social practice, the artistic field itself is ready and willing to create the aesthetic dispositions required for the functioning of this need. In other words, artists themselves have an interest in the function of the art field. Producers and consumers exist in symbiotic relation to each other; they need each other. There is, then, both a generative empathy and a mutually constituting relationship between artists and their clientele. Art, almost by definition, has to have an audience – an audience is where the aesthetic experience occurs.

To take the arguments sketched out above, therefore, Kantian aesthetics did not occur at an arbitrary point in time, but rather when socio-structural shifts (in a phenomenological sense) were altering the boundaries of what was and was not 'thinkable'. The notion of the 'pure gaze' was, for Bourdieu, true in as far as it goes, but only as a phenomenology of the aesthetic experience of someone who is already distant from social and economic necessity – the privileged. This development implied a certain autonomy. What Bourdieu saw in the changes of the art field during the nineteenth century was a social structural shift which created a new space for art, one which possessed a certain autonomy with regard to previous art–audience relations. Bourdieu discusses Flaubert and Manet in particular:

> Flaubert in the domain of writing and Manet in painting are probably the first to have attempted to impose, at the cost of extraordinary subjective and objective difficulties, the conscious and radical affirmation of the power of the creative gaze, capable of being applied not only (through simple inversion) to base and vulgar objects...but also to insignificant objects before which the 'creator' is able to assert his quasi-divine power of transmutation... [This formula] lays down the autonomy of form in relation to subject matter, simultaneously assigning its fundamental norm to cultured perception. (1993b: 265)

What Bourdieu is describing here is the separation of form and function which is a product of the autonomizing of the field of artistic production. It is in that separation that 'art-for-art's-sake', a field position analogous to the artistic process of the pure gaze, is born. There is, then, a mutually constituting relationship between the pure gaze of the privileged consumer and the independent creative gaze of the producer. Both implicitly assert an independence and therefore uniqueness. In the eighteenth and nineteenth centuries, the changes in social structures led to the growth of a new bourgeois class. Art, up to that point, had performed a social function in positioning those who consumed it, and hence those who produced it, with regard to particular social, political and moral values of traditional elites – aristocratic and religious. The new bourgeois almost 'invented' a new morality, which set it apart from the past. In the course of these developments, artists struggled to find a means of expression which gave them independence from the aesthetics of those they had served previously:

> Like pure painting which...is meant to be beheld in itself and for itself as a painting – as a play of forms, values and colours – and not a discourse, in other words, independently from all references to transcendent meanings, the pure gaze...is a result of a process of purification, a true analysis of essence carried out by history, in the course of successive revolutions which, as in the religious field, always lead to a new avant-garde to challenge orthodoxy – in the name of a return to the rigour of beginnings – with a purer definition of the genre. (p. 264)

The history of art here is viewed as a cumulative process of purification; in other words, the creative gaze analogous to the pure gaze is in effect a mark of distinction in which artists return to themselves the techniques, methods and subjects as an expression of their exclusivity and ownership over what they produce. A focus on form and the appropriation of particular subjects underlie this sense of autonomy which artists claim over their means of production, which must be structurally representative and analogous to the audience they were eventually to attract. The fact is, however, that this stance can only be understood as a position taking, a *prise de distance* from everything that has gone before. In other words, even the most radical avant-garde act of subversion is expressed in terms of opposition to something in particular within the established art field, and therefore carries with it its own seeds of conservatism. To enter the art world as a producer is therefore to enter an entire historical structure. However, Bourdieu argues that there is a paradox here. As what happens in the art field occurs more and more linked to its own specific history, it gets harder to analyse it in terms of the state of society. Modern art, for example, is only comprehensible in terms of the state of the art world itself. In fact, Bourdieu argues, deciphering art becomes increasingly a history of forms, so much so that the social history of the struggle for forms which underlies acts of decoding art is eclipsed.

In effect, what Bourdieu is arguing is that many art critics discuss the formal properties of painting in an 'ahistorical' manner in order to establish 'the exclusive validity of an internal reading' – in other words, reading and deciphering the development of artistic forms in a manner which occults the social conditions which produced them. However, he adds that this approach is a position which is itself a product of its own social conditions (position): 'what is forgotten...is the historical process through which the social conditions of freedom from "external determinations" get established; that is the process of establishing the relatively autonomous field of production and with it the realm of pure aesthetics or pure thought whose existence it makes possible' (1993b: 266).

The Field of Artistic Production

What Bourdieu is aiming to do is to define an approach which will be applicable to both artistic consumption and production. However, this also includes all elements within the artistic field and the relationship between the two. So any analysis of a work of art or an individual artist would include not simply their biography, but all agents involved – critics, collectors, curators – and the social space they occupy, both material and otherwise. Moreover, the logic of a field is hardly uncontested; rather there is a constant struggle for legitimation, power and dominance. For Bourdieu, this is why the very concepts and categories used (and here, the allusion to Kant must be deliberate) to classify art are indeterminate. His theory of knowledge sees a close match between social structures and forms of thinking; hence, he claims that we think as a condition of the way we are organized. With the caveat, again, that Bourdieu, of course, accepts that the class morphology and taxonomy of society and individual societies are dynamic and complex, his argument is that much that is identifiable in terms of our schemes of thought is also reducible to that basic division between the working class and the bourgeoisie:

> All agents in a given social formation share a set of basic perceptual schemes, which receive the beginnings of objectification in pairs of antagonistic adjectives commonly used to classify and qualify persons or objects in the most varied areas of practice. The network of oppositions between high (sublime, elevated, pure) and low (vulgar, low, modest), and spiritual and material, fine (refined, elegant) and coarse (heavy, fat, crude, brutal), light (subtle, lively, sharp, adroit) and heavy (slow, thick, blunt, laborious, clumsy), free and forced, broad and narrow, or, in another dimension, between unique (rare, different, distinguished, exclusive, exceptional, singular, novel) and common (ordinary, banal, commonplace, trivial, routine), brilliant (intelligent) and dull (obscure, grey, mediocre), is the matrix of all the commonplaces which find such ready acceptance because behind them lies the whole social order. (1984/1979: 468)

In fact, almost any of these words, or adjectival pairs, could be used in discussion about art. But Bourdieu makes the point that the fact that they are inscribed in the very language gives them a lassitude, that they can be used in and out of specialist and common discourse and therefore have a flexibility and vagueness which make communication 'ineffective'. This range of definition and usage allows the words to be appropriated at specific points in time to mean different things. For example, Bourdieu writes (1993c: 305) that a word such as 'provincial' can be the site of contestation. It can be used as a pejorative term – marginal – that is, as not centrist; or, avant-garde, to substantiate a claim to innovation. One thinks of the British abstract expressionists in the 1950s, who were based in St Ives, Cornwall, but used this position to claim that the 'centre' of the art world was now to be found there (a visit by the famous American painter, Mark Rothko, was evidence indeed of this consecration). Categories of thinking and the words used to talk about art are therefore bound to a particular socio-historical context, and marked by 'the social positions of the users who exercise the constitutive dispositions of their *habitus* in the aesthetic choices these categories make possible' (p. 262). Again, the allusion to Kant's categories can hardly be accidental, since it is the 'transcendence' of the terms, their lack of connection to the existing social world, which provides the 'fuzzy boundaries' needed for their redefinition. Bourdieu quotes the Greek word *kathegoresthai*, meaning 'to accuse publicly'. Such categories can become, for those who use them, veritable 'weapons and stakes' in the battle for power over defining the terms of the discourse on art. In actual fact, such overt categories are never contested and redefined anew; rather, they are used and reused in a process through which their social origins of production are also forgotten. They pass into the legitimate language of the field – the very way we talk and think about art (indeed, the very limits of the way we can talk and think). In this sense, Bourdieu rejects Kant, for establishing such 'categorems' as unconditional, giving them 'an air of eternity'. We might follow the logic of the argument and see Kantian a priori concepts and categories as the perfect theory to carry this claim to aesthetics, at once being an expression of the pure gaze, all the while passing over in silence the social conditions implied by their production and use.

The Science of the History of Art

We began by evoking the sense of an aesthetic gaze in front of a painting and asking what it was to experience art in this way. It is an image which haunts this book, and to which we shall return again and again. Clearly, from what we have seen so far, the charismatic property of art, the sense of the ineffable *au-delà*, is part of a form of aesthetic appreciation which Bourdieu seeks to question; not, he argues, because it should or might not exist, but because it implies a phenomenon that only exists in the imagination and beyond a sociocultural understanding of the same experience. What this approach implies for museums, photography and painting, we examine in the next part of the book, before returning to these questions of aesthetics and alternative aesthetics in the final chapter of our account of Bourdieu's approach to art. What, then, is Bourdieu offering as an alternative to Kant?

Aesthetics and Society

On various occasions, Bourdieu writes of the necessity of founding 'a science of the history of art'. He recognizes that there is indeed a 'history of art', but he clearly wishes to go beyond what normally passes in its name. The word *science* itself has a different connotation in French to that in English. It should not be equated with notions derived exclusively from the physical sciences relating to a theoretical predictive discourse of cause and effect. Rather, it must be understood as 'knowledge' and 'understanding'. If we can generalize with Bourdieu, we might say that the history of art has conventionally been concerned with the products of the artist and with their technique. In this world, actual social conditions are obscured. Rather, discussion of the art takes place in an atemporal realm, highlighting the particular characteristic subjects, themes and style of the artist concerned, as if out of time. Here, it is as if art proceeds in an evolutionary manner across history.

A modernist narrative would see art in terms of movement towards refined expression and technique, the uncovering of the muse, and the social function of art. Of course, Bourdieu was not the first, nor indeed the only one, to offer a more 'socially critical' account of art, in particular in response to the arrival of the modern world with its impact on developing mass communications and popular aesthetics. Although Bourdieu would eschew the Marxist tag, *La Distinction* needs to be read as part of a radical critical tradition of art and aesthetics which would include such writers as Meyer Schapiro, Frederik Antal, Theodor Adorno, Clement Greenberg, Arnold Hauser, Walter Benjamin and T J Clark. A classic Marxist argument would be that art can only reflect social conditions, themselves a reflection of the economy, for example, Arnold Hauser's (1892–1978) discussion of art which was published as *The Social History of Art* in 1951. His main thesis was that art should not be seen as a semi-independent entity, but as an integral part of life, as a way of coping with events and personal experiences. Culture is therefore a form of protection and therapy. For Hauser, art and social conditions were intimately linked. He takes the examples of Rubens and Rembrandt to distinguish between a courtly aristocratic society and the art it produced, and a more bourgeois, commercial one. These differences can be seen in the different styles, one flamboyant, the other sober. If different societies produce different arts, it is justified to have a 'sociology of art', which examines the social background to aesthetic trends. However, ideas derived from Marxism have also been applied in a broader way. For example, Clement Greenberg argued that art could indeed offer an autonomous realm with independent values. Furthermore, his social analysis of artistic movements saw leading painters of the seventeenth and eighteenth centuries as attached to literature rather than the painted objects themselves. Unable to 'liberate' themselves from literary subjects, he argued, by the mid-nineteenth century they instead revolted against modern bourgeois society. In effect, this led to a new stress on form – for example, in the work of Manet and the Impressionists – as a way of escaping from the ideas which had dominated their work up to that point (Greenberg 1940).

Later, Benjamin argued that the modern capacity to reproduce works of art for a mass market through photographic techniques had radically altered what we should understand by the nature of art. In effect, its 'aura' of uniqueness and inaccessibility was replaced by a form of mass consumerism (Benjamin 1969). Yet the modern mass art form – for example, cinema – could provide an 'art' for the new age as a way of raising consciousness, and even offering a potential liberating effect on individuals. Fisher (2001) extends this work, arguing similarly that modernist 'low' art in effect challenges traditional forms of 'high' art. The fuzzy boundary between the two means that in a postmodern age, even mass art, which is explicitly 'un-scarce', can perform a function akin to the traditional philosophical aesthetic.

The socio-historical critic T J Clark (1984) argued against Greenberg's view of the independence of art and for the need to go beyond a treatment of artistic movements in terms of technique alone, for example, in the case of Impressionism and pre-Impressionism. Clark's account is of the way these painters partly celebrated and partly critiqued the society that surrounded them. Clark is part of this largely neo-Marxist account of art which expresses itself in terms of new class structures and forms represented in art work and the new techniques and forms used in it. Clark does suggest that socio-conditions themselves should be seen as the prime generator of a certain artistic way of seeing the world. In sum, his approach seeks to see 'the encounter of painting with a certain myth of modernity, and the ways – the moments – in which that encounter put the myth on trial' (p. xxiv). That myth of modernity, as viewed by Clark, has itself been critiqued by feminist writers such as Griselda Pollock (see 1988), among others. Writing very much in a postmodernist mode, Pollock argues that women artists have been excluded from art history. Reintroducing them itself provides a feminist critique. However, simply reinstating women artists is not enough for writers from this perspective, who argue that the very categories of thought used in discussing art are 'androcentric': derived from and representing a masculine point of view. Thus, Pollock (p. 53) acknowledges that Clark 'nods in the direction of feminism' in his discussion of such paintings as Manet's *A Bar at the Folies-Bergères* (1881–82), by drawing attention to the implication that the viewer/consumer is masculine, with masculine interests. However, she argues that the way in which Clark does this rather compounds the problem by adopting a stance which sees this position as being 'normal'. For Pollock, therefore, a full historical investigation and theoretical analysis of the constitution and effects of such androcentricity is passed over, almost allowed to remain transparent, in investigating the history of Manet's painting. This argument is gender-based and challenges the narratives most commonly offered, even in Clark's class-based terms of the modernist world, both *of* and *in* the painting.

Other more forthright postmodernist critiques have been made – for example, Krauss (1997). In her line of argument, notions of singularity and originality are, of course, modernist myths to be expunged from any discussion of art. Even terms such as 'avant-garde' are suspect, since they presuppose progression. Eventually, 'class' itself is sucked into the vacuum of postmodernist deconstruction, as another narrative, another way of fictionalizing the world – and, as such, a modernist illusion. Bourdieu's own account overlaps with these approaches and distinguishes itself from them, while addressing the same concerns. However, in books such as *La Distinction* and *L'Amour de l'art* in particular, Bourdieu sought to locate his own critique within the artistic field itself, and derives his notions of social class directly from patterns of artistic practice emerging from extensive analyses of empirical data.

Bourdieu had argued that aesthetics, and the disinterestedness that it implied, had become a specific 'interest' of artists and intellectuals in the contemporary world. As is often the case for Bourdieu, at base he has a particular visual image in mind and a particular metaphor on which he hangs his analysis, in this case, the analogy between the artistic field and the religious field: 'Nothing is more like a pilgrimage to a holy shrine than one of those trips to Salzburg that tour operators will organize in the thousands for the Year of Mozart' (1992a: 86). Thus, consumers of 'high art', in this case Mozart, participate in the field in ways homologous to the devotee in the religious field. But this homology does not only apply to consumers of art. Rather, it is in the very structure of the artistic field of production that the transcendent sense of aesthetics is primarily produced. Values which are recognized as the 'highest' arise from a structure which is hierarchical: the dominated and the dominating. It is the particular characteristics of artists that they exist structurally located 'in between', as 'dominated members of the dominant class'. That position itself produces, in one aspect, a sense of 'normlessness' in the way that spiritual (artistic) greatness is structurally juxtaposed to social (class-based) greatness. A sense of singularity goes hand in hand with an affinity for artistic vision, the experience of which is a self-confirmation of an artist's own uniqueness. Artists are opposed to popular taste, but they are also opposed to dominant taste. They become avant-garde by denying previous avant-gardes. Bourdieu argues that this position is itself dangerous – artists have all or nothing to gain. There is therefore a struggle to establish and discredit, to occupy and displace, and to do so in the name of art, the high aesthetic sense (no matter, as we shall see, if that 'higher plane' is achieved in terms which deny its very existence, as is often the case in so-called 'postmodern art'). Artists have to 'make their own markets'. Because they are temporarily 'dominated', they are 'the predestined bearers of the eschatological hopes which, insofar as they support their "inner world asceticism" and their sense of "mission", are the true opium of the intellectuals' (1984/1979: 317). The analogy with religion holds true: 'in each case the indubitable transcendence with respect to strictly temporal interest springs from the immanence of struggles of interest' (ibid.). This struggle is played out in terms of, and with a sense of, what is missed and what might be possessed – of a 'not yet gained' other that is not even consciously articulated; simply, of some other 'unknown' who is structurally created, but whose creation is left unacknowledged, and is thus experienced as the only source of power it has over the artistic drive. Bourdieu concludes:

> Thus beauty is nothing but a fiction, condemned to be dealt with as such, against the Platonic belief in the beautiful as eternal essence, a pure fetishism by which the creator bows down before the projection of an illusory transcendence of what is lacking… (1996a/1992: 274)

One consequence is that an avant-garde artist, as a dominated participant in the dominant social space, might use a strategy of deferral to achieve a desirable field position. But what is lacking is not 'the spirit' itself, but what the artist might be in terms of their structural (valued) positioning in the social hierarchy. This misrecognition is at base a generating structure for the scholastic fantasy (*skholè*) of the intellectual who opposes the sacred and the profane, and the fine and the vulgar, without recognizing the structural generative provenance and *raison d'être* of such a mechanism, and who attributes to the artist an iconic role in expressing the sublime.

What, then, is Bourdieu's alternative? We set out the main tenets of Bourdieu's general theory of practice in chapter 2. It is now time to consider specifically what this theory buys us when applied to the world of art.

Bourdieu, Panofsky and the Field of Art

We asked earlier, where does art appreciation come from? The subsequent discussion has reflected on aesthetic experience of both the consumer and the producer of art. Bourdieu's own 'science of art history' takes its inspiration from Erwin Panofsky. In 1967 Bourdieu had published, with his own postface, a translation of Panofsky's *Gothic Architecture and Scholastic Thought*. In this text, Panofsky argued that the style and patterns of Gothic architecture did not come from the original mind of the artist as some form of translation of the artistic muse. Rather, they were the direct result of the socio-historical conditions of the time. Moreover, it was not even a question of current style, fashion of the spirit of the times, but rather that there was a direct homology between the structural patterning inherent in the scholastic system of the day and the ways these were reproduced in subsequent architectural practice. The key point here is that art does not depend on the individual characteristics or disposition of the artist, but arises out of structural meaning rooted in a particular time and place.

En passant, we might add that Bourdieu took this understanding of art and applied it to, or at least saw a direct resonance with, his own approach. Initially, he took this understanding of the way culture operated in prescribing what could and could not be thought (see 1971b) at a particular historical period and applied it to his work on education (see 1971a/1967). In such papers as 'Systems of education and systems of thought', Bourdieu provided a theoretical basis for his analysis of education (see also 1977a/1970). His main thesis was that education systems were not the site of education training in terms of some Platonic realm of discovery and personal development. Rather, they were social institutions saturated with a particular educational culture. This culture was self-generative in that it provided the means to ensure its own reproduction, albeit it in a transmuted form, and necessarily misrecognized as such. When those entering education came already endowed with cultural attributes which were homologous to the educational culture offered there, nothing else was needed for like to attract like, thus enabling its continuation – 'like a fish in water', Bourdieu was apt to say. Conversely, those not so culturally endowed found themselves already 'out of the game', unable to connect with a world which was already 'strange' for them. However, Bourdieu was going beyond a position which saw that in any diversified cultural field there are bound to be patterns of convergence and divergence set up when those originating from similarly diverse backgrounds encountered it. He argued rather that the nature of the homology was structural and was expressed in the structural matching of patterns of thought, scholastic thinking and the topography of social classes found in society. In other words, the very forms of thought themselves were an expression of social class. Bourdieu took this understanding to an analysis of the whole of society and the different cultural fields to be found there. The world of art is one of these.

Bourdieu begins his 'Outline of a sociological theory of art perception' (1993b/1968) by stating that 'any act of art perception involves a conscious or unconscious deciphering operation'. In other words, any response to art, unless it is simply that of the uninformed, naive viewer, implies a code of interpretation. If the naive beholder sees only in terms of immediate 'sensible qualities', content and form, there is a 'secondary' level of interpretation which is dependent on being familiar with conventional concepts and historic examples. Competence in art appreciation is therefore defined in terms of previously imbibed knowledge classified as appropriate for deciphering, or interpreting, art. This knowledge is expressed in terms of concepts, classifications, classes, representations and all divisions used in talking about art. In other words, art appreciation is a form of coding in time, which allows for and supports what is considered to be a legitimate way of thinking, responding and talking about art. Art is art because it is recognized as such by institutions with the socially acknowledged role of consecration: museums, art galleries, art schools, and so on. Value is consequently conferred and legitimated as one part of institutional control over its sphere of influence. Moreover, it is the same valuing, through repeated assertions and representations, which operates within the scholastic field in art education. So, there is a homologous matching between what is reproduced in systems of education and the culture at large. At this stage, Bourdieu was looking to establish the mechanism by which cultural capital acts as a means of social distinction and of the reproduction of advantage and disadvantage:

> To remember that culture is not what one is but what one has, or rather, what one has become; to remember the social conditions which render possible aesthetic experience and the existence of those things – art lovers or 'people of taste' – for whom it is possible; to remember that the work of art given only to those who have received the means to acquire the means to appropriate it and who could not seek to possess it, in and through the possession of means of possession as an actual possibility of effecting the taking of possession; to remember, finally, that only a few have the real possibility of benefiting from the theoretical possibility, generously offered to all, of taking advantage

> of the works exhibited in museums – all this is to bring to light the hidden force of the effects of the majority of culture's social uses. (1993b/1968: 234)

As we have seen, Bourdieu was to express this relationship between individuals and their cultural surroundings in terms of habitus and field. In other words, art appreciation and perception is a part of habitus, activated when it comes into contact with a specific field according to the mechanism of the theory of practice outlined in chapter 2.

At one point, Bourdieu asks: 'But who created the "creators"?' (1993a/1980). As we set out above, really, Bourdieu is applying the same epistemology, the same 'theory of practice', to all aspects of social life. So, from this point of view, if aesthetics, art appreciation and taste in general need to be understood as emerging from an interaction between individuals, their sociocultural origins and the fields in which they find themselves, the same thing can be said of the producers of art. We need to think of artistic creation as a product of the relationship between individual producers and the fields in which they operate. So, 'what is so-called "creation" is an encounter between a socially constituted *habitus* and a particular position that is already instituted or *possible* in the division of the labour of cultural production' (ibid.: 141).

For Bourdieu, any work of art cannot therefore simply be the work of an individual, or even of an identifiable movement; rather, it is the creation of the field of artistic production as a whole. Such a field would include all the arts in their positions relative to one another, as well as those allied to actual production itself, for example, journalism, galleries, museums. Moreover, the field of artistic production is related not only to the sub-fields which it includes, but to its position in the totality of all social fields, including economic, scientific and political fields. But this is not simply a system of relative relations. Bourdieu argues that what is produced and how it is produced needs to be understood in the precise details of these fields. In *The Rules of Art* (1996a/1992) he uses the example of the French author Gustave Flaubert. He remarks how Flaubert himself was an advocate of 'art for art's sake', defined in terms of a sort of neutral position with regard to both 'social (popular) art' and 'bourgeois art'. Flaubert denounces both and thus establishes an attitude of 'neutrality' in the literary field. Bourdieu seeks to show how this position and its consequent style is everywhere apparent in Flaubert's work. Flaubert is attempting a 'double' negation: against both the 'bourgeois' and the 'populace', and against 'bourgeois art' and 'social art'. This negation is experienced by Flaubert as a 'double refusal', necessary in defining himself as the 'pure artist'. Bourdieu's point would be that it is precisely by such a misrecognition, on behalf of the artist and those who behold him, that the artist himself is seemingly 'visited by' and expresses pure aesthetics. What is in effect a 'social construction of art' is taken to be something quasi-magical, divine and/or transcendental. Bourdieu seeks to show how it is that, in effect, what Flaubert did was a product of particular social conditions: first, the position of Flaubert and his family in terms of birth, rank and education; and, second, a particular position in the field of artistic and cultural production of his day. Bourdieu argued that the literary field exists as a 'dominated' fraction of the 'dominant class'. The logic of practice of the literary field is therefore organized in terms of a structural homology between it and the dominant class as a whole. It is therefore *apart* and *a part* of the dominant class. Bourdieu suggests that it is precisely this ambivalent relationship which is reproduced in Flaubert's own attitude to, and the consequent style in, his work. What is particular about Flaubert, and this is probably the root of his universally recognized genius, is that he was able to both fill and create the position he held within the field. In other words, it was not simply that the literary field existed in a certain state which suited Flaubert. Instead, there was something in Flaubert's background which enabled him to restructure the field in his own terms and then occupy its positions. We need to insist that such an occupation/position taking must not be understood in terms of Flaubert's strength of character and art, but rather how what he produced was itself an expression of a further struggle within social classes as a whole. Transformation in the socio-economic class structure of society repositioned the artistic field of production of which the literary field was a part. The consequent seismic pressures meant that the artistic field of production, including the literary field, needed to reconfigure itself so that this principle of homology could be honoured and the necessary homologies preserved. In that process, the avant-garde artist appears almost as a visionary in articulating the principle and logic of that reconfiguration in their artistic production. The fact that it is recognized as such is an indication of the way that immanent necessity is sensed before it is 'known', or explicitly named, among artists. It is then simply a question of who will name it first and thus occupy a position which is at once necessary and dominant within a larger dominant field in which it is dominated. Thus, the adjustment between producers and consumers being constantly played out in the artistic market 'results from the structural homology between the space of production (the artistic field) and the field of consumers (i.e. the field of the dominant class)' (ibid.: 143).

To understand artistic production, therefore, it is not enough to look at the individual work of art, however carefully, still less to understand the conscious decision made by the artist. Rather, aesthetics and the ethics which guide them must be examined in terms of the broader socio-political history of the field, namely, the common set of references which are used at any one time in conferring value on what is produced. These referents are 'demanded' from all those who enter the field – producer or consumer. Moreover, they are also themselves markers which define positions in the field:

> There is no other criterion of the existence of an intellectual, an artist or a school than his or its capacity to win recognition as holding a position in the field, a position in relation to which the others have to situate and define themselves; and the 'problem area' of the time is nothing other than the set of these relations between positions, which are also, necessarily, *relations* between aesthetic and ethical 'positions'. (1996a/1992: 145)

What this picture conjures up is the image of all those participating in a field struggling to occupy desirable positions which only occur when that occupation has been recognized as such by those in the field. The terms in which this struggle is played out are the referents which pose and propose 'problems' recognized as legitimate within the field. In this way, the past is displaced to make the present:

> the reaction against the past, which makes history, is also what makes the historicity of the present, negatively defined by what it rejects. In other words, the refusal which is the principle of change supposes and proposes and thereby recalls to the present, by opposing it, what it is opposed to. (ibid.)

Bourdieu offers an example of the way the Parnassians re-valorized science and integrated its results into their work as a reaction against antiscientific and individualistic romanticism. This picture of placements and displacements operating through a series of actions and reactions recalls Hegelian dialectics: of thesis, antithesis and synthesis. It also connects with the idea of 'paradigms' in Kuhn's *Structure of Scientific Revolutions* (1962). We will develop these issues in later chapters, in particular with exemplification in the chapters of Part II.

To summarize: a science of the history of art must, for Bourdieu, go beyond a straight examination of individual art objects (painting, photography, sculpture, literature, and so on), and artistic movements (Impressionism, minimalism, and so on) and their techniques. Moreover, a simple alternative account of an artist's biography and social context is equally insufficient. Rather, Bourdieu is looking to analyse the structure of social spaces: of products and producers, and of consumers. In effect, this approach requires that the analyst compares and contrasts thematic styles and features, the interests and views of producers as well as their social position and origins, and relates this to their choices of style. In other words:

> I think that the sociology of art has to take as its object not only the social conditions of production of the producers (i.e. the social determinates of the training or selection of artists) but also the social conditions of the production of the field of production as the site of work tending (and not aiming) to produce the artist as a producer of sacred objects, fetishes; or, which amounts to the same thing, producing the work of art as an object of belief, love and aesthetic pleasure. (1996a/1992: 147)

Bourdieu further makes the point that this means describing the social and economic conditions in terms of structural homologies, which are capable of attributing 'godlike' powers to successful artists. To do this, it is not enough to look at the individual subjectivities of the artists themselves. Rather, we must understand the entire field of production and the agents involved in their historical context. We must go beyond a simple linkage between style in its time and an account of the leading players in it. We need to look at the fundamental logic of the practice of fields and the principles and forms in which these are expressed at any particular time, and the way this derives from larger social forces, and then structures what is produced and consumed. In this sense, cultural products are arbitrary in so far as any object might be called upon to fulfil this role; but they are non-arbitrary in that what is expressed through the products – in terms of content, function and form – acts as an incarnation of attitudes, styles and beliefs. Of course, these beliefs and attitudes are immanent in the structure of thinking emerging from particular social groups at particular times and places, in response to past and future times and places. To this extent, there is a necessary logic to what is produced, even if it is misrecognized as such and appears *ex nihilo*, so to speak, inspired by a sense of what is beyond the humanly possible. The way to understand these processes more fully is to employ Bourdieu's 'thinking tools', especially habitus, field and capital.

In the last chapter, we referred to the way Bourdieu describes his approach as 'constructivist structuralism' or 'structuralist constructivism' (1989a: 14). There is some danger in employing such terms. Structuralism is often equated with Lévi-Strauss; with those underlying patterns of myth and taboo which are seen as fundamental to cultures in an anthropological sense. Bourdieu struggles to distance himself from this understanding of structure because he sees it as being too static, for example, in the way people are supposed to adhere to established marriage rules and rites in their choice of partners. For Bourdieu, structure needs to be understood in a much more dynamic way. It is less constituted as patterns and rules, but as 'objective structures independent of the consciousness and will of agents, which are capable of guiding and constraining their practices or their representations' (ibid.). It is less about 'following a rule', therefore, as about acting strategically. And this acting is mediated through habitus and field. It is the interaction of these two which is both cause and effect, producer and product, through a dynamic between them.

Another way of conceptualizing this relationship is as the interplay between the social and the psychological, the external and the internal, the outside and the inside of human facticity. This language attempts to capture something of what has been called 'the externalisation of internality and the internalisation of externality' (see Berger and Luckmann 1971). Bourdieu's approach aims to express this dynamic, and in so doing discover the principles of the logic of practice of social fields, as a way of explaining social action, social phenomena and their change over time. This is why he insists that it is insufficient to attempt to explain works or art in terms of 'internal' features alone; and by internal, we might be describing the art object itself or the particular characteristics of the artist. It is necessary also to analyse the 'external' features, but not merely in terms of the 'mood' of the time, the zeitgeist or the events of the day. Rather, as we have suggested in this chapter, it is necessary to consider the field of art in terms of the structured positionings within it and in terms of its relationship to other fields. It is necessary to consider the structural homologies between producer and consumer and the way these reflect wider socio-economic trends in society. Finally, it is necessary to examine the individual origins, background and trajectory of the artists in terms of what capital they possess to 'buy' themselves entrée to the field and to occupy desirable positions within it. Only such an approach, Bourdieu argues, takes us beyond both a naive transcendent view of art and a teleological narrative based on historical constructions and reduction. This is the 'fiction' of art history.

> It is true that 'art imitates art', or, more precisely, that art is born of art, and usually the art with which it contrasts. And the autonomy of the artist finds its basis not in the miracle of his creative genius but in the social product of its social history of a relatively autonomous field – methods, techniques, styles, etc. By defining the means and the limits of the thinkable, the history of the field causes what happens in the field to be never the direct *reflection* of external constraints or demands, but rather a symbiotic expression, *refracted* by the whole specific logic of the field. The history that is deposited in the very structure of the field and also in the *habitus* of the agents is the prism which intervenes between the world external to the field and the work of art, causing all external events – economic crisis, political reaction, scientific revolution – to undergo refraction. (1993b: 147)

This, then, is what Bourdieu is offering as an alternative, as a true 'science of the history of art'. But how do you undertake this apparently daunting task?

When asked explicitly by Loïc Wacquant to sum up his methodological approach, Bourdieu (with Wacquant 1992a: 104–7) describes it in terms of three distinct levels:

1. Analyse the position of the *field vis-à-vis* the field of power;
2. Map out the objective structure of relations between the positions occupied by agents who compete for the legitimate forms of specific authority of which the *field* is a site;
3. Analyze the *habitus* of agents; the systems of dispositions they have acquired by internalizing a deterministic type of social and economic condition.

It is possible to see how these three levels do represent the various strata of interaction between habitus and field.

In level one, we look at a field in relation to other fields, in particular, the recognized source field of power. Ultimately, this is political power and government, although there are a number of mediating institutions and fields: royalty, international business, and so on.

In level two, we consider the structural topography of the field itself: all those within it and the positions they hold. This positioning is expressed in terms of capital and its volume and configurations. In the last chapter, we described capital in terms of three forms: economic, social and cultural. Economic refers to financial wealth; social to useful or prestigious network relations; and cultural to symbolically powerful attributes derived from education, social background and dispositions. They are all capital because they act to 'buy' positioning within the field. Capital therefore has value derived from the field as the recognized, acknowledged and attributed currency of exchange for the field to be able to organize itself and position those within it according to its defining principles. The generating principles of a field have a logic of practice, a common currency expressed through the medium of its capital. It defines what is and what is not thinkable and what is doable within the field by systems of recognizing (or not) which give differential value according to principles of scarcity and rarity. In other words, that which is most valued is most rare, and thus sought after and therefore valuable; that which is most common is of least value.

In level three, we consider the actual particular agents within the field, their background, trajectory and positioning. This level is expressed in terms of individual features of the characteristics of individuals, but only in so far as they relate to the field, past and present. In other words, we are interested in particular attributes, which are social in as much as they only have value in terms of the field as a whole. We are not concerned with individual idiosyncrasies. Habitus then directs and positions individuals in the field in terms of the capital configuration they possess and how this resonates, or not, with the ruling principles of logic of the field. We can then compare individuals, groups and the way structures intersect and resonate in the homologies set up in the course of the operations of this field with other fields.

This chapter comes to an end, therefore, with a small set of thinking tools. The extent to which Bourdieu ever applied his three-level approach systematically to the many social contexts he studied can be argued, since he never followed through from level 1 to level 3, or from level 3 to level 1, in a strictly linear sequence. Rather, we have partial level analyses, or the mixing of all levels at one time, with him moving back and forth to draw out the connections. The next three chapters take a similar approach to the art world. In particular, they look at museums, photography and painting through the lens of Bourdieu's theory of practice. Why should we do this?

As we argued in the last chapter, for Bourdieu, what was at stake was 'truth' itself: 'if there is a truth, it is that truth is at stake'. Artists struggle for recognition in the field. Bourdieu is questioning in what terms that struggle is played out and on what basis there are winners and losers. What is implied therefore is a question of the legitimacy of art. Is there 'social art (fabricated)' and 'true art'? Bourdieu's critique of the art world begs this question. We shall return to it explicitly in the concluding chapters to this book.

Summary

We began this chapter by considering the nature of the aesthetic experience. We discussed briefly the tradition of philosophical aesthetics and the issues it raises about art appreciation. We then showed how Bourdieu's approach to aesthetics can be understood as an attack on the Kantian tradition of what might be called transcendental a priori aesthetics. A distinction was drawn in this between art consumers and producers. The implication of Bourdieu's social philosophy was considered for each in turn. We highlighted the need to understand art, as producers and consumers, in terms of a social construction immanent in the interaction between individuals and the contexts in which they found themselves. We showed how such an understanding is needed to go beyond a simple acknowledgement of context and agency. We examined the principles of the logic of practice behind the personal and social generating structures and how they interact. Exemplification was provided through the case of Flaubert and the homologies which existed between his position in the literary field and the way this expressed the dynamic of both an individual's social provenance and particular social conditions at one point in time; how art reacted to what was going on in society as a whole and how a certain art was needed by certain factions within it. Finally, we considered what methodology is required to study art in this way. For Bourdieu, it is necessary to put art under a social philosophical microscope; to employ, in general, a theory of practice as set out in chapter 2, and, in particular, to use such conceptual terms as habitus and field, and their related concepts. The next three chapters employ such an approach before returning to the issue of what it buys us in terms of understanding art, making sense of the possibility of aesthetics in a post-postmodern world, and, finally, addressing that overarching question – is art possible?

Part II

Practice

–4–

Museums

Introduction

This chapter is in three parts. The first part focuses on Bourdieu's own work on museums and art galleries, and the sociocultural relationships which exist between museums and their visitors. Key texts here are *L'Amour de l'art* (1991d/1969/1966), *La Distinction* (1984/1979) and *The Field of Cultural Production* (1993b). We show how Bourdieu used empirical evidence to demonstrate how an individual's experience of culture, in this case art museums, is structured by class, education and social origin, and how these have varied between sites and over time. The second part of the chapter presents three distinct national art institutions as case exemplars: the Musée d'Orsay in Paris, the Museum of Modern Art (MOMA) in New York and the Tate Gallery in London. Each art museum is considered in terms of the configuration of its symbolic capital, its position within the field of cultural production and its trajectory over time. For each, examples of a three-level Bourdieusian analysis (see chapter 3) are offered to show the structure of the field through the interrelationships of field participants and institutions. The third part of the chapter raises some specific questions about the present and future functioning of art museums within the artistic field, the broader social field and the field of power.

I

Bourdieu's View of Culture

Bourdieu's early work on museums and their audiences was written at a time of changes in French society. The issues of social class and access to education found in *L'Amour de l'art* would eventually come to a head in the student riots in Paris in 1968. His empirical work was undertaken at a time before the study of museums – museology – was an established field of knowledge. Since its publication, and its translation into English in 1991, it has become a key text in the sociological analysis of culture and in the study of museums. Bourdieu's findings could be argued to have shaped subsequent discussions between politicians, curators and art historians about access to culture, and its links to education and social class (cf. Sandell 2002; Smith 1998).

La Distinction was first published in France in 1979 and translated into English in 1984. This book continues Bourdieu's examination of culture and patterns of cultural practices, including art galleries and museums, and considers how individuals position themselves within French cultural space. As set out in chapter 3, he undertook extensive empirical work and used the strong correlations between patterns of cultural engagement and social and economic characteristics to show the structure of the artistic field in France in terms of the volume and the nature of agents' cultural capital.

The Field of Cultural Production, published in English in 1993, is a collection of papers written by Bourdieu between 1968 and 1989, in which he discusses the function and purposes of museums and museum visiting as examples of socio-economic participation within the field of cultural production. In one article, written in 1968, 'Outline of a Sociological Theory of Art Perception', he considers works of art as symbolic goods. In a later article, 'The Market of Symbolic Goods' (1993e/1985/1971), he offers a theory to account for the relationship between the art works themselves and the space of social possibilities generated by artists, their strategies, habitus and trajectories. These books form the backdrop to ideas presented in this chapter.

French Museums and their Visitors

Bourdieu's early work on art and culture includes a detailed study of museum attendance in the 1960s. *L'Amour de l'art* presents the findings of a series of systematic studies of European museums and their publics which Bourdieu directed between 1964 and 1965. Sixteen different survey instruments were used in the research, with approximately 25,000 museum visitors participating. These surveys were commissioned by the Ministry of Cultural Affairs, at a time of increasing social turmoil and change in France. Thus, issues of social equality and access to culture and education were targeted through questionnaires and interviews, which included such questions as: What is your highest educational qualification? What is your occupation? How many years of schooling have you received? How many times did you visit a museum during 1964? When did you go to a museum for the first time? With whom? Visitors to twenty-one French museums, ranging from small provincial museums to prestigious Parisian galleries like Musée des Arts Décoratifs or Jeu de Paume, were interviewed about the patterns of their visits, their experiences of museums and about themselves, their occupation, education and family. French regional museums were compared with each other and with their Parisian counterparts. The survey also extends to European art museums in Greece, Holland, Spain and Poland.

Museum Visits and Social Class

Bourdieu is most often quoted (e.g. Rice 1987) as finding that museum visiting was a product of social class. However, his findings are both more complex and more subtle than this simple correlation between class and museum attendance. He set out to establish empirically the relationships and patterns between experiences of museum visits and a range of distinct educational, social and economic characteristics, including social class. These characteristics constituted his notion of cultural capital and became key constituent aspects of habitus. In fact, Bourdieu does report that in France in the early 1960s, the middle and upper classes visited museums regularly, while those from the working class seldom visited. Typically, very few regular museum visitors were farmers or farm labourers (only 1 per cent), or industrial manual workers (4 per cent) (working-class groups); over a quarter of visitors – craft workers (5 per cent), clerical staff and junior executives (23 per cent) – were from middle-class groups, while almost half of regular visitors (45 per cent) were from upper-class backgrounds. This distribution across social categories in French museum-goers matched the profile of the population of French university students at that time, but was almost the exact reverse of the distribution of socio-economic categories across the total French population. Bourdieu concluded that there was significant differential engagement with culture across social class groups.

Museum Visits and Education

Bourdieu's data shows that there was a similar relationship between visiting patterns and levels of education, and visiting patterns and social class. However, it was in fact education and not class origins which determined an individual's pattern of museum attendance. He found that: 'Museum visiting increases very strongly with increasing level of education, and is almost exclusively the domain of the cultivated classes' (Bourdieu 1991d/1969/1966: 14). Visiting intensifies as level of education increases. In Bourdieu's survey, over half (55 per cent) of visitors held at least a baccalaureate. Only 9 per cent of visitors had no qualifications, but three-quarters of this group of visitors were children – too young to have taken any qualifications (p. 15). Regular museum-goers were, on the whole, well educated.

Bourdieu goes on to argue that it is the 'level of cultural aspiration' which is more influential than the level of qualification itself. In his survey report he found that some middle-class visitors claimed a higher cultural level than was indicated by their actual qualifications. For these individuals, visits to museums served to establish their cultural aspirations by mimicking the 'practice of baccalaureat holders' (p. 15). This idea is one Bourdieu later developed in *La Distinction*, where he writes about cultural choices: 'Taste classifies, and it classifies the classifier. Social subjects, classified by their classifications, distinguish themselves by the distinctions they make, between the beautiful and the ugly, the distinguished and the vulgar, in which their position in the objective classifications is expressed or betrayed' (Bourdieu 1984/1979: 6). This reflexive view of cultural choice making – in this case, which art museum to visit, when and with whom? – situates artistic consumption clearly within the struggle for position within a larger social space. As Bourdieu succinctly expresses it: '...art and cultural consumption are predisposed, consciously and deliberately or not, to fulfil a social function of legitimating social differences' (ibid.). Here, appreciation of established masterpieces, shown through visits to art museums, is constructed from social and cultural expectations, since recognition of membership of the middle or upper classes results from conformity to the cultural and artistic norms of that class.

Cultural Subgroups

In the surveys reported in *L'Amour de l'art*, Bourdieu found that the cultural practices of particular occupational groups do not always match their socio-economic grouping. For example, some individuals classified as craft workers and tradespeople belong to an atypical subgroup: they visit museums more frequently than their educational peers at all levels of education; they are better qualified than other craft workers and tradespeople; they present opinions closer to those of the upper classes than the middle classes; and 60 per cent of this atypical group are booksellers or fashion workers, or work in the art field, nearly all in Paris. In other words, social class is too simple a classifier because different strategies characterize differentiated intentions within the cultural space. In *La Distinction*, Bourdieu analysed empirical variations like this by distinguishing between the economic and cultural capital of distinct employment groups. He showed that higher education teachers (high-volume cultural capital, low-volume economic capital) prefer 'the rarest works of the past rather than the contemporary avant-garde', choosing Picasso, Braque, Breughel and, occasionally, Kandinsky. These choices differ from those made by people with highly consecrated cultural capital and high economic capital: professionals or executives with long-standing membership of the bourgeoisie, who inherited furniture, prefer traditional cooking and comfortable houses and who express preferences for Raphael, Leonardo and Watteau, and visit the Louvre and the Musée d'Art moderne. For these 'happy few' from dominant social groupings, the purchase of art objects from commercial art galleries is a material possibility. For social groupings where cultural capital, especially educational capital, is predominant, museums provide consecrated sites to view art in a social space where economic capital is neutralized; since art objects are not available for purchase, they can participate on an equal footing with those from more dominant fractions of society. Thus, teachers are strongly overrepresented in museum attendance, since these 'always offer the purified, sublimated pleasures demanded by the pure aesthetic... [and] ...often call for an austere, quasi-scholastic disposition, orientated towards the accumulation of experience and knowledge…' (Bourdieu 1984/1979: 272). Bourdieu found that teachers and other middle-class visitors are most likely to combine contemplation of a work of art with note taking (recording) and the purchase of reproductions (accumulation), indicating the valuing of knowledge over ownership. Hence, two distinct relationships to art objects, and to museums and art galleries, emerge. These are determined by material appropriation of, or knowledge about, art. These relationships vary with sociocultural groups defined by habitus – the balance, age and volume of economic and cultural capital. These patterns of consumption exemplify what is meant by field structures.

Age and Schooling

In *L'Amour de l'art*, Bourdieu was also looking at how museum visits varied with the age of the visitor. In France, museum-goers were relatively young – over a third (37 per cent) were aged fifteen to twenty-four, although this age group represented only 18 per cent of the whole population. He noted that 'the rate of visiting [which] remains constant up to the age of 65 after an initial decline around the age of 25 – is demonstrably explained by the influence of schooling' (Bourdieu 1991d/1969/1966: 19). This pattern was mirrored by surveys undertaken in Poland and Holland. In Greece, although the museum public was relatively young, attendance declined rapidly for those over thirty-five. Three-quarters of Greek museum visitors were aged between fifteen and thirty-four, with only a small proportion (10 per cent) over forty-five. In other words, Greek cultural patterns are distinct from those of northern Europe, perhaps because of differing patterns of parental visits to museums.

School visits were another significant factor in the high proportion of visits from young people. In France, survey participants with a baccalaureate typically visited museums three times a year while at school, but in later life only half continued to visit museums regularly. For higher levels of qualifications, attendance stayed the same after leaving school. In Greece and Holland, as in France, the proportion of museum visitors with secondary or higher education was much higher than the corresponding proportion in the whole population. In other words, few visitors had no educational qualifications or only primary education. A typical European museum visitor was relatively well educated – the cultural capital accrued through schooling is made manifest by regular museum-going. These patterns are further examples of field structures, since they are generated from specific logics of practice.

Habitus and Families

The empirical work presented in *L'Amour de l'art*, and later in *La Distinction*, showed that for any given level of education there were marked variations in cultural practices and artistic preferences according to the cultural level of the family rather than the social group of the individual concerned. The slowness of the process of acculturation in artistic matters means that the length of access to culture determines subgroups of individuals within the same social position and educational level. As Bourdieu puts it: 'Cultural nobility also has its lineages' (Bourdieu 1991d/1969/1966: 20). A 'taken-for-grantedness' of culture, which is associated with the middle and upper classes, is developed by early family experiences of art, art objects and visits to museums, and gives a surety of access to cultural and artistic heritage which is not developed through schooling alone. In Bourdieu's view: '...there is nothing better placed to give a feeling of familiarity with works of art than early museum visits undertaken as an integral part of the familiar rhythms of family life' (p. 67). Thus the conclusion was that parents' education affected the deep-seatedness of education of their children. Youngsters from the *haute bourgeoisie* are brought up to have an understanding of how to visit a museum and how to observe art. This understanding is more secure than that acquired through schooling or by autodidacts. Consequently, the length of education, including across generations, is as important as the level of education itself in determining knowledge about art and the acquisition of educational capital, which can be deployed effectively in the cultural field.

Bourdieu's study also investigated visitors' motivation and its relationship to education and social class. In France in the early 1960s, the proportion of individuals who visited museums as tourists increased with higher social class – 45 per cent of working-class, 61 per cent of middle-class and 63 per cent of upper-class visitors. Both income and social class factors also affected holiday taking. At the time of the survey, few working-class families would have taken holidays. Only a fifth of families with an income of less than 600 francs took a holiday, while almost all families (93 per cent) with an income of 2,000 francs or more took a holiday (p. 23). Since Bourdieu's findings closely matched the patterns shown in relation to education or social class, he showed that tourism did not exert a determining influence on museum visiting. Rather, he states that: 'tourism was seen as a permissive condition rather than a necessitating cause' (p. 24). In other words, the relationships observed between visiting patterns and socio-economic category, age or environment were almost totally reducible to a single relationship between frequency and pattern of museum visiting and the education characteristics of an individual. To use the terminology adopted later by Bourdieu, the strongest correlations to be found are between levels of cultural participation and the educational capital of the participants.

Social Class and Museum Collections

L'Amour de l'art showed that the proportion of visitors attracted to museums by historic, folk or ethnographic objects – furniture, for example – increased regularly and sharply with lower social class. When asked, 'Did you come to see anything in particular?', twice as many upper-class visitors (61 per cent) as working-class visitors (29 per cent) expressed a preference for 'major arts' – painting and sculpture. Conversely, four times as many working-class visitors (71 per cent) as upper-class visitors (17 per cent) wished to see 'objects' – furniture, folk objects. This overall pattern was repeated in the surveys in Poland and Holland, although a higher proportion of Dutch working-class visitors (59 per cent) preferred 'major arts' than in other European countries. Findings from Greece were again atypical, since here folkloric arts were much more popular than major arts overall. Only a fifth of upper-class visitors in Greece preferred 'major arts', while twice as many claimed an interest in folkloric arts (Bourdieu 1991d/1969/1966: 158). In general, a museum attracted the middle classes more if it presented folk and historic objects as well as painting. This pattern was also demonstrated in Bourdieu's analyses of attendance at regional museums in France, where there was a relationship between the nature of their collections and the proportion of each social class which chose to visit the museum. The greater the diversity of works exhibited by the museum, the more diverse the public visiting. Museums in Arles, Douai, Rouen, Lille and Marseille were predominantly exhibiting paintings, and received a restricted range of visitors; while museums in Dieppe, Laon, Moulins and Agen were visited both by art lovers and by those usually interested in historic objects, chateaux or local archaeology. In other words, the characteristic visitor to a museum depended on the nature of the collection displayed.

Bourdieu suggested that effective strategies for increasing visiting will vary with the purposes of museum curators. Increasing visits from art lovers – the middle and upper classes – may be achieved by rekindling their interest in painting by novel presentations of familiar paintings, by publicity and special exhibitions or through 'Friends' associations. Attracting new visitors from social classes who rarely go to museums is significantly more challenging. In the surveys undertaken in the 1960s, Bourdieu cites a particular example from Lille museum, where three exhibitions at very different levels were presented simultaneously: the museum energetically publicized a traditional exhibition of eighteenth-century painting, an exhibition of Egyptian art, sponsored by Lille University, and an exhibition of glass, crystal and furniture – 'The Art of the Interior in Denmark'. A socially diverse public might well have been anticipated. Visitors almost doubled, but their social profile closely matched that of the regular public of the museum. Bourdieu's analyses of the distribution of attendance by educational level confirmed that the privileged classes profited most from this attempt at popularization, since the proportion of visitors without a baccalaureate was markedly lower during these exhibitions than in the museum at other times (p. 90).

Visitors' familiarity with painters or schools of painting was also explored in these studies and found to correlate strongly with social class. Only 21 per cent of working-class visitors could name two or more painters or schools, compared to 55 per cent of middle-class visitors and 71 per cent of upper-class visitors. This pattern was repeated in questionnaires undertaken in other European countries.

Renoir was the painter most often cited by French museum visitors, while Mateiko was the best-known painter in Poland. Overall, Van Gogh was the most generally named painter, appearing in the top five for visitors in all four countries. Rembrandt, Cézanne, Goya and Picasso were cited less frequently, but were mentioned in all four countries. Citations of other popular painters varied by country, as shown in Table 4.1.

Table 4.1 Frequency of Citation of Painters in France, Greece, Holland, Poland.

Artists most frequently cited in France, Greece, Holland and Poland (arranged horizontally by popularity)					
Cited by participants from all four countries	*Van Gogh*	Rembrandt	Picasso	Goya	Cezanne
Cited by participants from three countries	Renoir	Da Vinci	Monet	Manet	–
Cited by participants from two countries	El Greco	Raphael	Toulouse-Lautrec	Gauguin	Rubens

Based on data taken from Bourdieu and Darbel (1991d/69: 60).

Overall, as shown in Table 4.1, European visitors agreed on a common hierarchy of famous painters. Although there were variations between the painters identified by each country's visitors, generally each country's public preferred their own national painters. Poland showed the most idiosyncratic and nationalist response. Polish visitors cited a high proportion of painters associated with their history (twelve out of twenty-one) and a correspondingly low number of more widely recognized painters – only six painters in their list of twenty-one were also cited by France, Holland or Greece. Bourdieu suggests that these findings related to the content of national art collections and, in Poland in particular, to the emphasis given to modern Polish painting in general education. Few non-European painters were cited, and no British or American artists were identified by visitors involved in these surveys. Nonetheless an agreed canon emerged. There are variations by education and by social class to the number and type of painters recognized. The lower the education level of an individual, the more likely they were to choose famous painters. In fact, Bourdieu found that only the most cultivated visitors living in very large cities cited modern painters. He suggests that establishing

> access to judgements of taste labelled 'personal' is another effect of education: the freedom to liberate oneself from the constraints of schooling is only available to those who have sufficiently assimilated academic culture to interiorize an emancipated attitude towards the academic culture taught by an educational system so profoundly

steeped in the values of the dominant classes that it appropriates for itself the worldly depreciation of academic practices. (p. 57)

For the most cultivated visitor, there was no need to conform to established norms. In *La Distinction* Bourdieu offered an example of a member of the *haute bourgeoisie* who had clearly achieved 'personal' taste. He visits museums, but only the Louvre, representing the artistic canon, and the Musée d'Art moderne de la Ville de Paris, representing the avant-garde at the time of writing. He looks for art objects to be aesthetically pleasing rather than valuable, but is able to buy paintings himself – he owns a Serusier and a Dutch master. This attitude contrasts strongly with the undifferentiated responses of the French working-class visitors interviewed in Bourdieu's earlier study. Quotes here included: 'It's very good. You couldn't present them any better than they are now'; 'I thought everything was very nice'; 'It's very good. It's really old…'; 'It's important to show the value of everything here, because it's the work of centuries… if they've preserved all this, it's to show the work done over hundreds of years, and that everything you do isn't a waste of time' (Bourdieu 1984/1979: 48). The age of an art work is recognized and valued by working-class visitors, but the critical understanding or appreciation of distinctive stylistic features of a painting which constitute the 'pure gaze' (see p. 6) of the middle and upper classes is not possible. The message is too rich, the code too complex to be decoded and, consequently, the working-class 'visitor feels drowned and does not linger' (Bourdieu 1991d/1969/1966: 39). Put more sharply, many of these visitors were at sea with the cultural expectations of the museums they had visited. They lack an independent vocabulary for judgement and are dependent on arrows, labels, guidebooks or guides in their interpretation of the experience. They lack the cultural capital to access this form of cultural experience. It is not surprising, therefore, if three-quarters of this group likened their museum visit to visiting a church. Only a third of upper-class visitors interviewed made the same comparison, and the same number saw museums as 'libraries' – places to access knowledge. In this, there is a marked contrast in attitude between social groups, and strong parallels between the acceptance demanded by religious belief associated with churches and the personal struggle needed to gain understanding and mastery of knowledge (stored in libraries). These trends can be seen as the causes and consequences of field structures.

Other Cultural Events

Attitudes and patterns of participation in other cultural visits, such as the theatre, concert going or cinema visits, were also investigated. Regular museum visiting was found to be very closely related to regular trips to the theatre and, if less markedly, to concert going. In general, cinema visiting did not follow the same patterns as museum visiting. With the exception of a minority grouping of aesthetes with a common avant-garde attitude to theatre, museums and cinema, cinema-going did not show the patterns demonstrated by 'high culture' and was only weakly dependent on education. However, clusters of cultural participation were found clearly linked to levels of education, so that

> a high degree of competence in areas of extracurricular culture, such as jazz or cinema, is very likely to be associated with competence in areas such as theatre that are taught and recognised in schools and is thus to be found amongst students most highly placed in the academic hierarchy, and, therefore, the most capable of applying a learned attitude to the cinema... (p. 64)

Here, again, is a demonstration of the correlation between educational capital and cultural practices embedded in the structure of the field.

French Art and Education

Given the determining influence of schooling on cultural practices, Bourdieu regrets the lack of direct action through art education in schools. Teaching of the history of art, including guided visits to museums, was weak and was most commonly left to the individual enterprise of teachers. Only 7 per cent of French visitors said they discovered museum visiting through school. Art teaching was seen as 'second rank', the teaching of drawing restricted and art history taught by historians rather than by art specialists. Bourdieu claims that: 'the academic institution...does tend to inspire a certain *familiarity* – part of a feeling of belonging to the cultivated world – with the universe of art, where one feels at home and among friends' (Bourdieu 1984/1979: 61). However, he argues that this largely coincides with going to university rather than school, since this 'marks entry into the cultivated world, in other words, access to the right and duty to appropriate culture'. Consequently, those with only primary or secondary education, including many of the middle class, are, practically speaking, excluded from the tools to access and develop a certain kind of relationship with art and culture which would give rise to cultural practices like museum visiting and, more significantly, are excluded from acquiring cultural capital for use in position taking within the cultural field.

Other Times – Other Countries

Much has been said in this chapter so far about museum attendance and field structures in France in the 1960s. Patterns identified in the social, cultural and economic characteristics of French museum visitors were closely related to those of other European countries at the same time, but do these same principles still apply today, and in other Western societies? In Britain in 1988 the reply would have been 'we do not know' (Hooper-Greenhill 1988). A large-scale survey of national attitudes was undertaken by Merriman (1989), who surveyed 1,500 people, randomly choosing names from the British electoral role. He found the annual rate of museum visiting to be around 47 per cent, but over 80 per cent of respondents claimed to have visited a museum at some time in their lives. As in Bourdieu's work, the most frequent visitors were found to be high status (two-thirds of those with high social status visited museums regularly), well educated (63 per cent of those with higher educational qualifications visited regularly) and employed (62 per cent of those in full-time employment visited regularly), or students (75 per cent of students surveyed were regular museum visitors). In contrast, only a quarter of the lowest social status group (social classes C2, D and E) claimed to visit regularly, with almost 40 per cent of this group never visiting a museum.

Merriman, like Bourdieu, found that museum visiting decreased with age, so that in Britain in the late 1980s, half of the over-sixties rarely or never visited a museum, while only a quarter of under-thirty-fives had never visited museums. These figures match Canadian findings (Sears 1983), which show that organized school visits account for a significant proportion of museum attendance, i.e. between 10 and 40 per cent of visits, depending on the museum. Another British project (Prince and Higgins-McHoughlin 1987) showed that, nationally, a quarter of visits could be accounted for by school visits, with the proportion increasing to a third for local museums.

In 1993–94, national statistics showed that, while a fifth of the UK population as a whole visited museums, higher status groups, including professionals and managers (social groups A, B and C1), were much more likely (34 per cent) to visit than people from social classes D and E (10 per cent) (Cultural Trends 1995). In other words, museum visiting continued to be a middle- and upper-class occupation in the 1980s and 1990s in Britain, as it was in the 1960s in France.

A study of 300 surveys of museum attendance (DiMaggio et al. 1979) found a very similar profile for museum visitors in America, so that here too museum attendance is a middle-class pastime. In a 1985 Survey of National Participation in the Arts, based on over 13,000 interviews, 22 per cent of the adult American population was found to have visited art museums in the previous year. Museum-goers were generally better educated and wealthier, with slightly more women than men visiting museums. This survey also found that African Americans were only half as likely to visit a museum as their white peers. More recent studies (1997) by the National Endowment of Arts in the United States have shown little or no change in patterns of arts participation. Participation rates increase with higher levels of educational achievements and with higher income. For example, in 1997 only 5 per cent of the American art public earned less than $10,000 a year. In other words, socio-economic patterns found in European and British museums are also demonstrated by art museums on the other side of the Atlantic.

These statistics show a remarkable geographic and chronological consistency to the socio-economic characteristics of museum visitors. Bourdieu's work in France in the 1960s has provided a secure and unvarying framework for other researchers interested in museums as sites of artistic consumption. For example, Sandell's (2002) book, which explores current issues of British social exclusion through poverty, ethnicity, gender or sexual orientation, uses Bourdieu's work to argue that inequality is passed from generation to generation by means of education. In his study of European National galleries, Prior (2002: 6) claims that: 'Bourdieu's work provides the most analytically sophisticated and empirically productive concepts available to represent the intricate mediations between aesthetic practice and social space'. Bourdieu himself broadened out his study of the 'museum-going' public to include more general patterns of French cultural consumption, including theatre and cinema, music, literature and newspaper choices. *La Distinction* offered a rich and complex picture of how individuals from different social strata, the dominated and dominant fractions of society, engaged in cultural activities. He was able to show empirically how the differentiated choices and strategies used by an individual to demonstrate mastery of culture (and who sought legitimation through it), reflect the age, education, social group and family heritage of that individual.

At its simplest: 'there is an economy of cultural goods, but it has a specific logic' (Bourdieu 1984/1979: 1). Here, the ordinary sense of culture has shifted to a more anthropological meaning. Relational thinking is necessary to understand how cultural engagement functions as a vehicle for establishing and improving socio-economic positions. Museum visitors are seen as active participants in the field of cultural consumption, whose success in the struggles for desirable field position are determined by their age, class, education, family and wealth, their cultural and economic capital or habitus (see chapter 2 for further discussion of these terms). As we have seen, a crucial element of cultural capital is the educational capital accrued through the family, through diplomas and through that acquired knowledge of how art objects are encoded which makes museums accessible. It is the need to match the complexity of the relations between cultural practice and the socio-economic field in which they occur which gives potency to Bourdieu's methodological stance and its resulting three-level analyses (see chapter 3). In this view, the production of an art work as 'a sacred, consecrated object' is, in fact, 'the product of the vast operation of *social alchemy* jointly conducted, with equal conviction and very unequal profits, by all the agents involved in the *field of production*, i.e. obscure artists and writers as well as "consecrated" masters, critics and publishers as well as authors, enthusiastic clients as well as convinced vendors' (Bourdieu 1993b: 81).What has this to do with museums and museum visitors today?

Museums themselves are active in the field of cultural production, as vendor, beneficiary or repository of art works – an institution which conserves the capital of symbolic goods – and also in the field of cultural consumption, as a provider of the site where individuals manifest cultural education and dispositions. Museums are highly consecrated sites, with high-volume cultural capital, where the habitus of field participants can be transformed. For instance, an art donor, in giving works of art to a museum, is making a contribution to a country's cultural heritage, but indirectly they may also seek to exchange the economic value of their collection for the invaluable cultural capital of public esteem and recognition. Conversely, their inheritors may 'trade in' the cultural capital of a masterpiece for the economic capital of reduced inheritance taxes. In other words, what can be achieved through an art museum is a transformation of the individual's configuration of capital – habitus.

President Pompidou's *grand projet* in 1993 sought not only to endow the nation with buildings of artistic and cultural heritage, but, by doing so, to exchange political capital at a national level for the more personal cultural capital of public acclaim. Not only did the Centre Pompidou initiate a cycle of urban regeneration for an area in Paris, but through its title, its named advocate acquired cultural distinction and long-term recognition, that is, he increased his cultural capital.

Similarly, the architects who designed the Tate Gallery St Ives, Evans and Shalev, increased their economic capital in the short term through fees, increased their cultural capital through the public recognition which designates them thereafter as the architects who designed Tate St Ives, and, in the longer term, increased their potential to earn further economic and cultural capital in the future.

It is in these sorts of ways that museums are able to endow cultural capital on individuals and institutions. As a culturally consecrated site, a museum also confers consecration on artists themselves – 'she has a picture in the Tate' – and on other field participants – 'they sponsored this exhibition'. Bourdieu writes of the various instances of consecration as: '…on the one hand, of institutions which conserve the capital of cultural goods, such as museums; and, on the other hand, of institutions (such as the educational system) which ensure the reproduction of agents imbued with the categories of action, expression, conception, imagination, perception, specific to the 'cultivated disposition' (Bourdieu 1993b: 121).

In Bourdieusian terms, the earlier question changes to one of: how does a museum function within the field of artistic production and within the field of power? We have seen that there is a strong correlation between education, social class and income, and individuals' patterns of engagement with art museums. But what of the field position of the museum itself as an institution which functions in the national and international fields?

How visitors' images of museums and their reasons for visiting them map on to the broader sociocultural field gives a preliminary picture of the field location of museums in general. When asked, 'What do museums remind you of?', respondents in Merriman's British survey mirrored those in the earlier French surveys: 61 per cent of non-visitors thought museums were like 'monuments to the dead' or a 'church', while over 40 per cent of frequent and regular visitors were reminded of a 'library'. In other words, the majority of museum-goers likened museums to other 'highly consecrated' institutions – sites with high-volume cultural capital. In Britain, as in France, survey results show a low incidence (only 12 per cent) of museum visitors who claimed to be visiting as tourists. Little seems to have changed since Bourdieu's surveys in the 1960s in France. Merriman (1989) claims that; 'a demonstrated boom in the heritage industry' is giving rise to the increasing popularity of museums with 'a wider range of people than ever before', and expresses optimism for the future widening of museum audiences. The theoretical construction underlying these claims is of a museum increasingly functioning as a tourist site – a place to visit for the day – an institution where pre-existing cultural capital is exchanged for economic capital by attracting visitors – the more visitors, the more (economic) capital generated. This runs entirely counter to the idea that: 'It is in the art museum that the aesthetic disposition becomes an institution' (Bourdieu 1984/1979: 30). Here, a museum functions as a highly consecrated site which confers cultural capital on its visitors through exclusivity and notions of 'distinction', 'taste' and the 'pure gaze'. A contradiction indeed.

It is against this contradictory background that the next part of this chapter explores how museums do function as cultural institutions. It does this through a consideration of three prestigious national museums and their role in a larger social space as sites of struggle for symbolic capital and for consecration. The museums are discussed in terms of three areas: founding and founders; their collections; and present-day activities. The founding of each museum is considered through examples of a level 2 (see chapter 3) analysis which relates key field participants and key institutions in the field of artistic consumption at that time. The field position of each museum is also suggested through a level 3 analysis which shows how fields relate to other fields and, in particular, to the field of power.

II

Case Example I: Musée d'Orsay

Founding and Founders

Opened in December 1986 amid great public controversy, the Musée d'Orsay, with a collection of about 4,000 art works, is the youngest and smallest of the three museum case studies in this chapter.

Museum's History: Building

This art museum is situated in a building with its own history. It is on the site of the Palais d'Orsay, which burnt down in 1871. The present structure was built around the time of the Universal Exhibition in 1900 as a prestigious railway station, the Gare d'Orsay, to bring people into the centre of Paris. Designed by the winner of an architectural competition, Professor Victor Laloux from the Ecole des Beaux-Arts, the building was considered to be the ultimate in 'académie' architecture (consecrated cultural capital from what is now considered a rear-guard school), with stone and stucco used to cover a steel structure of astonishing strength (symbolic capital derived from technological achievement). The nationalistic promotion of French cultural achievement, of which the Gare d'Orsay was a part, was a successful attempt to reposition Paris and its cultural practices as an innovative, high achiever within the international cultural and technological fields, and hence offers an instance of the reconfiguration of cultural capital. Here, the investment of both economic and artistic capital combined with symbolic capital derived from the political aspirations of a nation state to generate increased economic capital (income from visitors) and enhanced cultural capital with an international base (international acclaim of the quality of Parisian culture).

The use of the building as a station ceased in 1939, and after the Second World War was used only intermittently – as a clearing house for prisoners in 1945 and as a film set in 1962. In 1973 the Pompidou government made plans for the conversion of the building into an art museum. This task was adopted subsequently by Giscard d'Estaing as his *grand projet*, so he established a project group to complete the task. However, it was not until Mitterrand took power in 1981, and confirmed his interest in the initiative, that things started happening. A competition was organized for architectural designs for an art museum which preserved the grandiose character of the shell of the now disused railway station. As a socialist politician, Mitterrand chose to strengthen the historical and political aspects of the enterprise by appointing a historian of socialism, Madeleine Reberioux, as vice president of the project team. Thus, political logic played a significant part in determining the period of art to be displayed: from 1848 – a time of revolutions – to 1914 – the beginning of the First World War.

Transformation of Symbolic Capital

It can be seen from the preceding section that the origin of this art museum – and the building which houses it – is strongly political. As Barker put it: 'The Musée d'Orsay fits into a long French tradition of promoting the arts for the sake of the personal glory of the ruler and the prestige of the nation as a whole' (1999: 54). In this sense, the Musée d'Orsay project was a successor to the Centre Pompidou in converting symbolic capital derived from national political power into cultural capital within the artistic field. The volume of symbolic capital accumulated in these reconfigurations is prey to the conditions of the field. For example, President Pompidou fared rather well in terms of accrued personal cultural capital from his projects; better, perhaps, than President Mitterrand, whose key role in shaping the Musée d'Orsay is less widely remembered. Figure 4.1 shows key personnel in the founding of the Musée d'Orsay and highlights relationships between these agents and institutions, which contributed to the associated repositioning of individuals and organizations within the field of cultural consumption (level 2 analysis).

In Figure 4.1 we show how agents, participating in the French cultural field through diverse associations with the Musée d'Orsay, are also related to other public institutions within both the artistic field and the wider social space. The symbolic capital of the Musée d'Orsay itself is the sum of the individual configurations of capital it shares with its associated agents: founders, designers, political supporters, artists, donors, commentators and visitors, and, perhaps more impor-

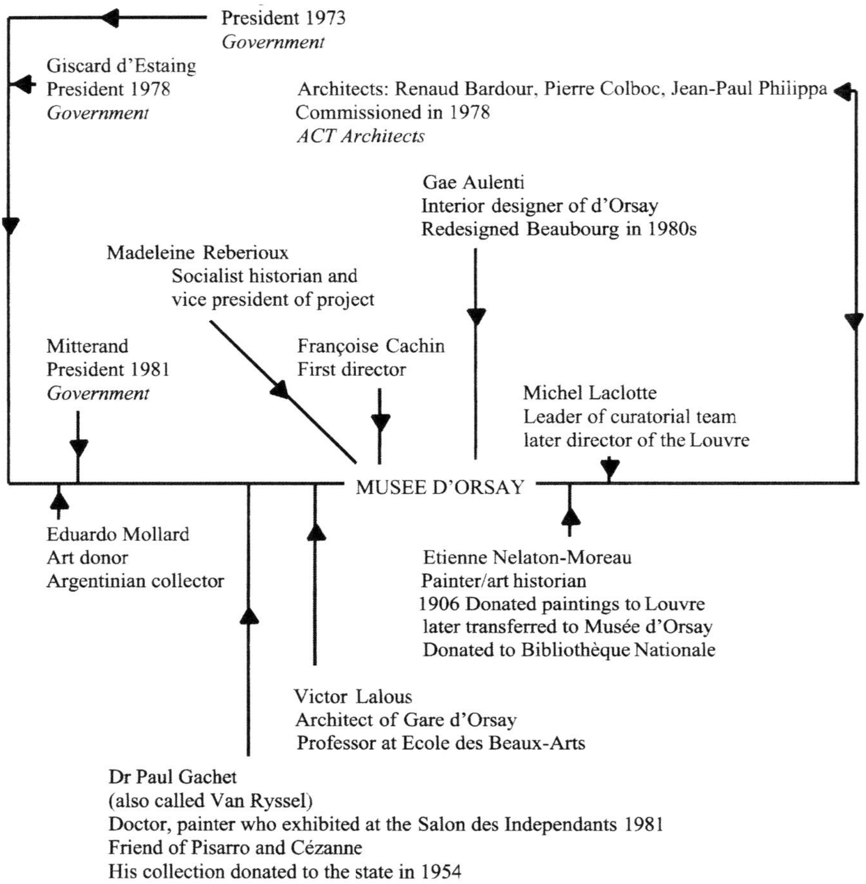

Figure 4.1 The Founding of the Musée d'Orsay. Level 2 analysis: key agents and some relationships to other institutions.

tantly, with the other institutions from which they in turn derive their symbolic capital.

Commercial institutions, such as architectural practices, increase their symbolic and economic capital through association with a highly consecrated institution like the Musée d'Orsay. More specifically, through their relationship to the museum, ACT architects benefited from contractual fees (economic capital), an enhanced professional reputation (greater consecrated cultural capital) and a broader network of political and artistic contacts (social capital). Similar symbolic and economic transactions occurred for all the participants and institutions in Figure 4.1.

Table 4.2 Musée d'Orsay.
Types of *capital*, *field* participants and *field* institutions.

Type of symbolic capital	*Institution*	*Field participants*	*Type of capital gained*
Political	Government	Pompidou, Giscard D'Estaing; Mitterand; Madeleine Reberioux	*Cultural and economic capital* from visitors
Artistic Capital	Louvre, Beauborg Ecole des Beaux Arts	Michel Laclotte, Van Gogh	Consecrated *cultural capital*
Education	Ecole des Beaux Arts	Victor Lalous ACT Architects	*Cultural and economic capital*
Economic	Art donors	Eduardo Mollard	*cultural capital*

In Table 4.2 we indicate the nature of the reconfigurations of capital which take place over time. For those who are successful position-takers within the cultural and social fields, individual symbolic capital moves towards capital derived from larger-scale social groupings, while new and unconsecrated capital matures into more powerful, old consecrated capital. These processes are clearly at work in the establishment of such a consecrated institution as a national museum. In analysing changes in configuration in capital, it is easy to forget that the history of any public institution is constructed from those position-takings, which proved successful over time for the institution or the field participant. The part played by a successful team leader is recognized and remembered. For example, Michel Laclotte, who established key cultural capital (art historic) for the Musée d'Orsay through his leadership of the first team of curators, increased further his personal symbolic capital by functioning successfully in a highly politicized context so that he went on to become the director of the Louvre, the most consecrated art museum in the French cultural field. The part played by less successful field participants is subsequently overlooked, for example, the unsuccessful architects in the competition to redesign the building. In the struggle within the field, there are both winners and losers.

Musée d'Orsay's Art Collection

The museum houses a collection of nineteenth-century art taken from a period of social upheaval – revolutions (1848) to world war (1914). The art ranges from recognized masterpieces – Manet, Van Gogh, Cézanne – with high-volume, consecrated artistic capital, to previously neglected or disdained work from the French Académie – Bouguereau, Cabanel, Carpeaux, who have less artistic capital, but aged symbolic capital associated with a style supported by an earlier French state. The collection is part of the French national collection and was achieved by the redistribution of art works already in other national galleries in Paris, in particular, the previously overcrowded Musée de Jeu de Paume and the Louvre. Thus the art works themselves provided both high-volume, consecrated cultural capital and the political capital which comes from government support. From the first, it was intended to display a broader range of art objects than had previously been seen as constituents of French cultural heritage, not only painting and sculpture from recognized masters and from the neglected 'official' art of the nineteenth-century establishment, but also furniture, photography and decorative arts. As Bourdieu had noted, art museums with historical objects as well as paintings were significantly more popular with the French working-class public. As there were strong socialist connections for the museum's key political founders (particularly Mitterrand and his appointee Madeleine Reberioux), the Musée d'Orsay's inclusion of art objects in its collection and displays is a product of the workings of a political will, intent upon education and widening access for the working classes.

Reberioux also sought to broaden the potential audience for art museums, particularly by increasing attendance from the working classes, by placing art works clearly in their social and historical contexts. In this, she was only partially successful. While historical artefacts of the nineteenth century continue to be on show, they have now been sidelined and are easily overlooked. As a single historian within a team of art historians, Reberioux probably lacked the necessary support (social capital) to achieve her objectives completely. Although the museum is arranged largely chronologically across three floors, painting is separated from sculpture and from furniture so that a visitor is easily aware of the art objects themselves, but must generate their own historical synthesis. The displays include several personal art collections donated to the French state, probably in lieu of death duties, so that the museum's chronology is further disrupted by a number of separate galleries named in response to donors' wishes to be recognized as artistic benefactors. These donations offer examples of how nineteenth- and twentieth-century establishment figures, such as Dr Paul Gachet or Max Kaganovitch, sought to exchange the economic value of art works for consecrated cultural capital. As a consequence, the museum display is a strange mix of traditional chronological arrangements of art works by genres, cut across by the display of individual collections, so that the experience of visiting the museum can be disjointed, if not postmodern.

Painters

With a mere 4,000 art works in the Musée d'Orsay, the range of the collection is diverse indeed: a specialist collection of art nouveau furniture by Thonet Frères, Mackintosh and Frank Lloyd Wright; paintings by the Nabis, Vuillard, Denis and Bonnard – prophetic of the modernism to come; or the early cinematography of

Louis and Auguste Lumière and Georges Méliès. However, the characteristics of the collection itself are fixed – frozen in time – 1848 to 1914. As a consequence, the latest developments in the artistic field pass the museum by and its rate of art acquisition is relatively slow – recently only nine new paintings in a year.

However, the collection of paintings is canonical, representing major painters of its time period – Courbet, Millet, Degas, Pissaro, Bonnard, Moreau and Puvis de Chavanne, among many others. If we return to Table 4.1, which shows the canon of works established in Bourdieu's survey by the recognition of the painters across different European countries, we can see that all the French painters from the time period – Cézanne, Gauguin, Manet, Monet, Renoir, Toulouse-Lautrec, Van Gogh – are represented in the Musée d'Orsay's collection. In other words, the museum's paintings will be recognized and popular in a large part of Europe. This is confirmed by the high proportion of foreign visitors to the museum (see Barker 1999: 68).

Musée d'Orsay in the Present Field

A number of internationally significant museums are situated in Paris. They can be considered in relationship to one another in terms of their artists and the avant-gardes to which they belonged, so the Louvre is clearly the oldest and most consecrated, with highly legitimated cultural capital from its works of art, old masters and its Parisian setting in an old palace.

The relative field positions of the state-funded art museums in Paris is controlled by the arts policy of a particular government. At one time, the Musée Luxembourg exhibited modern artists; now it exhibits the work of French regional artists. This museum, and others whose collections are determined geographically, not by artistic age, have not been included in Figure 4.2. (See chapter 5 for discussion of artistic age, and also Bourdieu 1996a/1992: 152.)

Activities and Funding

The Musée d'Orsay is a key tourist site in today's Paris and, as such, offers facilities to its visitors: a charming café is situated high above the galleries, near the station clock, and a smart restaurant overlooks the Seine. Elegant, nineteenth-century music is played in both café and restaurant, soothing and refreshing tired museum-goers. A cavernous museum shop, selling luxurious art books alongside more touristic souvenirs, is enticingly near the entrance. The museum has established partnerships with other Parisian cultural venues, including L'Opéra and Comédie Française. A website offers practical information about the museum, including special exhibitions, entrance fees and opening times. It can all be read in different languages, and information on specific areas is offered in dedicated sections of the website: students, education, the professional and tourism. Recent

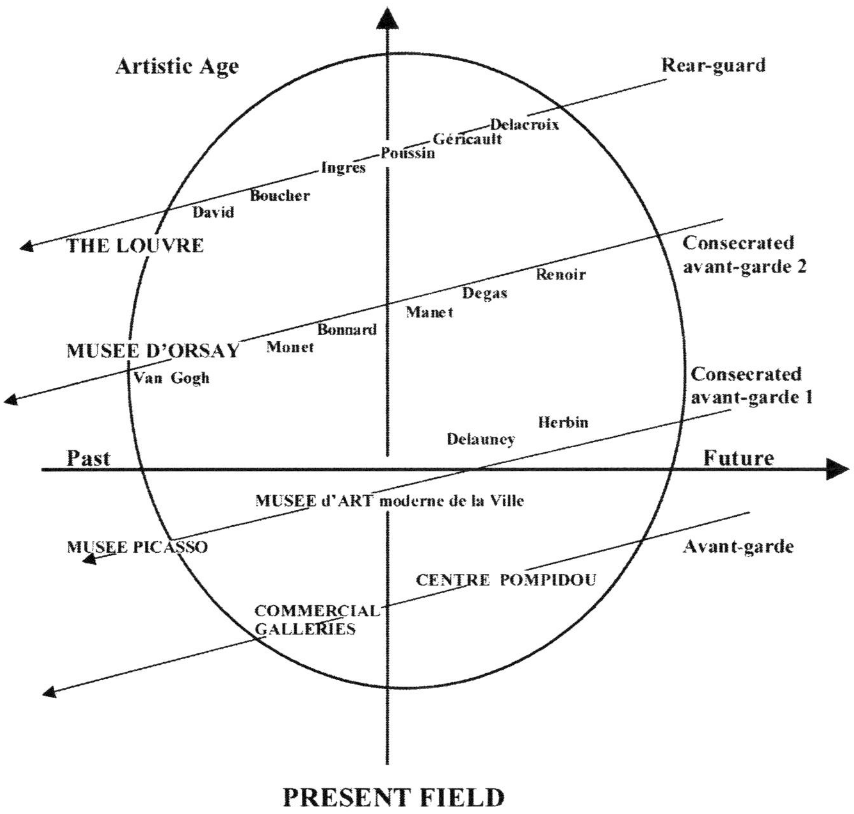

Figure 4.2 The Present Field of Artistic Production in France.

attendance figures show about 2.3 million visitors a year; most are foreign visitors, with over 70 per cent visiting for the first time. In contrast, the audiences for special exhibitions are predominantly Parisians. The museum has recognized and catered for the tourist nature of its largest audience.

The Musée d'Orsay is a charging museum – 1.7 million tickets sold in 2000. In other words, international tourism, with its resulting income generation, is an integral part of this museum's activities. Large-scale cultural capital derived from the nation state and from consecrated art works generates economic capital and symbolic capital from the international cultural field.

Education is not overlooked, however. Courses, educational visits, lectures and visual presentations of aspects of history relating to the collection take place regularly. A large auditorium supports regular conferences and cultural debates, which are later reported in the *Musée d'Orsay Review*. Education is a serious activity here, associated with study of high art (consecrated cultural capital) and, frequently, exclusively in French. Thus, the museum differentiates its response to its Parisian visitors, recognizing their different patterns of attendance and cultural competence. There are some vestiges of privilege available for regular museum-goers, probably French – Friends of the museum receive early access to the collection, thus avoiding the crowds. The *Review* itself is published in French only, thus implying that the audience for more serious discussion of art and culture is French-speaking. Is it the case that within the mass appeal of the Musée d'Orsay can be found a small kernel of Parisian visitors with a distinctive pattern of cultural participation – educational events, special exhibitions and published *Review*? With interests in educational capital and in the art historic, this is a group seeking social and cultural nobility. As Bourdieu reminds us: 'Social subjects, classified by their classifications, distinguish themselves by the distinctions they make, between the beautiful and the ugly, the distinguished and the vulgar, in which their position in the objective classifications is expressed or betrayed' (Bourdieu 1984/1979: 482). In the case of the Musée d'Orsay, Parisians are able to gain social and cultural consecration within the local field though their associations with the museum.

The museum's original intentions were to support education and widen access to a significant part of France's national heritage. To this end, what has been constructed is a spectacle, with its surprising and symbolic conversion of the nineteenth century – a technological and functional railway station – into a modern-day palace to aesthetic 'distinction'. Undoubtedly, the museum has popular, tourist appeal today, derived from its controversial birth and the 'middle-brow' art it displays, now considered a consecrated avant-garde. The museum's appeal to the middle classes makes a visit to the Impressionists in the Musée d'Orsay a necessity for any foreign tourist seeking confirmation of their cultural competence and distinction.

The field position of any museum is determined in part by its own history – its inherited economic and symbolic capital – but also by the structuring structures of the present artistic and social field. Although the Musée d'Orsay is a relatively young institution, both the building and the collection predate the museum itself. Hence much of the symbolic capital it has accrued is 'old' and consecrated – from the state and from other consecrated cultural institutions. The market value of its art works literally provides old economic capital. The museum has also accrued both large-scale cultural capital (the popular) and economic capital from the resulting income. The museum's field position shows a powerful configuration of the economic and symbolic.

However, today's mass audience for the museum, which gives it a dominant position within the field of national power as a prestigious and economically successful state enterprise, also makes it vulnerable to future changes in state policy and legislature – a dominated position. Most recently, discussions in France about allowing corporate backing for public institutions could radically change both the position and functioning of the museum within the social and cultural fields.

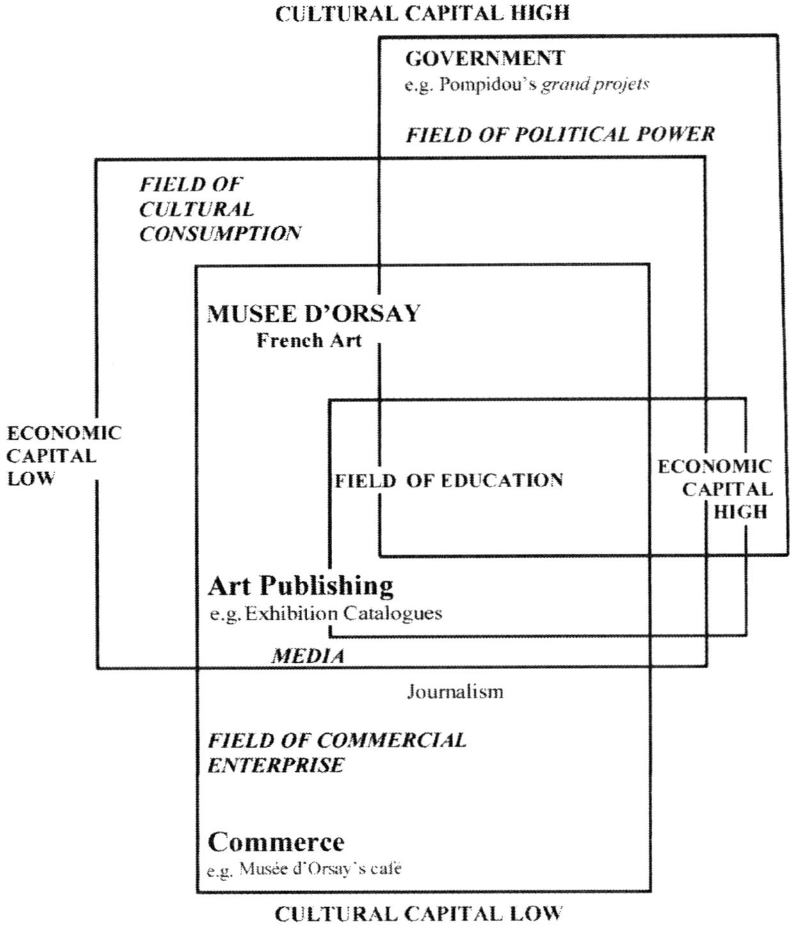

Figure 4.3 Musée d'Orsay. Level 1 analysis: fields in relation to the field of power.

Case Example 2: The Tate Gallery

This is the oldest and most complex of the three galleries we are concerned with here. From a single-site traditional museum, the Tate Gallery has evolved into a multi-site and multifaceted organization. It has buildings in three different geographical areas of England: two in London – Millbank, the original site, and Bankside, the most recent addition; one in Liverpool; and two sites in St Ives, Cornwall – Tate St Ives itself and a single-artist museum for Barbara Hepworth. A geographically diverse museum indeed.

Founding and Founders

The Tate Gallery opened in 1897, after several decades of discontent about the public presentation of British art and many heated discussions between government, key figures in the art establishment and potential art donors, most notably Henry Tate, a sugar manufacturer. Thus, even at its inception, the museum had access to significant capital, derived from diverse social and cultural fields: state political capital from the field of power, artistic capital from the cultural field and consecrated economic capital from the art works in question – albeit slightly 'tainted' by the 'trade' associations of their donor, Henry Tate.

In 1853, a parliamentary select committee discussed the purchasing policy of the National Gallery and ascribed two objectives to the potential gallery: '...one should be to elevate the public taste by exhibition of the highest works of the best masters, and the other to represent the progress of art in its various schools' (Edwards 1991: 56). We can see in this an early concern with the education of the museum-going public, which was to recur a century later when Bourdieu identified education as the determining factor in the cultural competence which results in artistic consumption such as regular museum attendance.

In 1857, Queen Victoria established a Royal Commission to determine the site of the new National Gallery and whether it should be combined with the fine art section of the British Museum. It was not until 1890, however, when Tate offered his personal collection of art works to the nation provided that a gallery was built to house them, that a British gallery for 'British art' became a practical, if hotly disputed, possibility. The national and art press, parliamentary commissions and the Chancellor of the Exchequer were involved in negotiations. Argument raged about the art museum's site, its purpose and about Tate's own intentions – his offer was described by *Society* magazine 'as the £80000 bribe of the sugar-boiler' (Unknown author 1892). In this, the establishment of a major public institution is seen to be a socio-economic project which simultaneously involves struggles for position in a number of diverse fields: the field of power, the field of cultural consumption, the field of artistic production and the endlessly contested British class system within the broader social field.

A site, formerly a prison, on Millbank in London, was eventually acquired and the museum designed and built by an architect of Tate's choice. The Tate Gallery thus began its tradition of building prestigious art museums in 'rundown' areas and, consequently, acting as an agent of social regeneration. This pattern was repeated in Liverpool where a converted warehouse was a focus point for the development of the Albert Dock area as a cultural centre. Again, Tate St Ives, a former gasworks, has changed the cultural geography of the town and its affluence. The Tate Modern, housed in a disused power station, has similarly acted as the initiator of major urban renewal, this time in Southwark, a poor and neglected area on London's South Bank. Thus, not only are the field positions of any museum the result of struggles for position between the field participants, but the establishment of a consecrated public institution – in this case, an art museum – changes the field structure of all the fields in which it plays a part – here, the British cultural field, together with the local economic and social spaces. We need to understand this analysis as an example of Bourdieu's 'structured and structuring structures'.

The opening of the original gallery in 1897 was attended by royalty (the highest consecrated social capital within the British field), including the Prince and Princess of Wales, and the Duke and Duchess of York; a ceremony in which Henry Tate presented the deeds of the gallery to the prince so that the gallery became the property of the nation. This 'gift' (see Bourdieu 1977b/1972: 6–7) established the gallery in a consecrated and dominant position within the cultural field and reconfigured the symbolic capital and habitus of many of the participants. For Henry Tate (and later for the Duveens), economic capital became consecrated cultural capital by establishing a reputation as an art donor – the same process used by Pompidou and Mitterrand in Paris a century later. In addition, Tate was created a baronet by King Edward VII and made a trustee of the National Gallery – cultural capital indeed. In Figure 4.4 we offer a level 2 analysis of the relations between some of the key agents and institutions within the sociocultural field during the establishment and early years of the Tate Gallery.

There are marked similarities between Figure 4.4 and the earlier level 2 analysis of the Musée d'Orsay (Figure 4.1), with a close correspondence between the characteristic agents – government representatives, art donors, artists, architects, curators – and the institutions active in the field – government, other art museums, art schools. Within the British socio-economic field, the most consecrated symbolic capital is associated with royalty and nobility rather than the political power of presidents. Nonetheless, as for the Musée d'Orsay, the Tate accrued economic and symbolic capital from its associated field participants and institutions. Hence, highly consecrated political (government), social (royalty) and cultural (art works) capital were key constituents of its initial highly consecrated habitus. A further ingredient in the strong field position of the Tate was economic capital derived from the field of commerce and industry through its earliest sponsor, Tate. As in France, association with the establishment of a national art museum had the effect of conferring significant cultural capital on individual field participants, but also on artists and British art itself.

The extensive press eulogies which followed the Tate's opening ensured that the public flocked to the newly opened gallery, mimicking the strategies of their 'betters' and seeking affirmation of their own social and cultural positions within the dominant field. From the start, social controversy, fuelled by active press engagement, industrial sponsorship and high levels of public participation, were features of the Tate's functioning within the cultural field. Despite myriad changes in site, scale and complexity, these remain characteristic of the Tate today, as, for example, in the annual media-fuelled debate which surrounds its Turner Prize, whose popular appeal is such that the London *Evening Standard* newspaper of 5 November 2005 offered its readers a free DVD providing a virtual tour of the Tate's exhibition.

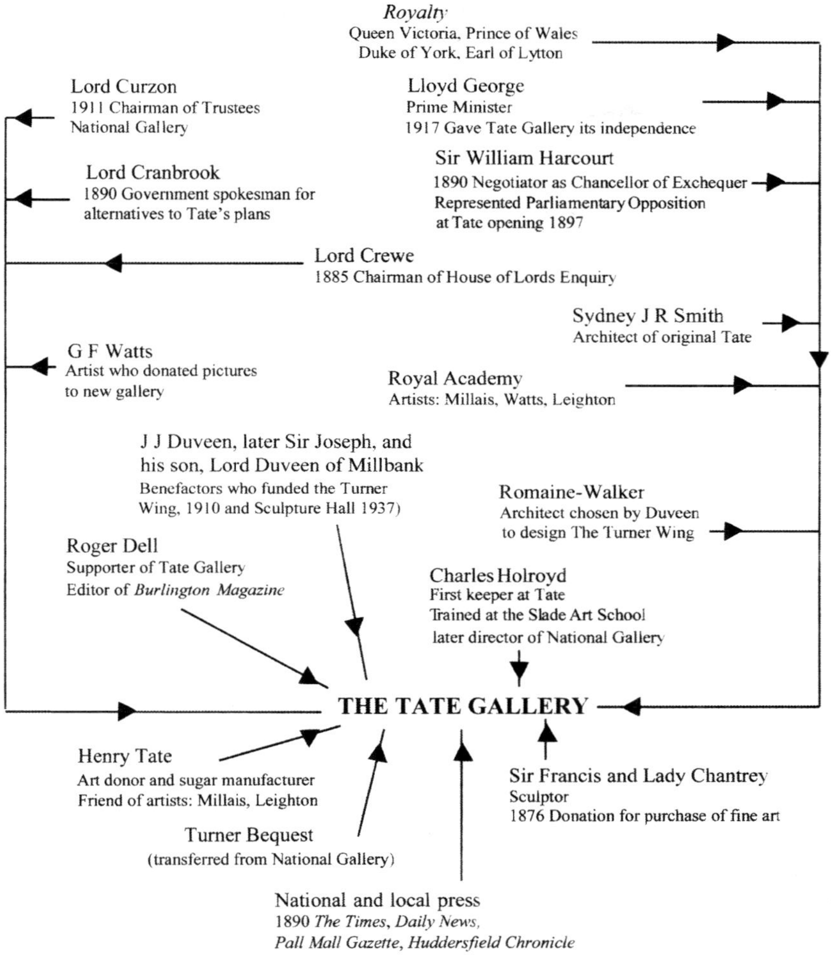

Figure 4.4 The Founding of the Tate Gallery. Level 2 analysis: key agents and some relationships to other institutions.

The Collection

The Tate Gallery was set up to display modern and British art (from 1790) and, with some adjustments, has continued in this purpose to the present day. Originally, its collection came about through redistribution of the existing national collection in the South Kensington and National Galleries. The Tate opened with a miscellany of art works – purchases from the Chantrey Bequest, the Vernon art collection, sixty-seven pictures from Henry Tate himself and ninety-six pictures from British painters born after 1890. From the first, the Tate had an active acquisition policy and sought to buy the works of younger British artists, perhaps because they were less expensive. For the first decade the Royal Academy had control of the Tate's purchasing policy through the Chantrey Bequest. As a consequence, the earliest gallery purchases were predominantly from Royal Academicians. A heated public debate then ensued about this purchasing policy, involving, among others, the *Burlington Magazine* (press), the Earl of Lytton (nobility), the Royal Academy (key artists and curators) and a House of Lords enquiry (government). Despite this controversy, it took until 1917 for the Tate to be granted autonomy from the National Gallery and to be given a new dual commission for 'the history and evolution of indigenous art' (Lord Curzon 1915, in Rothenstein 1963: 28–29) and for a new Gallery of Modern Foreign Art (now housed in Tate Modern).

The Tate's active acquisition policy has ensured that the collection has continued to expand and, with it, the constant need for a larger space and more galleries. By 1899, the art museum, with the addition of nine more galleries, was already the largest in London. The Tate Gallery has followed a cycle of acquisition and expansion, initially a new wing or two – the Turner Wing (1910), the Duveen Hall (1937), the Clore Gallery (1985) – and, latterly, new buildings on new sites – Liverpool (1987), St Ives (1993) and Bankside (May 2000). Each of the Tate sites has a distinctive exhibition policy, in support of the Tate's unique conceptualization of itself as 'a non-hierarchical whole comprising distinctive parts with independent curatorial expertise…'. In 2006, at the time of writing, the Tate collection is shared between the four Tate galleries and its other regional partnership galleries in Sheffield, Kendal, Stoke-on-Trent and Norwich. Thus, this national art museum occupies field positions within both the international and national (London-based) sociocultural fields, while simultaneously functioning within an expanding number of smaller, regionally based fields of cultural consumption.

At the time of writing, the Tate's collection includes 4,366 paintings, 4,307 unique works on paper, 1,544 sculptures, 11,066 prints, 37,463 works in the Turner Bequest and 3,734 in the Opie collection, plus an archive for twentieth-century British art. Photography is represented through a loan exchange with the Victoria and Albert museum in London and the Froelich Foundation in Stuttgart. As might be expected from any national art museum, the collection includes many canonical art works: Constable, Gainsborough, Blake, Turner, Millais, Sickert, as well more recent masterpieces by Burne Jones, Chagall, Nicholson, Epstein. Late twentieth-century artists, often controversial, include Gilbert and George and Michael Landy. The popular European canon, as represented in Bourdieu's study (see Table 4.1), plays only a small part in the Tate's permanent collection, but special exhibitions (such as the 'Turner, Whistler, Monet' exhibition, on display in 2005) serve to redress the balance.

Today, Tate Britain displays work from British artists from the sixteenth to the twenty-first centuries, including a gallery space called 'Art Now' – reserved for temporary exhibitions of the work of individual young British artists – and galleries dedicated to the work of William Blake and to paintings by Turner. Other

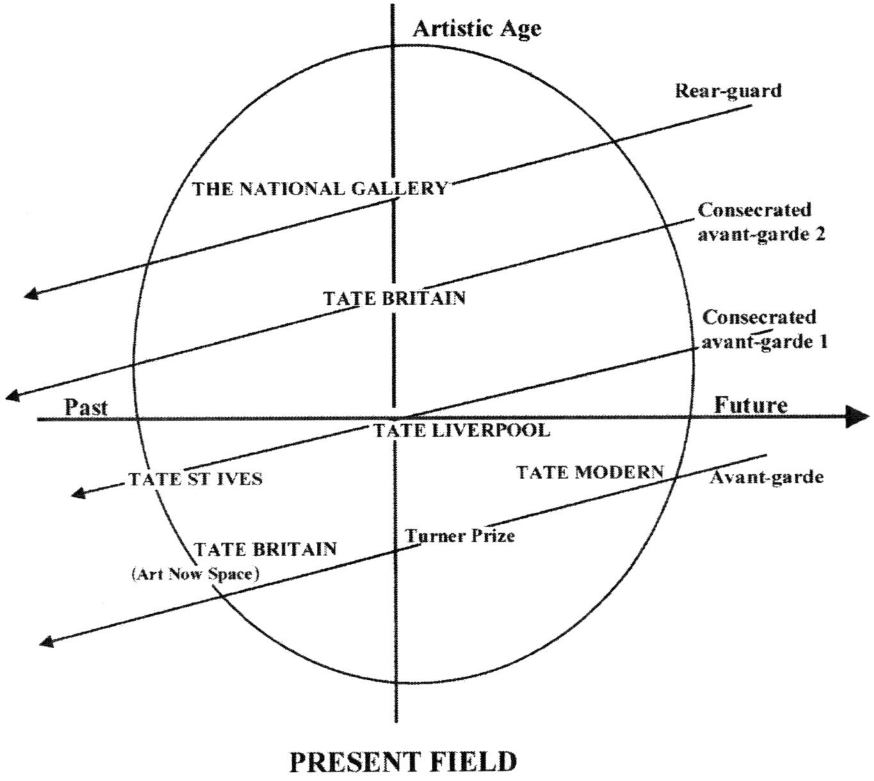

Figure 4.5 The Present Field of Artistic Consumption – Tate/London.

major attractions include the annual exhibition of the four artists shortlisted for the Turner Prize. This all gives a curious mix to the configuration of capital, of this art museum: consecrated cultural capital from the art historic seriousness of visitors to British rear-guard masterpieces; cultural capital associated with more recent avant-garde art; and, a high volume of capital (see chapter 2) relatively low in consecration from the mass audience drawn by Turner Prize controversy.

Tate Modern also displays international art from 1900 onwards. Here, the curators have broken with tradition, so that the permanent collection has not been displayed chronologically, but under periodically changing postmodern headings: recent examples are 'Nude/Action/Body', which includes works by Chris Ofili, Picasso, Bonnard and Modigliani; and 'History/Memory/Society', with installations by Thomas Hirkhorn and Boltanski alongside photographs from James Casebere and Thomas Demand. The Tate Modern houses the largest gallery space in world, which hosts spectacular and gargantuan installation and sculpture exhibitions; for example, Rachel Whiteread, Anish Kapoor, Olafur Eliasson and Bruce

Nauman. Here again, at this site, the consecrated cultural capital of the French avant-garde combines with symbolic capital from a more recent, restricted field, but contrasts with the large-scale audience attracted by the spectacle and novelty of the building itself.

A more parochial policy applies at Tate St Ives in Cornwall, where exhibitions have strictly Cornish associations. A small display of the works of local modernist artists, Ben Nicholson, Naum Gabo, Barbara Hepworth, Peter Lanyon and Bernard Leach, is supplemented by exhibitions of national and international artists, such as Rothko or Anthony Gormley. Here one finds a comfortable, middle-brow offering of second-generation modernism – in the local field these are high art (consecrated artistic capital), but the nationally debated building, with its beach panoramas, attracts crowds of one-off visitors (particularly when it rains!) – high-volume capital, low consecration.

Tate Liverpool displays twentieth-century art from the Tate collection on its first floor, complemented by thematic or stylistic displays on the second, typically, 'The Spirit of Cubism' or 'American Abstraction'. It is noted as a very user-friendly art museum and has claims to be a museum which 'actively listens to visitors' comments' (Stich 2000). Here again, the Tate shows a concern for the 'popular' (high-volume capital within the local field), mixed with artistic appreciation of established avant-gardes (consecrated cultural capital derived from an international cultural field).

Activities and Funding

As an organization that won national awards in marketing and public relations excellence in 2001, the Tate is unashamedly entrepreneurial. It combines the display of an ever-increasing art collection with a Public Record Office, library and research facilities and an active website. There is a Friends Association, registered as a charity. Schemes exist for art donors, company sponsors and American art donors. Distinct business operations – Tate Catering, Tate Shop, Tate Fundraising and Events, Tate Publishing, Education, Operations and Visitor Services, and Tate Enterprises Ltd – employ over 1,200 staff. Educational activities include a varied programme of talks, short courses and conferences. The website now includes not only access to the art collection, but a distance-learning course to encourage knowledgeable access. Interestingly, the website also now displays examples of web-art – a case of the technological field acting directly within the field of artistic production by changing the art form itself.

The Tate Gallery sites offer a range of facilities and activities beyond the scope of a traditional art museum, dedicated to providing public access to a national heritage. Restaurants, cafés, bookshops and visitor information are all provided with a keen eye on quality. Over one million visitors per year use the cafés and restaurants. A regular programme of guided tours and educational events is supplemented by audio guides, mini catalogues and extensive explanatory labelling for special exhibitions. Entry to the permanent collection is free – supported by government grant, but special exhibitions incur an extra charge. Nonetheless, queues and crowds are commonplace. There is even dedicated transport between the two London sites: an eighteen-minute journey in a boat decorated with a design by Damien Hirst. Few museums can claim to function in the field of transport.

Membership of Tate Friends offers a regular Tate magazine, free booked tickets to exhibitions and no queuing. There are additional catering facilities for Friends – a sedate and quiet café in Tate Britain, or a lively Cool Britannia tapas bar on the rooftop of the Tate Modern. Corporate membership gives access to a prestigious event venue for conferences and social events, with catering and privileged access to exhibitions. Nonetheless, the Trustees' Report for 2002 states clearly that national art treasures continue to go abroad because of lack of government funding.

Aggregated attendance figures for the Tate galleries typically run at 6 million visitors per year. Roughly 40 per cent of these are foreign visitors. However, while Tate Britain received over 1 million visitors in 2003–4, Tate Modern received about 4.25 million, and the website received 3.5 million visits in the same time period. With an income of more than £55 million in 2002, the organization deals not only with high-volume cultural capital, but in large-scale economic capital. This museum means big business!

The Tate's Annual Report for 2002 stated aims commonly associated with art museums: strengthen a world-class collection and improve public awareness of British art. It gives clear priority to developing new audiences and states explicitly its aim to broaden the social range of its audiences. It also uses language taken from a business vocabulary: build an organization, add new facilities, create partnerships to match the continuing engagement of the business sector in the museum. Exhibitions and other activities are regularly sponsored by a diverse range of companies – Volkswagen, BP, BT, Bloomberg, Barclays plc – including the media – Channel 4, *The Guardian*, the *Daily Mail*, the *Daily Telegraph* and, of course, Tate and Lyle plc. The distribution of the Tate's income matches the diversity of its activities: almost half from government grants (£27 million), a third from traded activities (£17.5 million), 8 per cent from donors and sponsors (£4.2 million) and only 6 per cent from admissions (£3.8 million). These figures show the diversity of social fields in which the Tate plays a part – the field of power (government), the field of charities (donors), the field of corporate business (sponsorship) and the field of tourism. The complexity of the Tate's field positioning is shown in Figure 4.6.

The Tate as an organization has engaged directly in the wider social field through a range of activities at different sites. Its claim is that each gallery has worked hard to contribute to and build relationships with the local community, for example, with Metropolitan Police and Southwark Social Services, with Cornwall's Traveller Support Service and with local prisons in Liverpool.

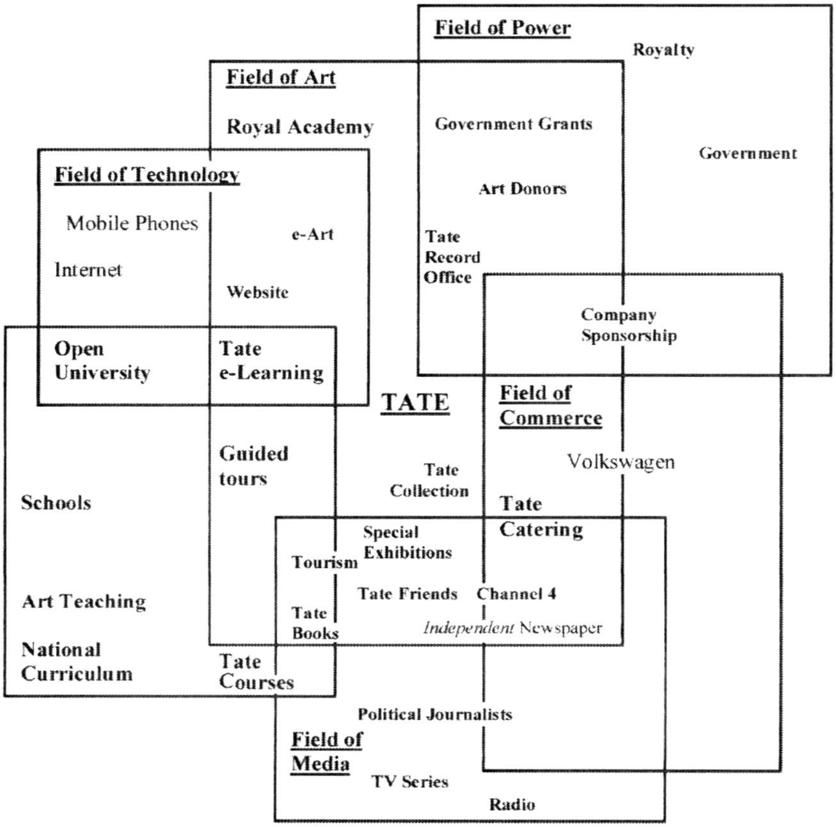

Figure 4.6 Tate Gallery. Level 1 analysis: fields in relation to the field of power.

Case Example 3: The Museum of Modern Art (MOMA), New York

This is the largest of the three museums discussed here and has the highest international profile. From the bright idea of a group of New York art collectors, committed to the avant-garde art of the 1920s, MOMA has become a multilayered organization, working with international partners and supporting an ever growing collection, a complex archive of modern art, a prestigious research and education programme and a huge website.

Founding and Founders

When MOMA was granted its charter by the New York State Education Department in September 1929, it had no obvious funding, no art works and no premises – in other words, no economic capital. What it did have was high-volume, highly consecrated social and cultural capital derived from the individual habitus of its seven founding trustees, and the determination and commitment to modern art of three rich and well-connected women, Lillie P Bliss, Mrs Cornelius J Sullivan and Mrs John D Rockefeller Jnr. As Nelson Rockefeller wrote some years later: 'It was the perfect combination. The three women among them had the resources, the tact, and the knowledge of contemporary art which the situation required' (quoted in Oldenburg 1984: 11). Although these female founders were not themselves active participants in the field of power – politics, business or state institutions – their own social capital, and the 'inherited' symbolic capital available through their families and friends, gave them strong connections with national and state government, the law, the military, the media, the world of avant-garde art and its collectors, and commerce and manufacturing, that is, capital derived from a broad spectrum of the most prestigious sociocultural fields. Unstoppable habitus indeed! They were art collectors in their own right, advised by key participants in the artistic field, for example, Arthur Davies, from the seminal Armory exhibition of 1913. Lillie P Bliss and Davies together wielded sufficient influence (symbolic capital) to secure, if reluctantly, an exhibition of modern art at the Metropolitan Museum of Art in 1921. Unfortunately, hostile press coverage reinforced the Metropolitan's caginess about modern art and the experiment was not repeated. Thereafter their zeal was directed towards establishing an American museum focused on modern art, and on art from living artists, in particular. However, it took another eight years for the three women to establish a committee for the proposed museum. With the strong relationships of the new trustees to highly consecrated institutions, the habitus of its seven founders was such that all would be said to occupy dominant positions within the social space. Suffice to say that the configuration of capital available to the proposed art museum, derived from the educational, political and commercial fields, ensured a powerful position within the artistic field. Figure 4.7 gives some exemplars of a level 2 analysis, showing how individuals were related to institutions within the field.

Our two earlier case studies were art museums whose origins were within the national fields of power, with highly consecrated political capital derived from government or royalty. This museum came into being with symbolic capital derived from both consecrated (New York State University, State Education Department, Harvard, Princeton) and pioneering educational institutions (Dalton School). Thus, MOMA was defined from the start as essentially an educational institution, highly consecrated and potentially avant-garde.

MOMA's founding trustees, however, were collectors of art, aware both of the aesthetic and economic value of an art object. These were participants in the artistic field, similar in kind to the 'Grande Bourgeoisie' interviewed by Bourdieu in *La Distinction*: '...the happy few in the dominant fractions who have the means of materially appropriating works of art' (Bourdieu 1984/1979: 273). Bourdieu goes on to say:

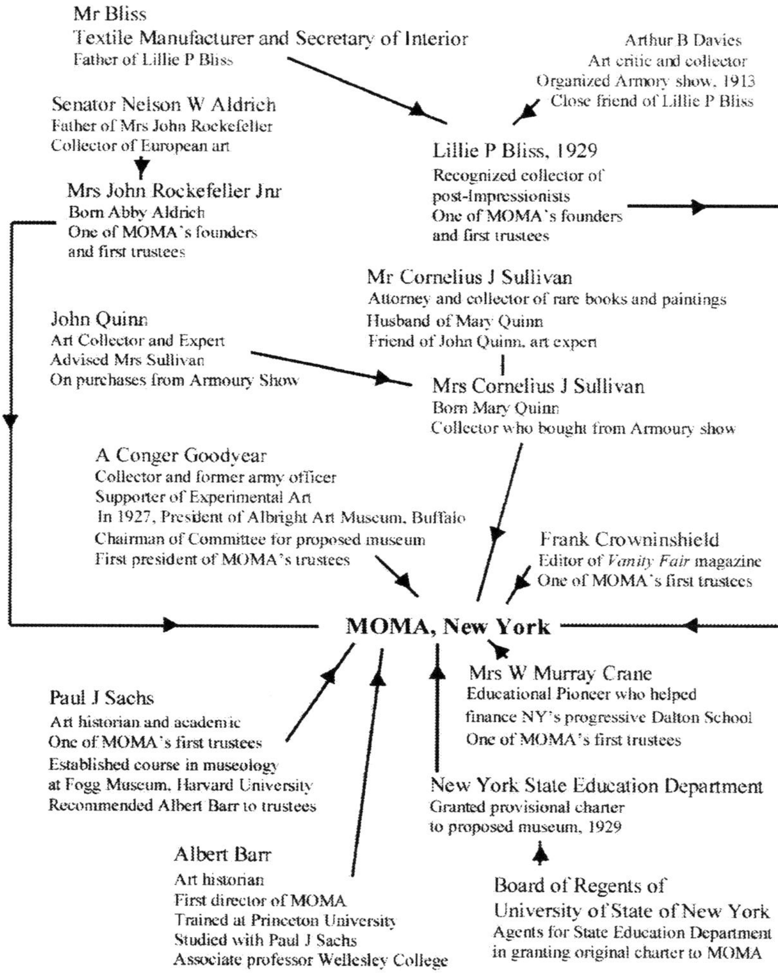

Figure 4.7 The Founding of the Museum of Modern Art, New York. Level 2 analysis: key agents and some relationships to other institutions.

> The whole relation to art is changed when the painting, the Chinese vase or the piece of antique furniture belongs to the world of objects available for appropriation, thus taking its place in the series of the luxury goods which one possesses…and which, even when not personally possessed, belong to the status attributes of one's group, decorating the offices one works in or the salons one frequents. (ibid.: 278)

Evidence that the founders did see art works as such luxury goods, at least in part, is given by the inclusion of Frank Crowninshield, editor of *Vanity Fair* magazine, as one of the trustees.

At their inaugural meeting in October 1929, the Board of Trustees elected A Conger Goodyear as their president. The trustees then swiftly and successfully undertook active fund-raising and a search for suitable exhibition space. With plans made for an opening exhibition in premises on the twelfth floor of the Fifth Avenue Heckscher Building, Goodyear scoured European dealers, collectors and institutions for the loan of art works to supplement those owned individually by trustees. This first exhibition, 'Cézanne, Gauguin, Seurat and Van Gogh', opened in November 1929, less than a fortnight after the collapse of the American stock market. It was a huge popular success – 49,000 visitors in five weeks – indicating that the artists identified later by Bourdieu's survey (1991d/1969/1966) as a popular European canon also had mass appeal in 1920s America. MOMA writing in the 1980s says of this first exhibition that 'the museum had clearly touched a nerve and need, bridging the gap between a few affluent collectors and amateurs who patronised the arts and the new democratic culture with its mass audience eager to unravel the mysteries of modern art' (Oldenburg 1984: 13). This exhibition did indeed set the tone for future MOMA exhibitions, which included Toulouse-Lautrec, Matisse and Corot. Unsurprisingly for an art museum with its roots in educational capital, MOMA has continued to this day to cater for mass audiences and to prioritize modern art education.

From the perspective of the broader socio-economic field, one observes that when a country's monetary and commercial systems flounder, the art market and works of art provide an alternative means of preserving economic capital. Thus, in America during the Depression, exhibiting one's own art works alongside other prestigious international art works, and hence adding to the symbolic value of all the works and to their consequent monetary value, preserved overall capital for the owner by increasing an art work's present cultural capital for later transformation into economic capital – a good investment of both time and money. As we commented earlier, a historical view of any field is structured from and by its survivors – in New York, both trustees and works of art thrived under this strategy of capital conversion. MOMA itself flourished, benefiting from the expanding symbolic capital of the trustees themselves and of their art works, and from the boost this gave to the cultural capital of its exhibitions. In 1932 the museum was able to lease a house from John D Rockefeller and, rather than purchasing its own art collection, continued its focus on an active and successful exhibition policy. It was not until 1936 that the museum announced plans to construct a new building. Despite the continuing Depression, trustees and associates were able to raise more than $1 million – a clear indicator of the dominant position within the socio-economic field of the individuals associated with MOMA.

At its inception, none of MOMA's trustees participated directly in the national and international political field, and hence the museum appeared to lack that form of consecrated symbolic capital which derives from the field of power. Strong social capital, often an enhancer of other symbolic capital (Bourdieu 1980) may well have provided the means of accruing this type of capital. But however it was achieved, during its first decade, MOMA was closely involved in the arts programmes which the government undertook in support of 'unemployed workers in every field of culture and the arts' (Oldenburg 1984: 19). During the Second World War, this engagement in the socio-political field was strengthened: thirty-eight contracts were executed for government agencies, for example, art therapy and a recreational centre for servicemen, and the detailed analysis of enemy propaganda films. Through these strategies, the museum accrued significant symbolic capital directly from the field of power, and, consequently, habitus which allowed MOMA to position itself as a nationally consecrated art institution, a benefactor of society and a democratic educator. This configuration of capital provided the means for the museum to confer consecration in its turn, in particular on a generation of post-war American artists – the abstract expressionists (see chapter 5).

The Collection

On his appointment as the first director in 1929, Albert H Barr submitted a plan for the art museum to the trustees. With no existing art works to accommodate, he used his academic experience to envisage a collection theoretically, using subject headings from the course he had taught at Wellesley College. He saw the collection as multi-departmental, combining the study and display of fine art (highly consecrated cultural capital from a field with restricted access) with the 'practical, commercial and popular' (high-volume cultural capital with low consecration) – a pioneering approach.

In 1929 Goodyear gave the museum its first sculpture, Maillol's *Ile de France*, but the museum's collection was not begun until 1934, when it had raised sufficient funds to meet the terms of the will of Lillie P Bliss. This demanded that an endowment be raised to maintain her collection of masterworks by Cézanne, Gauguin, Picasso, Degas, Renoir and others. With a collector's awareness of both the aesthetic and monetary value of works of art, Miss Bliss's legacy allowed the sale of any picture to acquire more desirable works – the transformation of cultural capital into economic capital, or into differently configured cultural capital.

Other early donors included Mrs Rockefeller, who gave almost 200 works, mainly American. She also donated money for Barr's first formal purchase funds. She followed Miss Bliss's example and allowed works to be sold in order to build the collection. From 1938 onwards, Mrs Simon Guggenheim proved to be a generous benefactor of paintings, providing funds for more than seventy masterpieces over a number of years.

At the end of its first five years, MOMA – originally intended to display modern art, particularly from living artists – owned an uncomfortable mix of nineteenth-century art and rather conservative choices in early twentieth-century art. Barr, however, was now able to realize sufficient economic capital from the culturally valuable, but 'disposable' art donations of his founders. Donations continued, but he could balance them with purchases and begin to implement his original plan of combining painting, sculpture, prints, drawings, photography, architecture, film and design in one collection. Although considered as less prestigious cultural artefacts at that time, a number of prints were donated, architectural drawings acquired, and early film – 1896 to 1916 – from the Biograph Company combined nicely with the gift of the Douglas Fairbanks collection in 1939. Hence the museum developed its Film Library, the Department of Prints and Drawings, the Department of Architecture and Industrial Art, the Department of Photography and a distinct department in support of the International Program. A uniquely structured and unusually diverse collection was established to complement the more traditional departments of Painting and Sculpture, the Library of Modern Art and MOMA's active education programme for children and adults.

Donations continued, along with periodic departmental restructurings. With its increasingly highly consecrated position within the artistic field, MOMA became a worthwhile repository for donations from artists themselves – those with an eye to posterity or perhaps seeking to enhance their own cultural capital within the future artistic field by a strategy of deferral of present economic capital. Alexander Calder's donation of thirteen of his sculptures in 1966 was the most consequential gift made by an artist.

MOMA's extensive collection today is indeed a realization of Barr's early conception of a multi-departmental museum. There are 6,000 drawings, 50,000 prints, 25,000 photographs, 24,000 architectural and industrial designs and 20,000 films and videos. MOMA claims its collection of 3,200 paintings and sculptures as both the largest and most comprehensive collection of modern art in the world. This is further supplemented by a well-established network of partnerships with other museums, such as the Louvre, and the recent affiliation with the PS1 Contemporary Art Center in New York.

The diverse nature and highly legitimated cultural capital of MOMA's collection overall serves to support works of less valued media (film or photography, for example) in adopting and maintaining field positions with higher cultural capital than would be possible otherwise. In other words, the volume and degree of highly consecrated cultural capital available to MOMA has served to change not only the possible field positions within the artistic field, but the boundaries between fields themselves, for example, between fine art and film. Bourdieu defines fields dynamically as both 'structuring of' and 'structured by' their participants' struggles for the best positions within them. Field changes between distinct artistic sub-fields are therefore the expected outcomes of human sociocultural activity over time. In 1929, when Mrs Rockefeller intended the new museum to reduce dramatically the time lag between the artist's creation and the public's appreciation of great works of art, she was a pioneer, but she may well not have fully anticipated that MOMA would be so successful in achieving this. This has had a more general effect within the international field of artistic consumption in accelerating the rate at which an art work accrues symbolic capital, and hence the potential economic capital for owner and artist alike. MOMA's collection has continued to grow steadily in size and in the time period covered by its collection. Thus, the museum premises have needed constant revision and extension in order to show its diverse art works to good effect and to provide opportunities to accommodate a constantly increasing audience.

Activities and Funding

The critic John Russell, describing MOMA's characteristics in the 1980s, writes:

> It is truly international. It covers not only painting and sculpture, but photography, prints, drawings, has its own publishing house, its own movie house and its own department of film and video. It has a shop in which everyday objects of every kind may be on sale provided they pass the Museum's standard of design. It is a palace of pleasure, but also an unstructured university. (John Russell, quoted in Oldenburg 1984: 11)

Since then, the museum has had to grow in size and complexity. MOMA's pattern of activities is similar to that of the Tate and, to a lesser extent, the Musée d'Orsay, but its scale and diversity are in a different league. Its education programme offers internships, academic conferences, courses and talks, high school programmes, a teacher information centre and an active programme of family activities. MOMA has established an award-winning website with access to its collection, library, archives, education programme and shop. It offers extensive advice about how to donate to the museum, how to become a corporate sponsor and use its prestigious facilities, and how to become a friend, associate or patron. There are online art projects, e-cards, an exhibition sub-site and comprehensive tourist advice. In contrast to the Musée d'Orsay's culturally conservative, French-only newsletters, MOMA offers any one of seven different monthly email newsletters. That the website should receive accolades from BBC Education is a clear signal that the museum has indeed maintained its educational mission, but similar praise from *Time Out* New York also confirms MOMA as a major tourist attraction.

This, then, is an organization which has adhered to its original aims to display the best of modern art and to prioritize education. In achieving a diverse collection which combined high and low art, and successfully seeking to increase its audience, it has had to adopt new strategies, such as its website and its recent affiliation to a gallery with exhibition space dedicated to the works of living artists. The highly consecrated field position of MOMA in the 1920s and 1930s as a pioneering institution has changed with the alterations to the field boundaries it sought to achieve. Now its field position has changed, so that it occupies a dominant position within the global artistic field. For MOMA, commerce was built in from the beginning – art is something to own. Its founding by art collectors demonstrates habitus derived from a highly consecrated socio-economic field, with a predisposition to see art works as luxury goods which may be owned and consumed directly. MOMA's emphasis on prints, photography and industrial design –

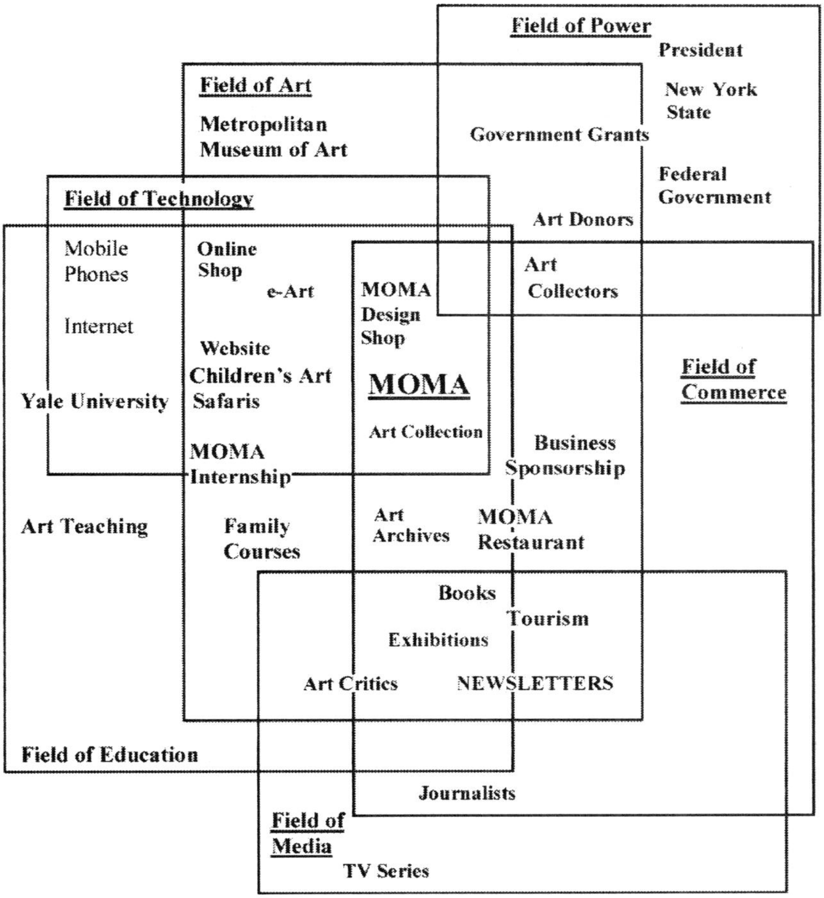

Figure 4.8 Museum of Modern Art, New York. Level 1 analysis: fields in relation to the field of power.

less highly consecrated art forms – and its shop selling 'good design' serve to broaden the socio-economic categories of the visitors who may aspire to distinction by exclusive ownership of art works or 'good design' (cf. Bourdieu 1979/1964: 280). While today's visitor cannot aspire to owning a work of art, they can afford a well-designed functional object from the shop or at least an e-card reproduction of one of MOMA's masterpieces. Thus, the museum has continued to reflect its entrepreneurial roots and educational values.

III

Concluding Remarks

Field Structures and Field Stability

In this chapter we have seen that three national art museums share common features in the symbolic capital needed for their successful establishment and for their functioning as a consecrated institution in the cultural field. Each of the art museums discussed has characteristics unique to that museum in the particular configuration of its economic and symbolic capital and its field positioning. Thus, the Tate, for example, derives some symbolic capital from regional artistic fields through Tate Liverpool and Tate St Ives – a characteristic not shared with MOMA or the Musée d'Orsay. The Musée d'Orsay has a distinctive high volume of socio-historic capital from the French cultural field through its building, its historically defined collection and its contextual displays. Within American society and its private enterprise values and beliefs, MOMA derives symbolic capital from the field of commerce as a privately established museum, with particular orientation towards private ownership of art.

Nonetheless, in the three-level field analyses illustrated in this chapter, the case examples show a remarkable similarity between the three art museums in terms of which sociocultural fields are the most significant to their functioning. As institutions, part of whose role is the legitimation of art works, artists and their donors, it is to be expected that the museums will themselves have accrued capital which is highly consecrated and of high volume. It was through field interactions between the very same four fields of 'culture and artistic consumption', 'education', 'government' and 'commerce' that each museum was founded. Although the relative importance of each field may have shifted over time, it is predominantly symbolic capital from precisely these fields which still constitutes the 'habitus' of each museum today. For the case examples here, high-volume symbolic and economic capital derived from the field of power (national government) is combined with highly consecrated cultural capital from the art historic field (educational institutions like Harvard and the Ecole des Beaux-Arts).

Each art museum has been, and continues to be, a site of field transactions where economic capital from the field of commerce can be reconfigured into more highly consecrated personal and institutional capital. Thus, the donation of economic capital in the form of art works (for example, Henry Tate's donation or Volkswagen's sponsorship of a Tate exhibition) or national grants and funding for buildings (for example, Mitterrand's support of the Musée d'Orsay project) has been transmuted into increased and consecrated habitus (sociocultural capital for the donor), while augmenting the museum's own economic and cultural capital.

There is consistency over time in the four fields in which the three museums are active participants, which strongly suggests that these relationships between fields and their field structures are themselves stable over time and across different settings. Is this true for other national museums? Are there cultural predispositions which are preconditions to this stability? Does this field stability continue to have explanatory power when applied to regional museums? Only further investigation would show the limits of this field stability.

Art Museums and Government

For any national museum we have seen that a strong relationship with national government is essential, since this provides highly consecrated symbolic capital from within the field of power, which is needed by a prestigious national institution. Government is also a source of economic capital. In Britain in the late 1990s, for example, a government decision directed substantial grants to national museums, including the Tate, to ensure free entry for all to their national heritage. The downside for an art museum of government-derived symbolic capital is the consequent vulnerability to changes in government or government policy. One example is the possible threat to the Musée d'Orsay's existing field position and capital which could result from discussions by the French government about corporate backing for cultural organizations. In cases like this, national policy change exacts major institutional change. As a privately established art museum, MOMA may have achieved more autonomy from government policy, but at the cost of exposure to any change in the interests of its donors and sponsors, for example, economic downturn or changes in the art market.

Museums and Educational Capital

In the first part of this chapter, museum attendance was discussed at some length as an example of artistic consumption, one particularly characteristic of the middle and upper classes. Cultural capital resulting from education – qualifications and inherited educational capital – was found to be a determining factor in the habitus of museum visitors. Since Bourdieu's work in the 1960s, museums have taken their educational role and the accessibility of their exhibitions as central to their development as public institutions. In each of our three examples, dedicated education departments and varied education programmes, including e-learning, are now integral to visitor provision. But here again, within a common strand of development, each museum demonstrates individual characteristics: the Musée d'Orsay's programme seeks to present art works as cultural artefacts within an overall socio-historic setting; the Tate makes extensive educational use of mass media, including art coverage by BBC radio and television, and programme series on Channel 4; MOMA has developed the widest range of education provision, from its web-based Family Safari to academic postgraduate conferences on art and its history. Audio tapes, gallery trails and publishing for a range of levels of artistic competence are all now commonplace in large museums, so that they are indeed educational places where one can find out about art, whatever one's prior knowledge – privately, through websites, or publicly, through well-labelled exhibitions, talks, courses and children's programmes. Today, an individual may acquire, with personal effort, art education sufficient to decode works of art and develop a strong, knowledge-based relationship within the field of art. What art museum education does not do is provide its audience with that easy familiarity with art works as luxury objects which can be bought and owned, which we saw was characteristic of the most dominant positions within the artistic field.

The Accessibility and Field Structures of Museums

Bourdieu's concern in France was for the cultural imperialism of art museums. The middle and upper classes visited regularly, unlike the working class, who associated museum visits with sanctified activities such as churchgoing. Today, the working class is no less disenfranchised, but this time by high entrance fees (for example, $20 for MOMA in 2005). Tate's public fares only a little better, since only access to the permanent collection is free, while special exhibitions are costly. The assumptions of middle-class values and income which lie behind the marketing of a museum as a pleasurable tourist visit further discourage the poorer or working-class visitor. Museum shops and online purchasing, proudly acclaiming objects of good industrial design, may be redolent of a comfortable upmarket shopping mall, but they effectively exclude the unemployed, the underprivileged and, sadly, those without access to a computer.

The three case example museums have all given priority to increasing their audiences. Their efforts to improve accessibility have been successful in substantially increasing the number of visitors. Despite curatorial resistance, marketing and communications departments have expanded and have taken visitors' responses seriously – from their eating habits to their reactions to exhibitions. As a result, museum provision is increasingly well matched to existing audiences (Schubert 2000). Unfortunately, museums in general, and our examples in particular, have been much less effective in broadening the distribution of their public across socio-economic categories. Davies (2005), reporting on a British survey of social class and museum-going, finds evidence that the proportion of middle-class visitors to art museums has actually increased. Barker (1999) argues that most of the visitors to the Musée d'Orsay are 'at least modestly affluent', since they are predominantly tourists interested in the canon of nineteenth-century art. The continuing exclusion from museum participation of specific subgroups, defined by disability, gender persuasion, ethnicity or religion, is also evidenced by Sandell (2002), when he argues for a museum's role in achieving social equality and for the desirability of privileged access for underrepresented sociocultural groupings. There have been changes, then, in the patterns of museum-going across the social space, but only to the scale of attendance, rather than transformation of the characteristic habitus of the audiences. Museums are popular, but they remain stubbornly middle class – those committed to the pure gaze!

Innovations such as virtual museum visits, images of collections on websites and timed visiting to special exhibitions can be interpreted as coping strategies for art museums with increasingly crowded gallery space (signifying high-volume, low-valued cultural capital), but with a need to preserve the museums' aura of exclusivity and social consecration (maintaining highly consecrated cultural capital). The tension between these two positions may well be a symptom of what Bourdieu calls hysteresis: a time lag between changes in the field position and field structures, and the modalities of discussion and analysis applied within the field. As Bourdieu states:

> Thus, it can be observed that to contradictory positions, which tend to exert structural 'double binds' on their occupants, there often correspond destabilised habitus, torn by contradiction and internal division...as a result of heightened consciousness associated with an effort of transformation, there is an inertia or hysteresis of habitus which have a spontaneous tendency to perpetuate structures corresponding to their conditions of production. (Bourdieu 2000a/1997: 160)

So, faced with contradictory cultural roles – highly consecrated cultural palace or pleasurable tourist spot? – art museums continue to use the same language to identify the same priorities, 'broadening its audience' and 'improving the visitors' experience' – issues which Bourdieu identified much earlier as at stake within the French cultural field. Curators are seen as successful if attendance is high, so, with blockbuster exhibitions, like Jackson Pollock's at MOMA in 1999, they seek to combine popular appeal with the exclusivity of artistic capital derived from the fine art field. Art museums' mass audiences, largely tourists, demonstrate clearly that they now occupy significant positions within the field of tourism and travel. Art historians are signalling this new position taking within the wider social space. For example, Barker (1999: 70) feels that: 'Not just Orsay...but central Paris itself functions today primarily as a glossy, nostalgic tourist attraction from which the poor of the region are effectively excluded'. Nonetheless, museums continue to market themselves as culturally consecrated institutions, seeking funds (visitors, trading or gifts) simply in order to purchase art works and further increase their artistic legitimation, but the ever increasing partnerships with mass media and business are running strongly counter to this classic field positioning. Whether there will be a complete and permanent change in national art museums' field position and position taking – from a habitus where highly consecrated cultural capital predominates to one where large-scale economic capital from visitors is the major constituent – is yet to be seen. Arguments about the relationships between these two field positions – art museums as sites which accrue cultural capital and consecrate its associated agents and visitors to varying degrees, or art museums as sites of popular cultural consumption and high economic capital as tourist spectacles – will certainly continue if what are occurring are fundamental shifts in field positions and boundaries. It will take time, however, for these field changes to be fully recognized and acknowledged. Alternatively, the two positions may continue in uncomfortable coexistence, since misrecognition of the functioning of symbolic capital may be in the interests of both institutions and agents in the field of artistic consumption.

More significantly still, there is evidence of shifting relationships between the fields themselves. Both the growing political vision of museums as agents of social and urban regeneration (cf. Sandell 2002; Smith 1998) and the increased entrepreneurial attitude and corporate sponsorship speak of a fundamental change in how the field of artistic consumption, the field of commerce and the field of political power interrelate. The advent of digitized images, copyright sales, digital art and museum's websites are all clear indicators that museums now also function within the field of technology and the field of information transfer. Thus, museums, always the sites of struggles for highly consecrated symbolic capital within the cultural and political fields, are developing increasingly complex field positioning within an ever greater number of fields, and with an ever greater influence from business and corporate sponsorship. Bourdieu sees all these changes as signifying that 'culture is in danger'. As he explains:

> ...what is currently happening to the universes of artistic production throughout the developed world is entirely novel and truly without precedent: the hard won independence of cultural production and circulation is being threatened, in its very principle, by the intrusion of commercial logic at every stage of the production and circulation of cultural goods. (Bourdieu 2001c: 67)

–5–

Painting

In various parts of this book we have evoked the picture of someone standing in front of a painting or a piece of visual art. We have also addressed the question of what constitutes 'aesthetic sense'. We have seen that art and culture appear in many guises, from the popular to the refined. They have in common an ability to produce a certain affective response, a relation between process and product, producer and audience. In some cases there is an other-worldliness, in others, a confrontation with self in the artistic transaction. We have also seen that Bourdieu sought to place aesthetics within its social conditions; this is especially true of his view of the 'pure gaze', the disinterested, a priori Kantian detachment which has characterized our contemporary understanding of aesthetics. In chapter 3, 'Art' was considered in two (interconnected) ways: from the point of view of the consumer and of the producer. In Bourdieu's *La Distinction*, evidence of the way 'taste' in cultural choice and consumption could be understood in terms of the structure of society was offered, and the way that cultural forms were distributed and apprehended within them. We have suggested that from a Bourdieusian perspective much of this differentiation operated in terms of dominant, legitimate cultural forms, which act as a kind of exchange rate for valuing all other forms. However, we also saw how a similar practical logic acted as a generating force for the cultural producers themselves. This chapter takes the latter point further forward, particularly with respect to painting.

We begin by considering the example of the pre-Impressionist, Manet, who is the painter Bourdieu himself considered most extensively. We do this in order to show Bourdieu's main arguments about the artistic field of painting and how it can best be approached. The mechanisms of change which 'produced' Manet will be demonstrated with particular reference to the morphology and functioning of the field of painting in the nineteenth century. This analysis leads us to a series of theoretical and methodological conceptions which we will then extend to two further examples, the young British artists of the 1990s and American abstract expressionism of the 1940s and 1950s.

A Temple of Art

Bourdieu often begins his analysis of social phenomena with one particular image in mind. It is as if Bourdieu captures a single picture which he then uses in an iconic fashion. The image leads to questions about what it represents and what the underlying social forces were which produced it. With a painting, there is also the personal sense of physically standing before it: the ineffable singularity formed in paint. Painting is subject to colour and form. It also has content – representational or abstract. What is represented can be viewed and used as simply decorative. The most significant paintings, however, suggest something beyond themselves: a rising above the mundane of the everyday lifeworld. Both the artist and the painting can be charismatic – classically defined as a gift from god. In other words, painting, and all art for that matter, offers a sense of exclusivity, a passage into a different way of experiencing. It becomes clear why, in Bourdieu's survey of museum visitors, many were keen to refer to art museums as latter-day churches. As we discussed in chapter 4, it is an analogy with some purchase on the social role, function and experience of these institutions. Little wonder, therefore, if art for Bourdieu could be considered as a 'collective act of magic' (2001d: 52). However, it was also a 'collective misrecognition'. In other words, art, and in this case painting, is not all that it seems. His approach is an attempt to uncover another more prosaic and socially functional reality behind this ineffability and beyond the mystery of art.

Manet

Bourdieu set himself the task of accounting for the changes in modern painting in France around 1870–80: the Impressionists. True to his own approach, Bourdieu argues that he can do this only by looking at the institution of art itself, in other words, the social and cultural conditions which produced art at that time. Such an account is not merely a historical contextualization of what occurred and what was produced, but is a structural constructivist's analysis of the interrelations of field and habitus, expressed through the medium of the artistic institution. It is not simply a historical narrative, but a sociological-phenomenological study of the logic of practice which constituted a field at a particular point in time, and of the effects this had on artists, painters and what they produced.

For Bourdieu, Manet was a pivotal figure. Up until this time, painting in France had conformed to conventions of moral exactitude or academic perception. With Manet, however, there was a break from all this. His style was novel: composition broke with normal rules, mixing in the same painting the classical and the everyday (as with the figures in *Déjeuner sur l'herbe*, 1863, for example). His subjects are frequently chosen to represent a certain social typology, often accenting the commonplace (as in *The Railroad*, 1873) or a particular incident in time and place (as in *The Artist's Wife at the Piano in Their Apartment on rue St Peterbourg*, 1867). His technique was highly innovative, apparently breaking with the established methods taught by the state-supported Ecole des Beaux-Arts, and seen now as a precursor to the later revolution of the Impressionists.

For Bourdieu, the fact that Manet was recognized *at the time* for what he did is evidence that what we are talking about here is not simply an abrupt challenge to

Panofsky

the conventional art of the day, but a veritable symbolic revolution in the way art was perceived. New categories of thought were necessary to support this revolution, analogous to a different way of seeing the world. No surprise, therefore, if Bourdieu sees such a revolution as being on a par with the great symbolic revolutions of the past. The task then is threefold: first, to understand what constituted this revolution in terms of the artistic product and the way it was expressed in terms of content and form; second, to apprehend the new forms of perception and thought that were required for this 'new art' to be accepted and appreciated; and third, to analyse the social conditions which constituted the symbiotic genesis of art and the categories of thought which both produced and consumed it. There is in fact a fourth stage also, which is about the categories of thought brought to this analysis: what theory of practice is at play in the above three-stage analysis; how it differs from the logic of practice to which it addresses itself; and how it is epistemologically placed in the present time with regard to these events of the past. This fourth concern will be developed further in chapter 7. For the moment, let us look further into the socio-conditions which formed (we might say 'allowed') Manet. In effect, this is to see Manet as 'historically necessitated without being historically necessary' (Bourdieu 1993b: 239).

Changes in French art throughout the eighteenth century were dramatic. Historically, this period moves from the height of so-called aristocratic painting, with its exaltation of divine immanence in Church and the Crown, to romanticism, with its stirrings of individual artistic autonomy, and finally a return to concerns with classical forms by way of revolution, nationalism and empire. The state-sanctioned French *Académie* in the nineteenth century operated a near monopoly over all things artistic. The Ecole des Beaux-Arts was one of the state training schools (*grandes écoles*) set up to ensure the production of a cultural elite in France. The trajectory of the conventional artist here proceeded analogously with that of any student in the *grandes écoles*: through preparatory schools, competition for entry and formal training in the *école* itself, where the artist learnt officially recognized techniques. Bourdieu makes the point that the painters emerging from this training were neither artisans, as in former times, nor artists, in the conventional sense of the word, but masters of the artistic field. These individuals often came from families already established in the artistic field (thus evidencing Bourdieu's own belief that habitus and cultural capital were largely the product of social background and determined trajectory). They would enter the ateliers of established academy artists, where they faced a life of harsh discipline and training, which demanded a certain disposition (habitus) to allow oneself to be inducted in the ways of the master. In effect, through imitation and copying, they were trained in 'his own image'. Success in competition led to entry into the Ecole des Beaux-Arts itself, which perpetuated the 'official' style and technique, finally to be rewarded in further competition prizes and exhibitions in the Salon. Indeed, Salon exhibitors in 1842 were required on entry to state the name of their master. In this way, there was a homologous match between training and outcome, official art and consecrated art, state structure and artistic hierarchies. Through these mechanisms, the art field was sanctioned and rewarded in terms defined by the state. Bourdieu (1993b: 243) makes the point that the subject of such art is a personification of the 'great principles': the True, the Beautiful and the Good. In an odd way, the attitudes and values of aristocratic art were also reproduced, in structurally homologous terms, in nineteenth-century art. Quoting Sloane, Bourdieu (ibid.) states:

> The ideas of moral grandeur which attached to the person of the king and his government were extended, in part, to apply to the art which was, so to speak, at their service. Irrespective of the quality of the results produced, a certain nobility was conferred upon any art which was related to these governmental ideas. Nationalism, love of France, respect for authority vested in the ruling power, and a desire to root the greatness of France deep in the past were all factors contributing to the undeniable strength of the academic system.

In style, it was an art of execution, an application of an established technique to a recognized historical subject. It was highly derivative in copying the masters, through belief in the subordinating of technique and subject to established method and canonical subjects. Bourdieu writes of painters being 'high level civil servants of art' in the way that the product and the process are controlled essentially by the state. The accent is on the accomplishment, virtuosity and techniques of the past masters. The idea was less to say something than to show how well it had been said. For Bourdieu, this was the style and approach of the French Academy – academic or scholarly art. As well as the accent often being on technique, the content of the paintings tended to favour literary content rather than pictorial invention. Effect is all: the expressive intention of painters is to present themselves as 'learned men and humanists' through the intellectual aspect of a work. Such an approach saw art as a way of expressing noble values, often literary in origin; as communicating something, 'a meaning transcending the pure play of forms and colours which merely signify themselves' (p. 245). Artists' expressive intent in execution was mirrored in the act of 'reading' a painting, which amounted to 'a scholarly decoding based on literary culture'. Bourdieu thus sees a 'minimized gap' between the artist and the 'bourgeois' middle class. The former caught up with development in technique through annual visits to the Salon after 1816, and relied on their knowledge of history and literary allusion to interpret what was being said. For Bourdieu, this is indeed the use of history to understand painting, but not history as he intends; not history as a way of situating the work in history. Rather, it is recourse to socially embodied history in the cultural capital available to 'read' the work as a learned individual. This history therefore 'ignores the perception which is based on a specific knowledge of the history of styles and manners in order to situate each painting, through the play of properly pictorial comparisons and distinctions, in the specific history of painting' (p. 246). In other words, Bourdieu claims that a 'science of the history of art' is needed in contrast to a purely naive one based on bourgeois aesthetics. Bourdieu sees the same logic of practice in the execution, content and appearance of painting as in its reception. The focus on technique itself leads to an 'ethical expectation' so central to the academic position. Indeed, orderly painting itself is a valued reflection of a certain social and moral order: 'hieratic, calm, serene...gentle colours, noble outlines, and idealized fixed figures' (p. 246). There is here an aesthetic of the 'finished' which Bourdieu argues is characteristic of bourgeois values of integrity and discretion.

Bourdieu sees Manet as flying in the face of all this. One of the major criticisms of Manet's work was that it was 'unfinished', a crude sketch, lacking in technique. The whole appearance of a painting such as *Olympia* (1863) was the very antithesis of 'orderly painting' and the 'academic approach'. As such, it was considered morally questionable. The accent given to line in relation to colour was 'deemed suspicious because of its carnal seductiveness', in other words, contrary to professional standards. Bourdieu quotes Albert Wolff (1869): 'Manet believes he is making paintings but really he only brushes in sketches'. Manet's paintings were therefore a challenge to the academic orthodoxy; a sort of ethical transgression not only in form and content, but in the values which underlay them. Such a challenge was therefore not simply one of technique and style, but, perhaps, of a whole lifestyle. Manet did not set up a painting to be 'read'. Indeed, in a painting such as *The Execution of Maximillian* (1868), conventional forms and narrative are absent: 'The unbearable lack of meaning leads either to indignant condemnation, when it is perceived as intentional, or to the arbitrary projection of different meanings' (p. 249). Manet refused to give a direct message to the viewer, or any depiction of the higher values, so characteristic of the 'academic approach'. In effect, Bourdieu argues that in taking this approach Manet broke with the artistic field as it existed at that time. Manet's revolutionary achievement was to be the thin end of an artistic wedge driving itself between the 'academic eye' and 'pure painting', since his painting expressed itself not through narrative and character, but by means of colour and form.

In sum, Bourdieu is arguing that, before Manet, painting had a certain academic style, which was characteristic of a certain social class – the ruling bourgeoisie. The state imposed its own aesthetic vision through the systems of state-controlled competitions, prizes and art training schools. Artistic success depended on conformity to a definition of artistic practice imposed by this field of cultural consumption. What was constituted was an artistic *nomos*, which ruled production. Entry into this was controlled by the state through its systems of consecration and rejection, most noticeably in those artists' works which were selected for exhibition in the Salon. The emergent style of the logic of this practice was immanent in the content and form of painting. Manet was the first to challenge this orthodoxy in a way that was recognized. His approach broke with the 'academic'; his style was its very antithesis. How did it come about?

For Bourdieu, the answer to this question has to lie in the social conditions of the times themselves. First, the sheer number of artists in the period led to a heightened sense of generational displacement. Bourdieu sees the consequences of these numbers as a greater competition for all forms of field capital, with the resultant necessity to revalue and reconfigure cultural capital itself. Second, the field of artistic production changed, involving not just painters but all those associated professionals, for example, writers, buyers, journalists, gallery owners and curators. Manet did not affect this artistic revolution on his own, but mobilized an entire professional network on his behalf (for example, the writer Mallarmé defended and supported Manet). Third, the state itself was changing. In 1863 Manet presented three paintings to the Salon. Although the jury rejected all of them, Emperor Napoleon III decreed that those rejected paintings could themselves be exhibited in what became known as the Salon des Refusés. Here we might see the state sanctioning the very challenge to its own orthodoxy. Why should this be so? Fourth, society itself was changing. New middle-class groups, with a distinct habitus, developed taste and a way of being in the world which required a new aesthetic. Manet's 'pure painting' can be seen as burgeoning in a new relation to art: 'art for art's sake'. We see in Manet, and in every artist thereafter, a new social positioning. No longer tied exclusively to established channels of state sponsorship, they asserted their own individuality and thus achieved free choice over their work. In a sense, nothing is more intimate to the artist than their craft, their technique. The assertion of independent control over that technique, and subject matter, was an assertion of artistic freedom and expression. It was also an individualism which matched perfectly that of the new middle classes: '"I am master over myself and over the universe" is an ethical profession of faith in which a dominant individual justifies his domination in his own mind by referring to his natural capacity to dominate nature' (Bourdieu 1988/1984: 110).

An artist such as Manet was similarly asserting his own mastery over his art and, by implication, lifestyle. In so doing, Manet was establishing a social position, complete with its own logic of practice, which was homologous to that of the new middle classes – his audience. The situation is therefore somewhat paradoxical. In many respects, Bourdieu sees Manet as a true revolutionary, and his achievement was a genuine heroic struggle to assert artistic independence. The fact that Manet's background was itself bourgeois, and that he had been trained at the Ecole des Beaux-Arts, makes his case all the more admirable. What he did, in effect, represented a double refusal: against the academic art of the establishment, and in opposition to social populism. He did this in paint and with art which defined a new status for the artist. However, one must never forget that Manet, as a kind of artistic intellectual, still represents a 'dominated member of the dominant class'. He is therefore still dependent on capital – social, economic and cultural – and therefore he had to create his own market in order to realize his artistic ambitions. This was possible because other factions within the field of power – society and the state – also sought a new art for their new society. The field of artistic production may have been reconfigured by artists, but it achieved temporal stability through corresponding reconfigurations in the field of artistic consumption.

The question implicit in all this is: To what extent does such an analysis of Manet provide the tools for the study of any other artistic movement? – in this case, painters and painting. In the rest of this chapter we will bring the same concepts – habitus, field and capital – to two other recognized painting movements: the young British artists (yBas) of the 1990s and American expressionism of the 1940s and 1950s. However, before doing so, we look in a little more detail at the 'rules of the art field'.

The Rules of the Field of Art

To sum up, Bourdieu argued that artistic production, in this case painting, must be understood in terms of its sociocultural conditions of production. Just as with aesthetic sense, art production needs to be understood as essentially immanent within the structures of society. With Manet, Bourdieu had a perfect example of someone who could only be understood in terms of what he struggled against and, in so doing, the space he opened up for what followed. However, such a position was not simply an individual assertion based on pure aesthetic sense, but was itself a product of the conditions of a particular place and time. Before Manet, the value of art – its content, technique and form – was defined in terms of the values of the state, through the intermediary of the art establishment and its institutions. Changes in the social structures, both within and outside of the field of painting, produced the forces necessary for change. In order to understand how this works in practice, we employ Bourdieu's conceptual thinking tools – habitus, field and capital – and consider painting in terms of the three-level methodology presented in chapter 3.

The traditional role of an artistic avant-garde is to challenge established hierarchies and the bourgeois values of the status quo. It is now almost a cliché to use the term avant-garde to designate the rapid succession of artistic groups or schools, particularly in turn-of-the-century Paris – the Impressionists and post-Impressionists, the Nabis, the Fauves, Cubism and Orphism, among others. Change in art necessitates a vanguard movement, which sweeps away the old and ushers in the new. Greenberg, writing in the late 1930s, expressed a view which seems to have contemporary relevance: 'the most important function of the avant-garde is not to experiment but to keep culture moving in the midst of ideological confusion and violence' (Greenberg 1939: 8). However, underpinning the notion of an avant-garde is a modernist view of change: collective in character, with artists assumed to be autonomous and able to adopt common subversive strategies to established art practices.

These arguments raise questions concerning the relations between tradition, modernism, postmodernism and the mechanisms of change in artistic movements. Furthermore, there is the issue of the role and status of the avant-garde. Their self-proclaimed *raison d'être* is to challenge. However, this mission is not to be confused with heroic altruism. Weiss (1994), for example, argues that artists' self-aware deployment of what we would call avant-garde strategies is merely a deliberate mechanism for establishing public recognition: 'the avant-garde is perceived as an on-going publicity stunt, and innovation in pictorial style is a promotional strategy' (p. 90). In other words, although avant-garde practice may well be aimed overtly at artistic recognition and the judgements made by cultural peers, it also has a clear economic basis in self-advertisement and marketing.

This complicity between artistic practice and economic aspiration fits neatly with Bourdieu's delineation of field positioning, where 'Social structures and cognitive structures are recursively and structurally linked, and the correspondence that obtains between them provides one of the most solid props of social domination' (Bourdieu (with Wacquant) 1992a: 14). These field structures are constituted through both symbolic cultural capital and economic capital – that is, cash. Avant-garde groupings occupy a dominated position within the dominating class. It is the relationship between the oppositionally defined practices and attitudes of each generation of artists and their artistic and social positionings which gives rise to field structures. Changes in attitude, changes in positioning and changes in field structuring are all mutually constituting phenomena, coincidental with the struggles for position within any specific field. The structure of the artistic field, and the way it changes, is graphically illustrated by Bourdieu in *The Rules of Art* (1996a/1992:

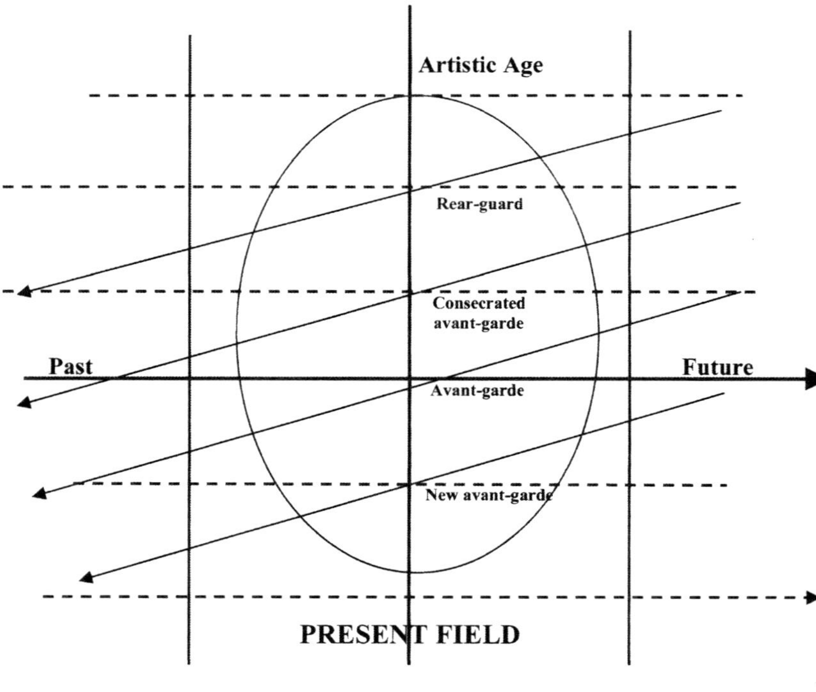

Figure 5.1 The Temporality of the Field of Artistic Production. Based on Bourdieu (1996a/1992: 159).

159), where he sets out the 'temporality of the field of artistic production'. His subject here was the literary field. However, it is applicable to any artistic field.

Figure 5.1 is based on Bourdieu's diagram and adapted for our own purposes. It can be seen as drawing attention to at least five dimensions of time, or temporality, in the nature of fields: first, real physical time – future, present, past; second, socially defined time, including months, weeks, years and *époques*; third, an individual artist's lifetime, in that they are born, grow up, age and die in time; fourth, the period a particular artistic generation lasts; and fifth, the time an individual artist remains recognized within a particular artistic generation. Each of these is defined in relation to the others. There are fields within fields, and individuals (habitus) within these fields within fields. The diagram offers a static presentation of what is a dynamic and ever changing process. An individual artist ages in physical and social time, but their passage through the field of their generation may be fast or slow, according to the degree of recognized legitimacy bestowed on them. And their generation itself may establish a consecrated position, or simply pass out of the current field, which contains the rear-guard tradition as well as successive generations of avant-garde defined in opposition to it and each other.

Figure 5.2 is an adaptation of Bourdieu's literary field to represent the field of fine art. It is illustrated with specific examples from successive generations of painters.

The data analysed for Figure 5.2 was taken from *Modern Painters*, an established British art review journal, which often favours a modernist and progressive view of artistic development. Key artists and authors featured in back copies over the 1990s are used here to represent that artistic field. It shows how artists fell into successive generational groupings:

- Tradition: Poussin, Donatello, Michelangelo, Giotto, Frans Hal, Velazquez, Titian, Vermeer, Tiepolo, Gericault, Goya.
- European avant-garde: Monet, Van Gogh, Gauguin, Bonnard, Cézanne, Picasso, Braque, Morandi, Matisse, Mondrian, Brancusi, Derain, Masson, Duchamp, Magritte, Chagall.
- American avant-garde: Hooper, Pollock, Rothko, Rauschenberg, Jasper Johns, Twombly, Motherwell, Stella, De Kooning, Ellsworth Kelly, Jeff Koons, Basquiat.
- British art: Sickert, Henry Tonks, Epstein, Stanley Spencer, John Piper, Barbara Hepworth, Victor Passmore, Henry Moore, Elizabeth Frink, Lucien Freud, Carel Weight, Eduardo Paolozzi, Howard Hogkins, David Hockney, Prunella Clough, Patrick Heron, Julian Schnabel, Tony Cragg, Gilbert and George, Anish Kapoor, Damien Hirst, Ron Muek, Richard Billington.

Figure 5.2 expresses this information in terms of a series of broad artistic generations. European avant-garde of the late nineteenth to early twentieth centuries defined themselves in oppositional relation to classical painting practices.

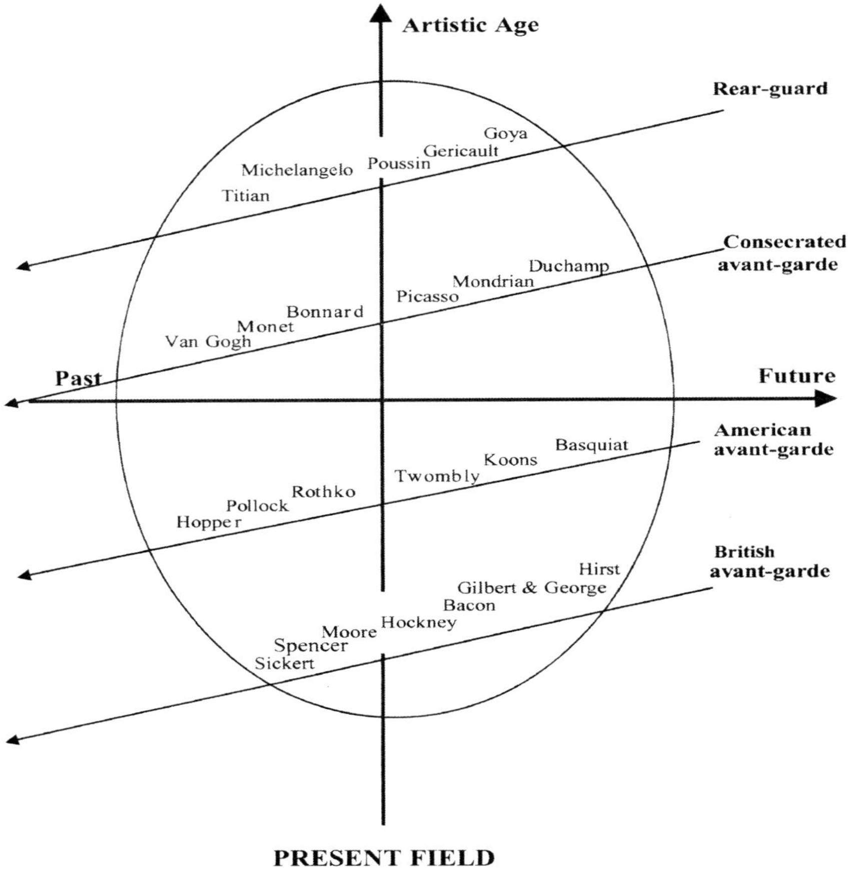

Figure 5.2 The Field of Modern Art from Art Review 1990s.

American avant-garde came to the fore after the Second World War, with the rise of abstract expressionism, minimalism, and so on. British art is the 1990s claimed to be at the forefront of artistic developments, superseding earlier American innovative practice, although some older artists are more closely related to the modernist practices on the European continent. These four groups of artists could, of course, be subdivided into more tightly defined groups in terms of their time-specific practices. For example, Edward Hopper sits uncomfortably in the same artistic generation as Pollack, Rothko and Rauschenberg; nor do the latter share artistic practice with Jeff Koons or Basquiat. In other words, the time scale used here for each 'generation' is a very broad one. Nevertheless, the diagram serves to draw attention to significant characteristics of artistic generations. First, it shows that artists and artistic generations define themselves in terms of what Bourdieu called a *prise de distance* between each other. Second, it shows that artistic movements do have boundaries and that these may have 'hard' or 'soft' definitions. Third, an individual artist or grouping is rarely recognized as being of note without legitimation within the field. In other words, artistic consecration can only be bestowed with the mobilization of an entire network of artists, critics, curators, dealers and gallery owners. As Bourdieu writes: 'To impose a new producer, a new product and a new system of taste on the market at a given moment means to relegate to the past a whole set of producers, products and systems of taste, all hierarchized in relation to their degree of legitimacy' (1996a/1992: 160). Manet's displacement of 'academic' art is an example of such a relegation.

In this way, the field of painting is seen as series of successive generations, where one established avant-garde is displaced by another. In effect, that is what Manet did: announce an avant-garde which displaced the academic art of the day. However, we have to stress that for Bourdieu this is not merely the genius of one individual, but something which is 'historically necessitated' by the socio-conditions of the day, in particular, the social topography of the intellectual and middle classes and their relationship to the artistic field and the state. The relegation of 'a whole set of producers', spoken of above, does not simply arise as the result of some utilitarian expression of originality, but is a kind of mobilization of an entire social aesthetic in the name of particular competing factions of the art field. To stress again, in order to create this space, an artist needs an entire set of capital – social, cultural and economic – in order to establish the value of the symbolic currency that is offered. Such a symbolic valuation occurs only as a result of recognition from others, which legitimizes and consecrates the product. As we saw in chapter 4, that is, above all, what an art museum does: it consecrates objects as 'art', as worthy of serious aesthetic consideration or of a visit.

We now consider two practical illustrations of how this process of legitimation takes place in the sociocultural field; first, the young British artists of the 1990s.

The yBas

'British art is booming' declared Louisa Buck in her *User's Guide to British Art Now* in the late 1990s (Buck 1998: 7). It certainly considered itself to be booming. Arguably, half a century had passed since the last time British art attracted the attention of the international art markets. Recognition of its significance was evidenced in late 1997 by the lively media coverage given to the controversial 'Sensation' exhibition, which was held in London at the Royal Academy of Arts (the home of the British art establishment). *Sensation* (Rosenthal 1997) exhibited work of the leading yBas: Hirst, Whiteread, Hume, Gormley, Wearing and thirty-eight others. Its claims to be a movement of international significance were further supported by the notoriety and interest it attracted across the world as it toured to Berlin, Sidney and Tokyo. In New York the mayor threatened financial sanctions if the exhibition took place – a threat which confirmed the 'avant-garde' challenge of the yBas, and hence their cultural status.

What follows is a systematic analysis of the yBas in terms of our three-level methodology. To recall, this entails: first, the positioning of the artistic field vis-à-vis the field of power; second, a mapping out of the objective structure of the relations between the positions occupied by the agents of institutions (art galleries, museums, art schools) who compete for the legitimate form of specific authority of which the artistic field is a site; third, an analysis of the habitus of artistic agents, the different systems of dispositions they have acquired by internalizing a determinate type of social and economic conditions, and which find a definite trajectory within the field under consideration and a more or less favourable opportunity to become actualized. This case example is therefore presented in terms of three distinct levels in order to focus on operations across and within the artistic field. The three levels range from the formal socio-political relations in society itself to field structures derived from the activities of agents and institutions and from individuals' habitus.

A further methodological aspect concerns 'insider accounts'. What matters in establishing the structure of any geographical or temporal field, and an artist's position within it, is not how, with hindsight, we make 'objective' judgements to establish relative values for social, cultural and economic capital, but what functional value each configuration of capital has contemporaneously within the practical logic of the field. Genet Delacroix (1986) uses data about particular French artists to illustrate, or 'test', some general classifications of types of nineteenth-century art. She insists on using only historically contemporary 'insider accounts', such as reviews, letters and diaries. We might even argue that Bourdieu himself made use of such insider information on a number of occasions in his work: the Béarn, the state training schools, higher education, even Algeria to an extent, were all areas where Bourdieu was intimately involved at the level of the empirical subject. The fact was, however, that he sought to make use of these contexts and his insider knowledge of them, while developing the 'impartial view' of the 'scientific subject'; and to offer the whole as an alternative paradigm grounded in his theory of practice and the reflexive objective 'truths' it provides (we develop these themes in chapters 2 and 7).

In collecting data for the current case example, a range of contemporary insider accounts were used: reviews, magazines (*Flashart*, *Art Review*, *Modern Painters*) and a number of commentaries (for example, Buck 1998; Kent 1994). None of these offer data which is objective. It is the writers' very subjectivity – their familiarity with the field – which is useful for this analysis, since it reflects their own artistic habitus gained as participant observers in the field. Every writer's account of the field demonstrates how they perceive its sociocultural structures and their bases for valuing within the field of British art in the 1990s. They represent both a position taking within the field and a personal construction of the relative positions of others within the same field. What is presented here is a snapshot in time of how one part of the British artistic field was structured in the 1990s, based on accounts written at that time rather than a post a priori reconstruction of the yBas' place in history. An account using documents written at a different time could well show significant differences. We approached the three-level analysis systematically in this case.

Level 1: The Field of British Art within the Field of Power

Figure 5.3 is based on the insider accounts referred to above. It demonstrates the way that the field of contemporary art connects with other media fields and, ultimately, the field of politics, and with audiences of all these. It is indicative of this level of analysis.

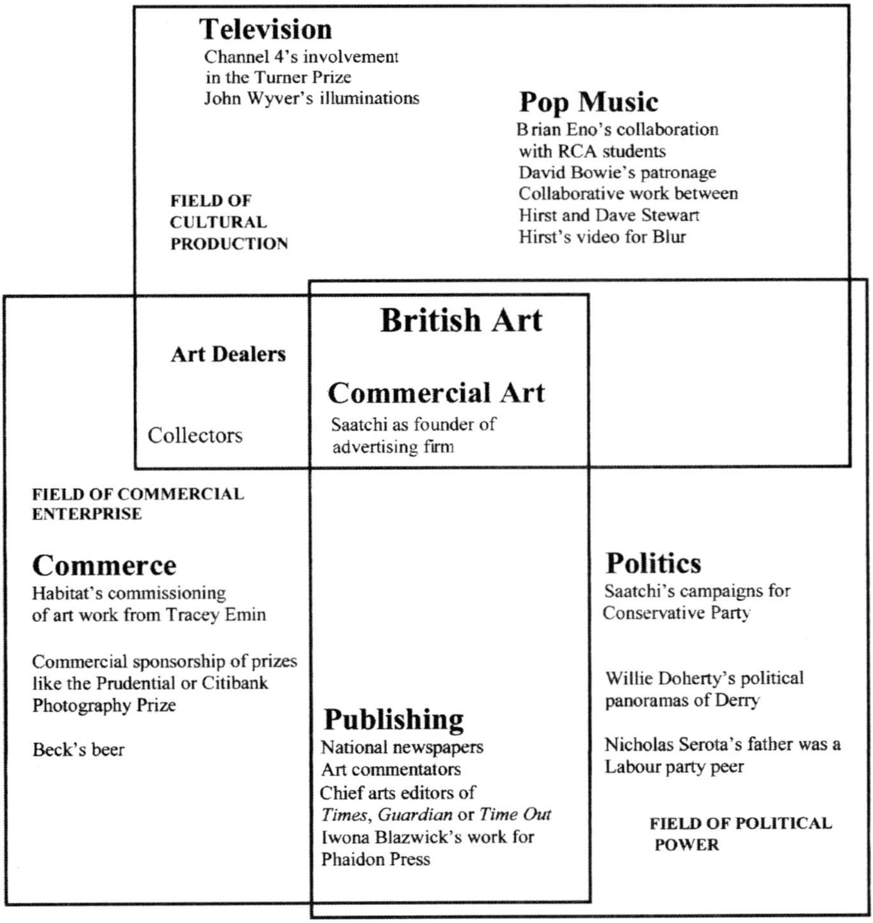

Figure 5.3 One Part of the Field of Young British Artists. Level 1 analysis: fields in relation to the field of power.

Bourdieu defined the field of power as: 'the set of relations of force between agents or institutions having in common the possession of the capital necessary to occupy the dominant positions in different fields (notably economic or cultural)' (1996a/1992: 215). Any cultural field occupies a 'dominated' position within the field of power since, despite the ambiguity of their relationship to the bourgeois, ultimately, cultural producers are dependent on their patrons, be they wealthy art buyers or fine art institutions.

Furthermore, Bourdieu writes: 'the relationship of homology established between the field of cultural production and the field of power (or the social field in its entirety) means that works which are produced with reference to purely "internal" ends are always predisposed to fulfil external functions as an added bonus' (ibid.: 166). We can see this dual function in practice. A commentator such as Buck writes of artists' shared 'desire to use whatever means are at their disposal...to make work that speaks of what it is to be human and live in this world' (1998: 7). Such ends are internal to the art world and the functioning of the field of artistic production. Simultaneously, however, such internal ends have external consequences. For example, the international lawyer, Stuart Evans, is identified by Buck as an important art patron. He had purchased work by Matt Collishaw and Rachel Whiteread to enliven his company's headquarters. The art works therefore fulfilled an external function of art as a luxury good within the social field: used to support a prestigious corporate image and to position the company strategically within the more general field of power. The dynamic nature of these field interactions was further demonstrated when Stuart Evans bought art from Tracey Emin. She then used his services as a lawyer when she leased property and subsequently donated further work to the firm as payment – a mutual exchange of cultural and economic capital, and an instance of structured structuring within both the artistic field and the broader social space.

Bourdieu writes further: 'It is a very general property of *fields* that the competition for what is at stake conceals the collusion regarding the very principles of the game. The struggle for the monopoly of legitimacy helps to reinforce the legitimacy in the name of which it is waged (1996a/1992: 167). For example, in a position taking similar to Manet's, the leading yBa, Damien Hirst, overtly challenged the hegemony of orthodox artistic hierarchies, 'when he mixes up disparate elements from TV series, children toys...with such art historical influences...as the pristine Minimalism of Donald Judd' (Buck 1998: 47). However, the overall result was that his own practice was further legitimated by assimilation of cultural capital from his consecrated source – Judd – and from the avant-garde position shown by his appropriation of elements of popular culture. Thus, paradoxically, he joined the fine art hierarchy that he appeared to challenge. Many contemporary artists challenge fine art practices with their hybridization of traditional forms, by their foregrounding of commodification and popular culture, and by their oppositional stance to bourgeois values in prioritizing novelty, shock and taboo breaking. However, despite the 'novel' form of their art works, they necessarily have a dominated positioning in relation to their markets and audiences, which is directly homologous to the previous field positioning of the fine art artists and practices which they apparently oppose. These struggles between field participants for stylistic domination of the field disguise their necessary accumulation of economic and cultural capital. In the longer term, the same struggles may well result in these oppositional cultural producers, the yBas, altering the structures of their own field of production and of their relations to the established field of power, in the same way that Manet's practice was the meeting point of change in the artistic field and change in society at large. Some of these successful avant-garde artists are becoming 'establishment' figures of the future, to be opposed and deposed by younger artists in their turn.

A wide variety of other factors are relevant to the positioning of the field of British art within the field of power. These include the wide circulation of products from the various fields as fashion objects or popular ideas; for example, Monet's *Waterlilies* was used as a design for Royal Academy carrier bags, and Hirst's *Shark* and Emin's *Bed* were used as artistic icons in a range of popular cultural contexts. The art world's relationships with politics is also significant; for example, in the social and family connections of key players such as Nicholas Serota (director of the Tate and son of a Labour peer), and when the British prime minister, Tony Blair, supports British artists like Gary Hume at the Venice Biennale. The political and social views and attitudes of key individuals influence their relationships and position taking as field participants in the field of art; for example, the photographer Willie Doherty's views on Northern Ireland, and art critic Sarah Kent's changing relationship to feminism. Commercial partnerships and sponsorship by business also influence both individual habitus and positions in the artistic field and in the field of power itself; for example, Beck's beer used British contemporary art for publicity, and Habitat commissioned designs from established British artists. There are also strong relationships between the British art field and the fields of media, publishing and music. Examples include interactions with art editors of major newspapers, collaborative projects between artists and musicians such as David Bowie and Brian Eno, and media sponsorship of art prizes and exhibitions, such as Channel 4 for Turner Prize. (This discussion recalls the references to 'high art' and 'low art', as perceived by such writers as Benjamin and Fisher, referred to in chapter 3.)

The key factors here are coverage in the popular media rather than the traditional elite appeal of fine art; personal politics rather than national politics; and individual commercial enterprise rather than the stereotypical view of an unrecognized artist struggling in poverty. Today, the media do mediate the value of artistic field capital, but artists deploy media attention to increase their symbolic and economic capital. Many yBas – Damien Hirst, Chris Ofili and Tracey Emin, among others – have knowingly used public controversy in the popular media to gain recognition for themselves in the broader social space, and hence have accrued symbolic cultural capital which can then be deployed within the artistic field itself.

Level 2: The Field of Contemporary British Art

The next level of analysis looks at a mapping of the field of contemporary British art itself. Such a map is to show the structural connections between those involved, for example, artists, critics, teachers, curators, museums and institutions of art, gallery owners and buyers. Such relations occur at both a personal and an institutional level, and are both formal and informal. The medium of these relations can be understood as economic, cultural and social capital.

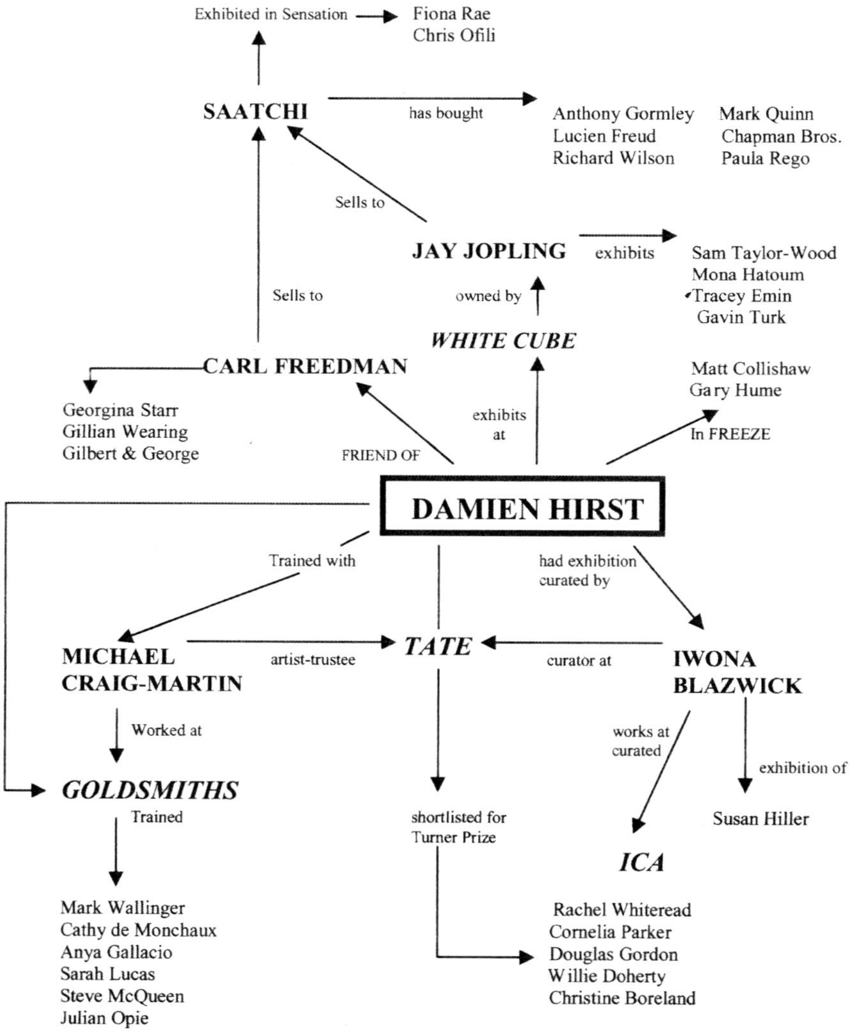

Figure 5.4 Damien Hirst. Level 2 analysis: the field of contemporary British art.

Rather than offering a depersonalized 'map of the field', Figure 5.4 uses the artist Damien Hirst as an anchor. Hirst is described by Buck (1998: 199) as an artist with 'ubiquitous star status', and has been seen very much as leader of the pack of the yBas. The figure starts with Hirst and shows some of his interactions with other active participants in the field. By doing so, it demonstrates the interrelations and symbolic capital referred to in the last paragraph.

One can conclude that Damien Hirst is well placed within the field. He has connections to three key institutions: Goldsmiths, the Tate and the Saatchi Gallery. Goldsmiths is a leading art school in London, where Hirst trained under the mentorship of the influential teacher Michael Craig-Martin. His relations with Goldsmiths, with other Goldsmiths students (the 'Freeze' exhibition), with Carl Freedman (the 'Modern Medicine' exhibition) and with Jay Jopling (owner of the White Cube gallery and fundraiser for Hirst) are important for his subsequent positioning in the field. Inversely, his success is important for the field positioning of these individuals – a mutually beneficial and self-constituting field relation. Unsurprisingly, perhaps, success begets success, and aspiring artists might well aim (and do) to establish similar field networks. Where they succeed, cultural consecration results. To return to Buck's commentary of the British art field in the 1990s, over 80 per cent of the artists she lists as 'Rising Stars' are associated with exactly the same key institutions and individuals as Hirst.

At this point, it is worth emphasizing how these institutional links are actually expressed at the level of individual or personal connection. The habitus of those involved with legitimated institutions is crucial in the institutional power they wield over the artistic field. Let us take the three key individuals associated with Hirst: Iwona Blazwick, Michael Craig-Martin and Jay Joplin. Iwona Blazwick curated Hirst's first solo exhibition. She exemplified habitus which is particularly strong in terms of institutional cultural capital, with connections to ICA, Phaidon Press, the National Trust, the Henry Moore Sculpture Trust, Tate Gallery Liverpool and, most recently, Tate Modern.

Michael Craig-Martin demonstrates an equally strong pattern of capital, but this time mostly derived from educational capital gained by association with consecrated institutions of art. He is Professor in Art at Goldsmiths, but also taught at Canterbury and Bath. Such habitus offers not only institutional consecration, but places him in a powerful position to offer institutional consecration to others. Craig-Martin's own education at Yale provided him with significant educational cultural capital, from the institution itself, but also from more content-specific artistic capital. He was taught by the American avant-gardist Frank Stella, among others, and had experience of teaching based on Bauhaus principles. His own successful experience as a conceptual artist bestows artistic capital on him, as has his subsequent involvement as a Tate Gallery artist-trustee. In other words, he is a key field participant with a dominant position in the artistic field, well placed to assist others in their struggles for field position.

Jay Jopling has a very differently constituted habitus. He was educated at *the*

English public school – Eton – before going on to graduate in art history from a university which is part of the British establishment. In other words, he entered the field with a high volume of social capital arising from his social origins. Bourdieu refers to this type of capital as 'embodied' in the personality and character of an individual. This image of a well-connected young man is further evidenced by his active involvement with celebrated good causes like Band Aid and Save the Children in 1986. Jopling also accrued social and cultural capital when he visited New York in the 1980s, making contact with key avant-garde artists such as Julian Schnabel and Jean-Michel Basquiat. Thus, social and economic capital combined with Jopling's friendship to position him as an effective fundraiser and dealer for Hirst's early career.

The habitus of each member of this trio is essentially distinct, but taken together, they offer an unusually potent configuration of social, cultural and economic capital that could be used on behalf of Hirst to accelerate his trajectory through the field. Bourdieu writes of the effect of social capital as an 'enhancer' (Accardo and Corcuff 1986: 94). In other words, this trio of artistic field players offered Hirst a royal flush in terms of structural positioning; a sound choice of collaborators on Hirst's part, with capital he could assimilate and which could be utilized to achieve successively more powerful field positions.

Level 3: Artists' Habitus

Fields themselves change as individuals activate configurations of capital within them. The last section showed how vastly different capital backgrounds, habitus, can come together to establish a new legitimate configuration, thus establishing a 'new' form according to an 'old' process. The section also illustrated the mutually constituting effect of key players' habitus and their positions in the artistic field. The next level of analysis examines how artists' habitus maps on to the field configurations identified in the last section.

Buck's 1998 review of the British artistic field categorizes over a hundred artists under three rubrics: Presiding Forces, Current Contenders and Rising Stars. We considered all the artists listed under each heading in terms of their backgrounds and the scope of artistic activity – their habitus. Basic signifiers of habitus in this artistic field are taken to be age, geographical and social origins, gender and ethnic origins, artistic education and commercial connections.

Each element of the artists' habitus is discussed in turn to show the patterns found between successive generations of artists. These patterns reflect the principles which structure the artists' field.

Age. The rear guard grouping, Presiding Forces, contains artists who are all over fifty. All the other artists were in their thirties. These generational groups are a consequence of Buck's perception, as a field participant herself, that the structures of the artistic field are age-related.

Origins and Centre of Activity. The group of artists as a whole is predominantly English, white and London based, but, as the artists' age decreases, there is a strong trend towards centralization in London. Presiding Forces artists live mainly in London, but have varied international origins. Current Contenders are largely British-born and living in London, while over half of Rising Stars are born in or around London. Almost all of this youngest group live in London.

Gender and Ethnic Origins. There has been a steady, if somewhat unspectacular, increase in the participation of women across the groups. Ethnic minority groups are dramatically under-represented in all groupings – 10 per cent at most.

Education. Patterns of educational cultural capital vary little with age. Over time, a small increase to the already high proportion of art school trained artists has occurred. Training in fine art has continued to be almost exclusively London-based. Variations are on an individual basis rather than following an overall pattern. However, within the Presiding Forces, clear mavericks exist; for example, Francis Bacon had no formal art school training, while Susan Hillier trained abroad, initially as an anthropologist. In the other two groupings, Rising Stars and Current Contenders, there is a provincial sub-pattern of educational capital, with a small minority of successful artists training in Ireland, Scotland or Wales, for example, Willie Doherty, Douglas Gordon, Christine Borland and Melanie Counsell. Effective educational capital for this artistic field is therefore an art school training.

Art Schools. The SLADE (a school of art in London) recruited the most stable proportion of artists over the three generations. St Martins (again, London-based) recruited 30 per cent of Presiding Forces but none of the Current Contenders. Comparisons are difficult here, since St Martins, Chelsea and Camberwell amalgamated in 1986, but 30 per cent of the Rising Stars trained within this new grouping. The Royal College of Arts in London (RCA) trained few of the Presiding Forces or Current Contenders, but offered postgraduate training to 40 per cent of the Rising Stars. Goldsmiths trained over 50 per cent of the Current Contenders and 30 per cent of the Rising Stars. This suggests that in the late twentieth century Goldsmiths may have been losing its field position as the incubator of the avant-garde. Still, a contender in the artistic field who is white, in their thirties, art school trained (preferably at Goldsmiths College) and London-based, is well positioned in this field and is likely to be successful. By examining both artists' habitus and the field of art in which they participate, it has been possible to identify both field structures and the constituents of a successful field strategy, for yBas at least.

And Painting?

We noted before that Bourdieu wrote of an 'ontologic complicity' (1982: 47) between habitus and field, and the above analysis shows briefly how this might be so for an art field. It demonstrates how field patterns and habitus configurations mutually collude to sustain processes of capital accumulation for all concerned, and how symbolic capital can have very real economic consequences. In *Distinction*, Bourdieu made what he called a 'deliberate refusal' to appeal to the tradition of aesthetics. However, having offered a social analysis of aesthetics, he writes: 'we must now allow the return of the repressed', here aesthetics, 'in order to prevent the absence of direct confrontation from allowing the two discourses to coexist peacefully as parallel alternatives' (p. 486). Bourdieu posits a double structure between the social and the aesthetic. In other words, it is possible to follow up with a second field analysis, which shows how habitus and these field structures are identifiable in the products of art, in other words, the artists' work itself. Here, the field structures are more familiar to us through the practices of art critics and art histories.

Let us consider just three major sources of artistic consecration for artists in Britain in the 1990s: those who have been nominated or won the prestigious competition for modern art – the Turner Prize; artists whose work had been bought and exhibited by the millionaire collector Charles Saatchi; and artists listed by Buck in her survey of British Art in the 1990s. Here, the data shows that a rear guard can be defined as those artists who won the Turner Prize, but were not included by Buck or Saatchi as 'art now'. This group of artists shows similar configurations of symbolic capital, that is, habitus: they are all middle-aged, all were born outside London, but almost all of them trained at London art schools; artistically, they all work in sculpture with large-scale, strong geometric shapes – the New British Sculpture of the 1980s.Tony Cragg and Richard Deacon were leading members of this group. Anish Kapoor's sculptures of primary colour and spiritual interests distinguish him from the New Sculpture movement, but the scale, simplicity of shapes and rough use of stone in his work are common to many artists in this group. While sharing these stylistic characteristics, the artists seek to distinguish themselves from each other. For example, Richard Long and Tony Cragg both work with simple-shaped geometric sculptures: Long – natural and pastoral; Cragg – urban and mechanical. Cragg claims that his work implies a criticism of the romantic pastoralism of Long (Lucie-Smith 1996: 322), but they share a preoccupation with man's relationship with his environment. This grouping of artists was identified here by the similarity of the capital configurations of their habitus. In this case, at least, individuals of similar habitus also share strong similarities in their artistic practice. This dual structure between the sociocultural characteristics of a field and its artistic products shows the interpenetration of artistic character and habitus as located within the field of British art.

The most prestigious group of British artists, and thus those endowed with most symbolic capital, are chosen by all three of the consecrating agents used here: the Saatchi collection, the Buck review and those who have won the Turner Prize. Only four artists appear in this grouping: Gillian Wearing, Damien Hirst, Chris Ofili and Rachel Whiteread. All were born within the same five-year period; all trained in London (two at Goldsmiths); all are London-based. In terms of artistic output, the group uses film, photography, painting and sculpture. Where paintings are produced, they might include collage, popular icons, plastic, pins and elephant dung (Ofili). Art objects are not necessarily crafted by the artists themselves, so issues of uniqueness of art work and authorship are blurred (Hirst). Rachel Whiteread literally turns inside out one of sculpture's fundamental assumptions about the relationship between surface and volume. Wearing uses video and photographs in a format derived from documentaries, but blurs distinctions between reality and fiction, between public and private, and between voyeurism and collaboration. These artists share with each other defining characteristics of postmodern practice: appropriation, site specificity, impermanence, accumulation, discursivity and hybridization. But, of course, none of the four artists demonstrates all these characteristics. Each shares a spirited willingness to subvert previous fine art characterizations in terms of their use of media and in their onslaught to the boundaries of fine art categorizations. The absence of a purely visual stylistic similarity does not preclude a shared postmodernist aesthetic and corresponding field positioning: subversive in intent and challenging to previous assumptions about fine art.

'Practices have double truths, which are difficult to hold together' (Bourdieu 1998c/1994: 95). The resulting ambiguity is only manageable, since we more often discuss the artistic field as a site of aesthetic judgement rather than the site of socio-economic relations. Bourdieu calls a system of exchanges such as this British artistic field an 'economy of symbolic goods', and writes that: 'This duality is rendered possible, and viable, through a sort of self-deception or self-mystification. But, this individual self-deception is sustained by a collective "self-deception", a veritable "collective misrecognition", inscribed in objective structures... and in mental structures, excluding the possibility of thinking or acting otherwise' (ibid.). It is this collective misrecognition of and by the field participants which allows strategies of notoriety and controversy to be deployed effectively to maximize exposure of an artist, and hence, accumulation of cultural and economic capital; for example, when Saatchi copied the cultural orthodoxy of avant-garde naming and somewhat arbitrarily called an exhibition 'Neurotic Realism' – a collective self-deception indeed.

We have seen previously that, for Bourdieu, a structuring aesthetic was not an a priori one. If Manet's 'pure painting' was dependent on a particular social condition – in his case, a double refusal of academic and popular art – the 'pure gaze' itself was, similarly, a social by-product of the times. What they shared, however, was the notion of autonomy. One might argue that the aesthetic of the pure gaze was a necessary attribute of the bourgeois individual making a claim to legitimation as original, and seeking warranty of their social prestige and of their inherent worth: a kind of independent assertion of personal value and social standing. Similarly, with Manet, Bourdieu sees that we need to understand the move towards artist-centred painting (pure painting) – in technique and subject – as a characteristic of the movement towards autonomy in the artistic field of production:

> (the fields of cultural production) are at any one time the site of a struggle between two principles of hierarchization: the heteronomous principle, which favours those who dominate the field economically and politically (for example, 'bourgeois art'), and the autonomous principle (for example, 'art for art's sake'), which leads its most radical defenders to make of temporal failure a sign of election and of success a sign of compromise with the times. The state of relations of forces in this struggle depends on the autonomy which the field *globally* disposes of, meaning the degree to which its own norms and sanctions manage to impose themselves on the ensemble of producers of cultural goods and on those who – occupying the temporally (and temporarily) dominant position in the field of cultural production (successful playwrights or novelists) or aspiring to occupy it (dominated producers available for mercenary tasks) – are the nearest to the occupants of the homologous position in the field of power, and hence the most sensitive to external demands and the most heteronomous. (Bourdieu 1996a/1992: 216)

There are, then, two countervailing forces – field dependency and field autonomy – through which the internal and external dynamic of the art world is regulated. On the one hand, there is art (painting) which is mercenary, totally defined by the consumer; on the other hand, there is art which is totally free of any consideration of audience (art for art's sake). The message of Bourdieu's 'science of a history of art' must ultimately be that 'art' is often not as free as it presents itself. Certainly, in the case of the yBas, it is difficult not to see their activities and work as an expression of economically self-serving individuals in the use which they are able to make of their social origins, education and consequent social networks – social and cultural capital – to shorten the time span to the legitimation of an avant-garde generation: a consecration which ultimately leads to the acquisition of economic capital – money wealth.

For Bourdieu, the principles of autonomy and heteronomy at play in the dynamic of the field lead to paradoxes, where success is considered failure and vice versa:

> The degree of autonomy of a field of cultural production is revealed to the extent that the principle of external hierarchization there is subordinated to the principle of internal hierarchization: the greater the autonomy, the more symbolic the relationship of forces favourable to producers who are the most independent of demand. (ibid:. 217)

In other words, a truly autonomous art field would direct its own affairs, independently of a value hierarchization derived from outside. However, another paradox is that the field has to be dependent on an audience or, perhaps more pertinently, a market. It is in this sense that artists and painters must truly be considered the 'dominated members of the dominant class'. No matter how corrosive the artistic avant-garde is, it is still dependent essentially on a leisured and monied class for its recognition, and, ultimately, for financial sponsorship. Nevertheless, it is the unique principle of artists to misrecognize this dependency. They do this, among other means, by elevating to the highest point the principle of art for its own sake, a kind of mystical allusion which acts as both source of and justification for aesthetic transcendence – feeding back to the consumer a sense of uniqueness transmitted in the originality of artistic expression. What must be misrecognized are the economic and associated social structural ramifications of this aesthetic. Ironically, as in the case of the avant-garde itself, while challenging the status quo, it does so in terms of pseudo-intra-Nicene battles of displacement which disguise the close homologous affinity that any Rising Stars must hold with the political field. It is worth recalling that the Salon des Refusés at which Manet exhibited was in fact sanctioned by the emperor. And, with the yBas, it is worth noting that this 'new' generation of artists resonated with the 'New' Labour political culture of the decade. Bourdieu argues that there is often a 'structural affinity' between the avant-garde and the political vanguard, and that 'internal struggles are to an extent arbitrated by external sanctions' (ibid.: 252) – in this case, in the way galleries themselves and the prizes they confer are part of this sanctioning, as we have seen. New groups of painters struggle to displace a whole aesthetic scheme of perception, and, in so doing, to transform the structure of the field. The point is that it is not only ways of judging what is and is not 'good' art which is at stake, but an entire world view and perspective. To this extent, what takes place in art and painting should not be seen as parochial. Rather, what is presented is a representation of what is potential, possible and permissible. In this way, it can also be seen to be political. To gain acceptance in these terms is indeed to gain legitimation for an aesthetic which must be understood, as Bourdieu wrote, as 'historically necessitated', if not historically necessary.

American Abstract Expressionism

Let us pursue these relations with another example – American abstract expressionism. Unlike the yBas, whose place in art history is as yet undecided, abstract expressionism and its artists have already been recognized as an important international artistic movement, if a rather sterile one. The name 'abstract expressionism', invented, like 'cubism', by an art journalist (in this case, most probably by Robert Coates of the *New Yorker*), reveals little of either the practice or the artistic products. Much of their work is not abstract, but unapologetically figurative (de Kooning's painting, for example). Nor would all the artists be happy to be called 'expressionists' (Franz Kline, for example). Alternative names were used by the two art critics, Harold Rosenberg – 'action painting' and Clement Greenberg –

'American-type painting' (Greenberg 1955). A more accurate, if less evocative name for these artists would be 'The New York School', since all these field participants worked in New York during the 1940s and 1950s. Since abstract expressionism was therefore at its height in post-war America, the course of its development and the social and artistic trajectories of its artists were deeply embedded in the socio-historic changes of the time: the Depression, the Second World War and the rise of Communism.

During the Depression the art market had collapsed. President Roosevelt was persuaded by his advisors to include artists and sculptors in social support programmes through the Works of Art Project (WAP) and, later, the Federal Arts Project (FAP). Artists therefore received a worker's pay for producing art works: paintings, murals and sculptures which reflected the values and achievements of the country. This move created unusual socio-economic conditions for America's artists, providing them with sufficient resources to live and eat, while at the same time offering them a high degree of artistic freedom. They were thus highly autonomous, freed from market restraints in a way unknown before or since. These projects were of major significance in positioning the field of artistic production in close relation to the fields of politics and power. Further relationships between significant fields of socio-economic activity have been identified and located in the broader social space, by studying the key institutional participants in the American field of the day. In particular, a level 1 analysis (as described in chapter 3 and employed above) of the interrelations of the field of power and other fields in which the abstract expressionists participated exemplifies a number of distinctive features.

Level 1: Field of Art within Other Fields

First, as Figure 5.5 shows, the interpenetration of the field of power with the field of artistic production was particularly marked at this time and place. Second, the role of religion, myth and philosophy was unusually explicit in both the work of this group of artists and their individual relations to the institutions associated with these ideas, for example, theosophy and the Museum of Non-Objective Painting; Jungian psychoanalytical theory and its New York practitioners; or religion itself, in the Russian Jewish Old Testament inspirations of artists like Mark Rothko. The third feature was the effect on American society as a whole, and on the field of artistic production, in particular, of the large number of European immigrants – many Jewish – who had fled from German fascism. Thus, almost overnight, New York acquired an active European subculture, transposed from the fields of cultural production and consumption brought by the émigrés. As a result, many leading surrrealists, Max Ernst and Duchamp, were to be found in New York in the 1940s and became an 'imported' consecrated avant-garde generation for younger American artists. Major exhibitions of European painters such as Picasso, Cézanne, Mondrian and Kandinsky took place in New York, so Pollock and others were able to see and respond to this work first-hand. Instead of simply developing in opposition to the American home-grown art of the social realists and regionalists, younger artists, supported economically by participation in federal arts projects, were free to respond to the culture of these avant-garde masters, their artistic products and their underlying philosophies.

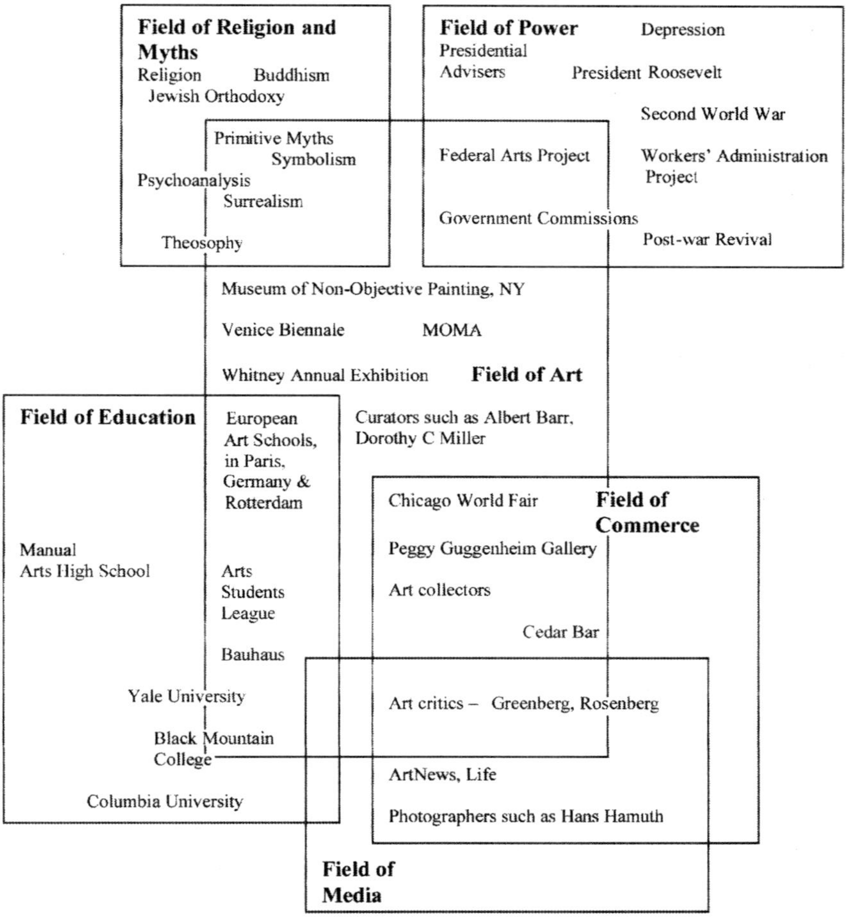

Figure 5.5 American Abstract Expressionists. Level 1 analysis: fields in relation to the field of power.

Level 2 Analysis: Relationships between Field Institutions

Four different types of field institutions played key roles in the development of abstract expressionism: government projects – FAP and WAP; the art schools – Art Students League and the Black Mountain College; the art galleries – MOMA, Art of the Century and Museum of Non-Objective Painting, and, less formally, but no less influential, Cedar Bar in downtown New York.

Field Institutions: Art Schools and Their Teachers. Several key artists – Rothko, Pollock, Krasner and Barnett Newman, among others – studied at the Art Students League, where Thomas Hart Benton and Hans Hoffman were teachers. Benton, a leader of the American regionalist painters, taught and acted as father figure and mentor for Jackson Pollock, in particular. Hans Hoffman, often categorized as an abstract expressionist himself, was a teacher and a formative influence on many of the younger artists, including Lee Krasner and Pollock. He was described by Clement Greenberg, the art critic, as 'in all probability the most important art teacher of our time'; 'the insights into modern art of the man himself have gone deeper than any other contemporary' (Greenberg 1945). The other educational establishment to have a major influence on abstract expressionists was Black Mountain College, and through it the Bauhaus School. Motherwell, de Kooning, Franz Kline and the art critic Clement Greenberg all attended this college and came under the influence of one-time member of the German Bauhaus School, the colourist Josef Albers.

Field Institutions: Art Galleries and Museums. Art galleries in New York, including MOMA, exhibited many European masterpieces, including Picasso, Léger, Miró, Mondrian, Matisse and Cézanne. Younger American artists were therefore very familiar with the European avant-garde painters of the 1920s and with émigré surrealists such as Duchamp, André Breton, Max Ernst and Roberto Matta. Peggy Guggenheim's presence in the city also had a profound effect on the field of artistic production in New York in the 1940s and 1950s. She funded the Museum of Non-Objective Painting, which was run by theosophist Baroness Hilla Rebay, and where many of Kandinsky's works were exhibited. Peggy Guggenheim, at this time married to Max Ernst the surrealist, also established the Art of the Century Gallery for abstract and surrealist artists under forty. Here, many abstract expressionists exhibited paintings as early as 1943 and 1944, including Jackson Pollock, William Baziotes and Robert Motherwell.

Level 3: Individual's Habitus

The configuration of symbolic capital and, hence, habitus of artists has been analysed in much the same way as the yBas presented earlier in this chapter. Since dispute continues about which artists can properly be put under the name 'abstract expressionist', the habitus of a long list of twelve artists has been examined in terms of their ages, geographical origins, family status, education, friends, supporters and patrons, and the galleries with which they were associated. Visual characteristics of their paintings have also been examined, together with the artists' own claims and critics' commentaries about their paintings and the influences on them. Artists considered were Jackson Pollock, Lee Krasner, Robert Motherwell, Franz Kline, Mark Rothko, Barnet Newman, Clifford Still, Adolph Gottlieb, Ashile Gorky, Willem de Kooning, Hans Hoffman and John Graham. Josef Albers, although better known as a colour theorist, was also included, since he intended his geometric abstractions to be meditative and to represent human relationships; he thus shared spiritual intention and artistic form with many abstract expressionists. An extract of these analyses is given in Table 5.1.

As we saw in the level 2 analysis where institutions were discussed, above, there were also a number of key players in this field of artistic production who were not artists themselves: gallery owners, Peggy Guggenheim, and her successor, Sally Parsons, those responsible for exhibitions, such as Baroness Rebay or Dorothy C Miller at MOMA, and art critics and journalists, among them Clement Greenberg, Harold Rosenberg and the photographer Hans Namuth.

Unlike the analysis of the yBas, where the artists were initially selected by age, here the habitus of all twelve artists has been examined and the resulting patterns and correspondences noted. As we did for the yBas, these patterns, which reflect the structures of the artistic field, are discussed below in terms of each element of their habitus.

Age. The artists split neatly into three age groups: the oldest artists are born between 1880 and 1886 and are all three 'artistic influencers' – Hans Hoffman, John Graham and Josef Albers. There are then six artists born between 1903 and 1905 – Rothko, Newman, Still, Gottlieb, Gorky and de Kooning. Those in the youngest group were born between 1910 and 1915 – Pollock, Krasner, Motherwell and Franz Kline.

Origins and Centre of Activity. As we indicated earlier, all the artists worked in New York during their active painting careers. However, the geographical origins of the group are much more varied. Only 60 per cent of the artists were born in America, including all of the youngest group of artists. Unsurprisingly, in light of the Second World War, all three of the oldest artists were born in Germanic countries and emigrated to the United States. De Kooning and Gorky were also immigrants – this time from the Netherlands and Armenia. Rothko came to America as a small boy from Lithuania. Overall, more than three-quarters of these artists were first- or second-generation migrants. Several changed their names, in fact.

Gender and Social Origins. Only one woman, Lee Krasner, is included as an abstract expressionist painter. Her tenacity and varied style would have earned her a place, but marriage to Pollock, while it inhibited her artistic development, did ensure that her name was remembered. Since many of the artists' families were recent immigrants from Europe, they needed to deploy symbolic capital acquired in one sociocultural field within a new and unfamiliar field. Social positioning was

Table 5.1 American Abstract Expressionists.
Level 3 analysis: artist's habitus.

Habitus of individual artists	*Jackson Pollock*	*Lee Krasner*	*Robert Motherwell*	*Franz Kline*
Age	Born 1912	Born 1911	Born 1915	Born 1910
Place of Origin	Wyoming, US	New York	Aberdeen, Washington, US	Pennsylvania, US
Family	Farming; owned small hotel	Russian Jewish émigrés	Father a San Francisco bank president	Mother was Cornish, father a German salon keeper
Education	Expelled from Manual Arts High School for drinking, but was introduced to Kristnamurti and Rudolph Steiner	Incomplete study at All Women's Art School, New York	BA at Stanford PhD Harvard (abandoned), studied art history with Meyer Shapiro at Columbia	Boston University
Art Schools and Groups	Art Students League, Federal Arts Project	Art Students League, Federal Arts Project	Black Mountain College	Black Mountain College, trained as an illustrator, art college in Boston and in London
Artistic Supporters and Patrons	Thomas Hart Benton, John Graham, Clement Greenberg	Hans Hoffman, Harold Rosenberg's wife was witness at her wedding	Joseph Albers	Patrons I David Orr, Dr Theodore, J Edlich Jnr
Art Galleries and Exhibitions	Peggy Guggenheim Gallery, Whitney Annual MOMA, Venice Biennale	Whitney Annual, 1973, Whitechapel Gallery, London, 1975	Raymond Duncan Gallery, Paris Arts Club of Chicago San Francisco Museum of Art, MOMA 1946 Royal academy, London 1978	Egan Gallery, New York, 1950 Venice Biennale, 1956, 1960
Artistic Output	Action painting	Varied and changing styles included collage	Psychic automatism, torn paper collage	Bold gestural strokes, black + white painting similar in appearance to Zen calligraphy, but actually premeditated painting
Influences	Picasso and Guernica, Jungian psychoanalysis	Matisse, Mondrian	Émigré Surrealists in New York	Japanese art

therefore relatively unstable and could change rapidly; for example, when Newman's father's business went bankrupt, or when Rothko's father died unexpectedly, shortly after Rothko's arrival in America.

Robert Motherwell, the youngest artist in this group, was also the most socially and economically secure. His father was a San Francisco bank president. This status was reflected in his study at Stanford, Harvard and Columbia – all prestigious universities.

Education and Art Schools. None of these artists was self-taught. They were all dependent on educational capital for their participation in the field, but the volume and nature of that capital was very varied. Less than half had studied art to first degree level. Two of these, de Kooning and Kline, initially undertook commercial art training. But, as noted above, Black Mountain College and the Art Students League in New York were influential institutions for this group – two-thirds of the artists were involved with one of these. Only a third of the group had attended European art schools (Académie Colarossi in Paris, for example).

Artistic Approach. The visual output of the painters falls into three rough groupings: aggressive gestural brushstrokes were the mark of about a third of these painters (action painters); another third painted large areas of luminous, emotion-laden colour (colour field painters); the remainder were more representational, but equally concerned with automatic painting, gesture, emotion and colour. Religion, myth and primitive art – including Navaho sand painting, Eskimo images and Zen calligraphy – also played a significant part in the artistic products of all of these artists.

What does this analysis tell us about the structures of the field of artistic production in post-war New York? A successful abstract expressionist was most likely to be male, living in New York, probably with parents who had emigrated from Europe, to have undertaken some art training and to be interested in action painting, colour field painting or gestural art. It was better to define his own art work in relation to European avant-gardes, particularly surrealists, and to oppose American art of the social realist or regionalist styles. It also helped to have an explicit philosophical underpinning to art works: Jungian archetypes, Native American myths, theosophy, the Old Testament. It seemed to matter less what it was – more that there was one! These, then, were the constituents of habitus which allowed an artist to occupy a desirable field positioning in New York in the 1950s.

Concluding Remarks

In this chapter we have analysed the components and configuration of artists' symbolic capital. For a yBa artist in the 1990s, an art education at Goldsmiths (educational capital), work exhibited in the Tate or the Saatchi Gallery (consecrated artistic capital) and living and working in London (social and cultural capital) were key constituents of the habitus of the most successful. For an abstract expressionist, the strongest capital constituents were paralleled by art education, ideally at the Art Students League in New York or at Black Mountain College (educational capital), work exhibited at MOMA or the Art of this Century Gallery (consecrated artistic capital), and living and working in New York (social and cultural capital). For Manet, the equivalent constituents of successful habitus were the Ecole des Beaux-Arts (educational capital), the Salon des Refusés (consecrated artistic capital) and living and working in Paris (social and cultural capital). In other words, although the particular constituents of habitus are field-dependent, the successful configurations of symbolic capital are the same across different fields at different times and in different places. The particularly successful trajectories of both Damien Hirst and Jackson Pollock may be accounted for by the strong connections they developed to the key teachers, gallery owners, curators and critics of their respective artistic fields. For the field of artistic production, at least, it may well be the case that volume of social capital – a symbolic capital which enhances the efficacy of other capitals – is the decisive factor in an artist's success or failure.

We have considered three different artistic groupings: Manet, the yBas and abstract expressionists. We have examined the interactions between individual artists' habitus and the fields of artistic production in which they each struggled for success. In all three examples we have seen how the policies and actions of government, the Salon des Refusés or the Federal Arts Project, have directly and indirectly served to structure subsequent field interactions. The part played in successful field manoeuvres by the symbolic capital accrued from legitimated institutions such as art schools and art galleries has been noted in all three settings. Gallery owners, curators, art teachers and art critics have been identified as field players of significance who are able to offer consecration to artists through exhibitions, educational qualifications and good reviews. For each of the three artistic groups, struggles for desirable field positions are enacted through the interactions of the same sociocultural fields – education, government, commerce – with the field of artistic production. In chapter 4, where the field of artistic consumption was considered through three art museums, it was these same fields which were actively involved in each case. While for each case museum and for each group of artists, the precise nature, volume and configuration of capital is different and distinct, it is perhaps reassuring to find a homology between the functioning of the field of artistic consumption and the field of artistic production. We now take this analytic approach and these conclusions to the field of photography.

–6–

Photography

Introduction

Bourdieu's relationship to photography was a complex one. He was himself a proficient photographer and used photographic techniques in his work as a sociologist. Examples of this aspect of his work are found in *Travail et travailleurs en Algérie* (1963), *Images d'Algérie* (2003) and 'The Peasant and Photography' (2004b). He also explored photography as an element of French cultural practice in *Les Etudiants et leurs études* (1964b), *Les Héritiers* (1979/1964) and in *La Distinction* (1984/1979). He undertook extensive empirical investigation of photographic practice in France in the 1960s, presented in his major work on photography, *Un Art moyen* (1965), translated as *Photography: A Middle-brow Art* (1990a). This collection of works is addressed in the first part of this chapter. In the second part, individual photographers and specific settings or periods are examined, as in chapters 4 and 5, by applying Bourdieu's three-level analysis of fields, in this case, to the photographic field.

As a cultural practice, photography is particularly diverse in its techniques, purposes and products, ranging from the amateur holiday snapshot, preserved lovingly in an album, through the high society portraits of glossy coffee-table books, to the cutting-edge photo-montage displayed in prestigious art museums. Photographers are themselves equally varied: the war photographer, the photographer taking pictures for art reproductions, the cookery photographer, the camera club fanatic, the artist using a camera to make fine art images, the anthropologist recording his findings or the five-year-old using a digital camera in school. As a visual practice highly dependent on technology, photography changes rapidly. At a time when mobile phones are capable of capturing still and moving digital images, it is surprising to think that it is less than 200 years since the first photographic images were fixed on paper. This, therefore, is a cultural field where change is routine and diversification is commonplace. Photographic practice is consequently well matched to the dynamic nature of Bourdieu's field theory, where habitus of different individuals interact with one another and with the structuring structures of cultural, economic and social fields to generate new structures, emergent field positions and reconfigured habitus. This process is illustrated in the second part of this chapter by considering a number of notable photographers, their habitus and their field positions. The evolution of photography as a field is explored through examples from photojournalism, fine art practice and pop culture, in order to see it in terms of its changing interrelationships with the field of cultural production and consumption, the field of technology and the larger socio-political space.

I

Bourdieu's Relationship to Photography

Bourdieu was himself an avid photographer, using a camera to record the people he met and their culture, specifically in Algeria and in his home region in France, the Béarn. These early photographs from the 1950s and 1960s were not published until much later (Bourdieu's Algerian photographs were published in 2003), or were presented anonymously; examples are included in *Travail et travailleurs* (1963) and *La Distinction* (1984/1979). Consequently, the extent and quality of Bourdieu's photographic practice was not widely recognized until after his death in 2002. This is just one example of what we referred to in the previous chapters as Bourdieu exploiting his own 'insider experience' in order to gain information on the topic of his subject.

While on national service in Algeria in the 1950s, Bourdieu photographed the local people, their homes and their daily lives. He made friends with local photographers, whom he also consulted and hired, so that together they recorded the social and cultural consequences of the tragic events of the colonial war. Bourdieu's photographs contrast the subtle decoration of traditional Kablye dwellings with the regimented functional buildings of the resettlements. His pictures show people in the towns engaged in their everyday tasks – buying, selling, travelling, talking – dressed in worn and mended garments, a strange mix of the traditional Arab and modern European dress. Ladies with covered heads and flowing white traditional robes reveal strappy stilettos and slingback shoes (2003: 204) as they walk down an urban street. Rural life – men gossiping and drinking coffee under an ancient olive tree (p. 31) – is juxtaposed with the bustle of the town where poverty predominates and traditional culture is fragmented by colonial interventions. Quoting Schultheis, Frisinghelli writes of Bourdieu: 'Photography captivated him because it expressed the distant regard of the researcher who records, but who remains always aware of what he is recording, with its capacity to fix immediately, and at a familiar distance, the details which, at the moment of perception, pass by unnoticed or escape from a more in-depth examination…' (p. 205). Bourdieu here describes a use of photography which is essentially anthropological.

Photographs from the same Algerian settings were published earlier in the second part of *Travail et travailleurs* under the title 'Etude sociologue'. They illuminate the text by offering images of the economic necessity of work, the diversity of work tools, traditional and modern, and a fragmentation of traditional cultural modes of living. A spice seller in a bustling market kneels on the ground beside his scales, offering a sharp contrast to the solitary factory worker surrounded by sparks. A cobbler sits quietly in the Casbah d'Alger waiting for trade, while a group of workers attacks a steep dusty bank with spades, pick axes and pneumatic drills. On a busy street, a beggar, wearing a darned and mended overcoat, holds out his upturned hand towards us, his eyes modestly averted.

Half a century on, the archive of these Algerian photographs was used by Camera Austria and Bourdieu himself to form an international travelling exhibition. It opened in Paris at the Monde d'Arabe and later was shown in London at the Photographer's Gallery in October 2004. The exhibition catalogue was published in the same series as the work of Robert Doisneau and Jean Cocteau, and combines photographs, interviews and textual extracts from Bourdieu's books in a textual collage. The exhibition and its associated events, a videoed interview, commentary, talks and a film, *Bourdieu – la sociologie est un sport de combat*, presented a neat twenty-first century field positioning for Bourdieu as an acclaimed high-brow photographer, a sociologist and a social activist.

In a research paper, 'The Peasant and Photography', recently republished in English (2004b), Bourdieu undertakes an ethnography of his childhood region, Béarn, and the uses made of photography by the rural peasant population in the 1960s. He found that peasants used photography strictly as consumers, since taking photographs was seen as a frivolous urban luxury and an innovation at odds with maintaining rural tradition – showing a wish to rise above one's station. Bourdieu describes a typical photograph of a family celebration – often a wedding – two families newly united, aunts, uncles, nieces and nephews, arms around each other, formally and symmetrically arranged and squared up to the camera: it represents a social ritual 'to solemnise and materialise the image a group intends to present of itself' (ibid.: 1). Inclusion in the photograph grants the legitimacy of one's presence – 'I give my image'. Absences were noted and disapproved. Buying the wedding photograph was mandatory – a gift to those who made the invitation: 'Such pictures capture behaviours which are socially approved and socially regulated… Nothing may be photographed besides what must be photographed' (p. 606). In short, photography was used collectively to confirm social practices, and individually to objectify the self-image. As Bourdieu explains: 'Photography is the situation in which the awareness of one's body-for-others reaches its highest acuity. One feels subject to a gaze and to a gaze that fixes and immobilises appearances' (p. 614). For the peasant, photographs were not for display, and were usually stored in a box specifically for that purpose. Photographs were taken out on family occasions – given a social reading. The photograph as an object was not recognized. Technical and aesthetic aspects of a picture were ignored since its purpose was to 'situate' each person in their lineage. Bourdieu juxtaposes the view of the rural peasant: '…it would be indecent or ostentatious to display pictures of members of the family to anyone who happened by…', with the view of the petit bourgeois town dweller for whom, '…they acquire a decorative and affective value: enlarged and framed they adorn the walls of the living room, along with travel souvenirs' (p. 606).

A camera was the sign of a 'vacationer'. A rural farmer might allow himself to be photographed with his livestock 'in the expected pose', but would do so with irony: 'These people have time to waste and money to squander' (p. 608). Unmarried bachelors, already marginal participants in village social practices, or teenagers – expected to be frivolous – might be tolerated as photographers. Generally, local inhabitants who took photographs were treated with disapproval, since an innovation like photography was regarded as a denial of traditional values which may suit outsiders, but them alone.

Bourdieu's Photography and the Field of Visual Anthropology

When he used photography in his fieldwork in Algeria and Béarn, Bourdieu followed in the footsteps of noted visual anthropologists and ethnographers. In the 1920s, sociologists from the Chicago School used photographic techniques in their fieldwork, for example, Anderson's study of the American hobo in 1923, or Thrasher's 1927 work on the gang. Like Bourdieu's photographs, these pictures focus on the everyday activities of participants rather than the visually spectacular. Claude Lévi-Strauss also took more than 3,000 photographs in his Brazilian fieldwork between 1935 and 1939, most not published until 1995. Lévi-Strauss did not use these images directly in his theoretical arguments. Bateson and Meade (1942) were the first to use photography as a source of anthropological theory. Their 800 photographs of Balinese culture recorded social rituals and routine behaviour together with dwellings and farming techniques. The first text to offer practical suggestions for photographing traditional field studies was not published until 1967 (Collier), some time after Bourdieu's major fieldwork was complete. It was not until 1974 that the first arguments were presented by Howard Becker (1974) for photography as a key constituent in a visual sociology concerned with the critical examination of a society.

Thus, Bourdieu's photographic work in the 1950s and 1960s could well be viewed as pioneering work in the field of a visual anthropology and sociology. Certainly, after Becker's formulation of 'visual ethnography informed by traditional sociological concerns for validity, reliability and sampling' (Harper 2003: 244), the 1970s and 1980s saw a flurry of documentary studies based on photographic images. These included studies of Harlem family life (Davidson 1970); social stratification in suburbia (Owens 1973); hippy lifestyle (Simon and Mungo 1972); European migrancy, based on the labour market (Berger and Mohr 1975); and pervasive American poverty (Harrington and Adelman 1981) – these all sought to bring out a fuller picture of the culture in question. Later, visual ethnography made a more dialogical use of photographic material, as did Bourdieu himself when he employed photography in what he called a 'discursive montage' to inform and complement the analytical text and empirical case materials of his study of French taste in *La Distinction* (1984/1979). The temporal development and succession of these generations of visual anthropologists are shown in Figure 6.1.

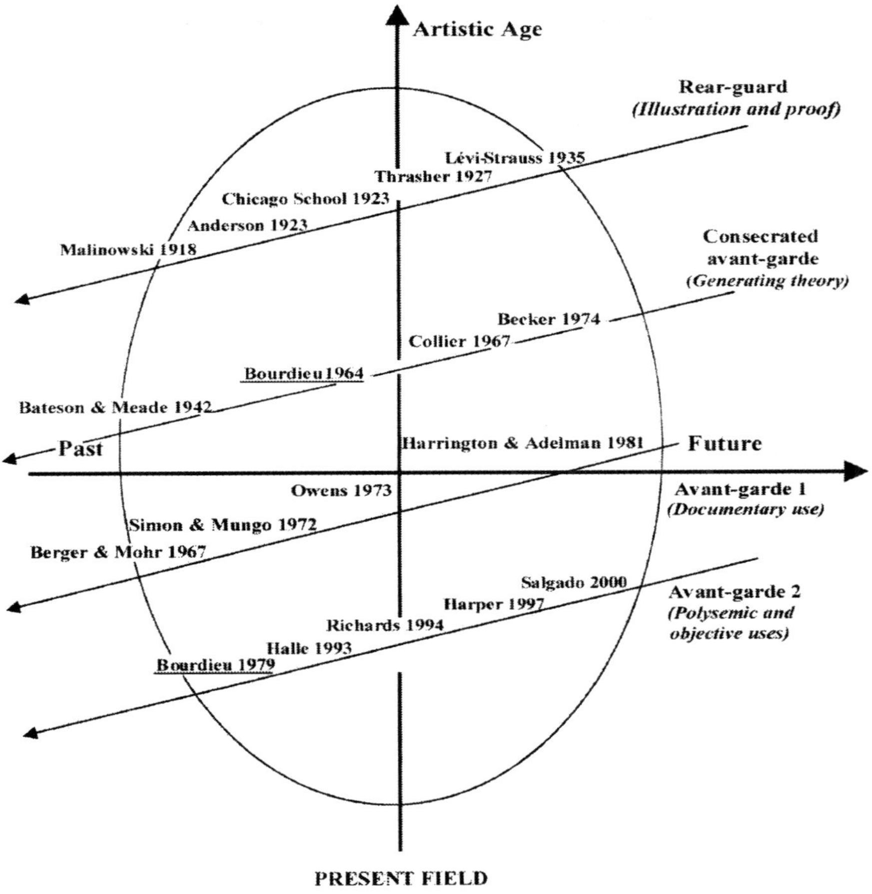

Figure 6.1 The Present Field of Visual Anthropology. Based on Harper (2004).

It will be noted that Bourdieu occupies a position both within a consecrated rear guard of early visual sociologists (Algerian and Béarnaise photographs) and, through his use of photography, within 'discursive montage' (*La Distinction*) as a representative of the later, polysemic approach to visual sociology. In *Images d'Algérie* (2003), Bourdieu was asked if it is altogether logical to think that 'there is an intrinsic rapport between the means of objectification of the photographic gaze and the ethnographic approach' ('la façon d'objectiver à travers le regard photographique et l'approche ethnologique que vous étiez en train de construire, et les deux yeux, l'oeil de l'ethnologue, de l'anthropologue, et l'oeil du photographe, doivent avoir une affinité élective') (Bourdieu 2003: 27). Bourdieu replies: 'Yes, you are probably right. There was in each of these cases this type of rapport at the same time objective and affectionate, distant and close, something which should be understood with a certain humour' (ibid.)

The recent publication of the archive of his Algerian photographs by Camera Austria re-presents this photographic work within a changed cultural and political field and demands that they are read anew. What has changed is not the images themselves, but the nature of the attention we give to photography. Our present reading of these photographs has changed because the society to which they related, of which they are a chosen sample, no longer exists, but continues to have consequences in the social unrest of immigrant populations in French cities. Bourdieu's Algerian photographs, poignant images of the poverty and fragmented culture of the displaced Algerians, are no longer quaint or picturesque, since one must now read them politically as clear colonial precursors to the riots which took place in 2005 in the immigrant quarters of major French cities. This fresh reading is in line with Bourdieu's own renewed political activism in the years leading up to his death (see Grenfell 2004).

The Range of Bourdieu's Uses of Photography

As noted above, Bourdieu makes extensive use of photographs in *La Distinction* as one element of the 'discursive montage' he used to present his findings of investigations – in 1963, 1968 and 1975 – of French cultural practices. In his discussion of patterns of cooking and eating, and how they vary across gender and social class, he offers the outcomes of his empirical evidence: '...the working class is chiefly distinguished by the inclusion of salty, substantial, clearly masculine foods, such as soup (eaten almost exclusively by farm workers, meat (46% farm workers, 17% manual workers) and cheese' (Bourdieu 1984/1979: 382). This text is juxtaposed with a newspaper article and a photograph of François Bruat, a bean-eating champion – a middle-aged man sitting behind a plate of beans and looking slightly nauseous. In this case, a picture (p. 383) is indeed better than a thousand words.

Similarly, in Bourdieu's discussion of marriage patterns, he says: 'Taste is a match maker; it marries colours and also people, who make "well-matched couples", initially in regard to taste... Hence the astonishing harmony of ordinary couples, who matched initially, progressively match each other by a sort of mutual acculturation' (p. 243). Here he provides exemplar photographs of three different couples. First, a fashionably but casually dressed young couple sit sideways on a bench, leaning towards one another, both looking thoughtful – a symmetrical and balanced picture suggesting a symmetrical and balanced relationship. The second couple are of the same age, both wearing long, full-sleeved white shirts, and face each other across a wooden table, each resting one elbow on it – equally matched, but oppositional. The third couple are older; a man sits in a chair eating with a spoon, while a woman one presumes to be his wife sits behind him smiling –

contently asymmetrical, but with the same perspective on the world. The photographs, with their images of how the couples relate to each other in physical space, reinforce the message of the text.

Photographs also formed part of Bourdieu's research methodology in the survey of cultural attitudes which he undertook. As part of an interview, he showed the photograph of an old woman's hands – twisted knuckles caught in the light. This picture is presented in the text of *La Distinction* (p. 44). When interviewed about the photograph, Bourdieu reports that none of the most culturally deprived of his subjects ever made an 'aesthetic judgement' about it, but confined themselves to ethical or emotional comments: 'The old girl must've worked hard', or, 'I feel really sorry seeing that poor old woman's hands…' (p. 44). Only those from the higher levels of the social hierarchy commented on the photograph as an object itself: 'I find this a very beautiful photograph. It's the very symbol of toil. It puts me in mind of Flaubert's old serving-woman…' (p. 45). How a photograph is understood, Bourdieu concludes, is therefore a matter of social position rather than an aesthetic absolute.

Bourdieu further explored the aesthetic disposition of his respondents by asking if a range of objects or scenes – including a sunset, cabbages and a little girl with a cat – would make a beautiful photograph. Here, he found that technicians offer the best example of middle-brow taste: 'They are particularly drawn to objects most typical of middle-brow photography – the weaver, the still life…' (p. 58). Almost half of technicians and upper-class groups thought that a photograph of tree bark could be beautiful, while only 17 per cent of the working classes thought this possible. All groups liked sunsets, but to differing degrees: working class (90 per cent); middle classes (84 per cent) and upper classes (64 per cent). Few upper- or middle-class respondents (4 per cent and 1 per cent) and none of the working classes thought that a car crash could be beautiful. In contrast, higher education teachers and artists form an atypical group of the upper classes: 17 per cent thought a car crash could be beautiful; 49 per cent that a metal frame could also be so. This highly educated group were the most inclined to state that all the objects mentioned could make a beautiful photograph. This is the group which Bourdieu found to be most likely to possess '…the practical mastery of the relationships between objects and groups which is the basis of all judgements of the type "ça fait"…' ('it looks…') (p. 60), while the middle classes preferred photographs with '…explicit reference to a pictorial tradition or a visible stylistic intention combining the human picturesque…with gratuitous form' (p. 58). A working-class aesthetic recognized only those things previously defined as 'nice or pretty' – calendars or postcards, for example. Working-class hostility to innovation and to formal experimentation was strongest in photography – and in cinema – because they have least legitimacy and present the greatest social risk for those whose habitus has the lowest cultural capital.

This strong relationship between social origin, with its associated habitus, and the nature of the reading given to a photograph demonstrates clearly differentiated patterns of cultural consumption reminiscent of the distinctions drawn by Béarnais peasants between their own uses of photography and that of their more innovative, urban neighbours.

Bourdieu's Study of Photography as a Cultural Practice

In several of his early books, Bourdieu presents the findings of a series of empirical studies of photography in France. For example, in *Les Etudiants et leurs études* (1964b), he collaborated with Jean-Claude Passeron and Michel Eliard to investigate the cultural and educational attitudes and practices of French students, including photography. He found less variation by class origin than was the case for their other cultural activities, such as music making. While 58 per cent of the students from middle-class homes took photographs themselves, over 40 per cent of students with agricultural backgrounds did the same. Bourdieu also concluded that student photographers came from predominantly middle-class backgrounds. In the same study he investigated how students' practice of photography varied with level of education, and again found relatively little variation – educators (67 per cent) and secretaries (62 per cent) were most likely to practise photography. Serious engagement in photography – those able to give the make and format of their camera – varied with level of educational study: from 20 per cent for sixth-formers to 52 per cent for those in higher education (*polytechniciens*). Bourdieu found that educators, often autodidacts, were an atypical group, being more serious photographers than others with similar levels of qualification. Thus, for French students in the 1960s, the most highly qualified and the most artistic adopted similar patterns of cultural consumption in opposition to the social norms of their peers and were the most likely group to practise photography seriously.

In the same study, Bourdieu also asked 156 students which of a range of cultural phenomena they felt most merited a sociological study. Choices were made from a list of twelve possible projects, which included juvenile delinquency, industrial work and housing, as well as amateur photographic clubs. Amateur camera clubs were judged to be of no sociological interest by all the students from the working-class and upper-class groups, and by all but four middle-class students. Despite this almost unanimous view that camera clubs were of no sociological value, Bourdieu's subsequent large-scale study of photographic practice in France included the study of amateur camera clubs and their members. The project was funded in part by Kodak, as Bourdieu explains: 'Some twenty years ago, when I wanted to undertake a study of photography, I accepted support from Kodak not so much for the money which was an insignificant amount, but rather for information, especially statistics, that only the company could provide' (Bourdieu (with Haacke) 1995a/1994: 15). It is to this study, published in French in 1965 as *Un Art moyen: essai sur les usages sociaux de la photographie*, that we turn now.

Photography: A Middle-brow Art

In his introduction to this study of the practices of photography, Bourdieu argued that 'if a break is to be made with naïve familiarity and the probable deception of immediate understanding, a detour is necessary to establish statistical regularities and formalizations in order to achieve a properly anthropological project of re-appropriating, previously reified meanings' (Bourdieu 1990a/1965: 2). In this, Bourdieu is describing the empirical methodology which he and his team of researchers adopted when they undertook their investigations of how photography was in fact used. Consequently, this book, like *L'Amour de l'art* (1991d/1969/1966), presents the empirical findings of a complex series of interviews and surveys undertaken in Paris, Lille, Alsace and beyond, between 1960 and 1965. For an English-speaking readership, *Photography: A Middle-brow Art* is an awkward book to place chronologically in Bourdieu's thinking, since it was not translated until 1990. Since the findings appear to have general applicability, it is easy to assume that the surveys are recent, when, in fact, the work which gave rise to them was undertaken in France in the early 1960s. As noted in chapter 2, Bourdieu, at that time director of studies at the Ecole des Hautes Etudes en Sciences Sociales, established a team of researchers at the Centre de Sociologie Européene and also made use of a number of studies undertaken by private organizations, including Kodak. The book therefore offers a particularly rich mix of perspectives on photographic practice, ranging from Bourdieu's own study of photography in the Béarn (discussed above), an extended discussion of domestic uses of cameras and detailed surveys conducted by his collaborators, including the photographic practices of amateur camera clubs and the attitudes and practices of professional photographers.

Amateur Camera Clubs in the Field of Photographic Production

This investigation of amateur photographers and camera clubs was undertaken in the early 1960s and was based on a number of separate studies carried out in Paris, Lille, Alsace and Bologna. Co-researchers in this study, Castel and Schnapper, saw photographic practice as 'both an index and a means of social integration' (Bourdieu 1990a/1965: 103). Photographers who belonged to these camera clubs distinguished themselves from other photographers by the consistency of their claim that 'real' photography did not involve taking pictures whose sole function was the consecration of family events. Here, photographers no longer represent social relationships as in the pictures so valued by the rural workers in Béarn, but desire to take photographs in a different way. Camera clubs were much less cohesive in their definitions of a new purpose for photography, swinging between norms derived from artistic practices and technological principles. Unsurprisingly, these photographers took significantly more pictures than the rest of the population. Their clubs gave them 'a means of moving from naïve practice to a more scholarly practice within a group which supplies formulas and tips in order to intensify photographic activity' (p. 104). Thus, camera clubs are of two types: those with interests derived from the aesthetic, and those from the technological. The choice was a principled one which reflected an awareness of individual and group position within the broader social space (field and habitus). The groups, predominantly middle class, that adopted an aesthetic disposition towards photographic practice did so in order to mimic the cultural models of the upper classes to which they aspired. Camera clubs with more working-class members tended to valorize the camera itself as technical object and technique in general.

In the study represented here, two camera clubs were of the aesthetic type, but each with distinct relationships to the artistic field: the Bologna Photographic Club, in a city where art is a highly valued attribute of the dominant faction, had members who had achieved national and international acclaim. In contrast, Trente et Quarante was an avant-garde Parisian club with both amateur and professional members. As interviews with member photographers illustrated, both clubs emphasized the aesthetic over the technical: 'In photography, the technical aspect is fairly slight and you can learn it straight away' (Trente et Quarante) (p. 107); and, 'Before, when you took portraits, you wanted, say, the girl you were photographing to be as beautiful as possible; now we want the photograph to be as beautiful as possible' (Bologna) (p. 108). It is not therefore the choosing of the object to be photographed, but the style and artistic strategies of the photographing subject which generate the structures of the field of photography for these clubs. As one member of the Trente et Quarante camera club said: 'If the photographer has a personality, he will have a way of taking photographs so that you recognise him' (p. 109). For these clubs, then, aesthetic value is created through the stylistic decisions of the individual photographer – success or failure is personal, driven by social aspiration.

Camera clubs which recruited from more working-class environs had a membership which was younger (average age of twenty-four) and showed a more technical bias. Several youth clubs (*maisons de jeunes*) were studied, together with adult groups like the camera clubs associated with Renault factories. Data collected from both age groups showed the same patterns and structures to photographic practices. Technical matters and the darkroom are often the centre of these groups: 'More members turn up at the darkroom than at the meetings' (member, Mouffetard) (p. 121); 'You should see the new arrivals and their eagerness, their excitement when they first see the pictures appear on the film' (member, rue Mercoeur) (p. 122); and, 'Photography is very simple, it's a matter of adjustment and lighting' (ex-group leader, Vincennes) (p. 123). For many of its members, a camera club overcomes the economic obstacles which otherwise limit access to the specialized technical equipment needed to make a photograph, and provides a means of actively participating in a technological culture.

Rules of practice are communicated. The organizers 'provide tiny little formulas' (p. 127), so that a club member not only achieves mastery, in this case of photographic practice, but, at the same time, learns the pedagogic value of imitation and careful attention to technical processes. For the youth club organizers, photography is one of several morally healthy leisure activities and forms a part of a programme of 'popular culture'. As the organizer of the Vincennes camera club states: 'The purpose of photographic practice is to teach the young person to see, to be a witness to his time and to have no hesitation in taking photographs, for example photographs of demonstrations' (p. 117). Photography is offered not as a valued practice in its own right, but as a means of communication and emancipation, 'to let them discover the world through it and to say something about it' (organizer, rue Mercoeur) (p. 118). The camera club thus has both a pedagogical and a political role, derived from a relation to the broader social field. Direct comparison with art and artistic practice was underplayed – 'Photography is an art, if you like' (group leader, Mouffetard) (p. 123) – since these are the very social groups who lack the necessary cultural capital to access art for themselves. Artistic experimentation in the shape of abstract photographs was most firmly refused in these technically proficient and politically committed clubs, in strong contrast to the aesthetic aspirations of the camera clubs with strong middle-class memberships – Bologna and Trente et Quarante. What was at stake here was rather a matter of emphasis – technology or art? – and of differing solutions to the pendulum swing between 'imitation of painting' and an 'interest in technology'.

In all this there is clear evidence that patterns of photographic practice result from the interactions of a broader socio-economic field, sub-fields of the field of cultural production – the photographic – and an individual's attitudes and practices – habitus. Whatever its definition of photographic practice, the amateur camera club provided a protected space within which an individual's socio-economic capital was mediated and transformed into cultural capital, recognizable within the field structures of the group itself. The study itself concludes that: 'this analysis confirms the inability of photography to establish an autonomous aesthetic of its own, and that the pursuit of justification is determined, via the image of photography itself, by the social image of art and technology, their roles and their conditions' (p. 128). In other words, in 1960s France, the photography of the amateur, even at its most culturally elevated, took second place to art.

Professional Photographers and the Field of Photographic Production

Some 200 professional photographers were surveyed during 1964, and their attitudes, aspirations and patterns of practice were analysed. Overall, photographers were found to be individualistic, isolated, jealous of each other, independent, unable to cooperate and likely to 'pinch other people's ideas' (Bourdieu 1990a/1965: 149). The photographers interviewed always 'defined themselves in terms of their uniqueness and originality, comparing themselves more often with other photographers than with professionals from other areas' (p. 151), but few of them claimed to have other photographers as friends. However, the study concluded that the lack of unity in the profession was not so much the result of photographers' own characteristics as the consequence of the wide range of social and economic conditions of the profession itself. The profession included employees, independent photographers, business managers employing a dozen workers and small craftsmen working alone. Initial investment in equipment varied as much as income from photography. The nature of the tasks performed by 'photographers' was equally varied – selling cameras, developing amateurs' pictures, as well as taking photographs for newspapers, magazines, advertisements, fashion, portraits, art photography or more specialist scientific and medical purposes. In other words, diversity in photographic practice itself equated to the diversity in the external conditions in which it was practised.

Photography and Education

Unlike many other professions, entry to photography is unregulated. Buy a camera, take a photograph and you are a photographer. No training or apprenticeship is demanded. Indeed, in the study, the acquisition of a school qualification did not increase the likelihood of achieving a better paid or more prestigious role as a photographic craftsman or as a successful manager of a photographic business. The survey found that for employees, at least, 'the hierarchy of incomes varies in inverse ratio to qualification' (Bourdieu 1990a/1965: 152).

With continual changes in technology – more technically sophisticated equipment and emulsions – the skills base of the profession was diminishing all the time, so that photography could be practised professionally with 'lower levels of knowledge more quickly acquired' (p. 153). The survey found that the higher the level of educational qualification photographers obtained, the less frequently they acquired a professional photographic qualification. The only exception to this was in industrial or medical photography, where specialist training – the short course – was a prerequisite to employment. The diversity of careers and tasks encompassed by the profession of 'photography' was matched by the diversity of the qualifications of its practitioners. Two-thirds of all photographers had no qualification in photography, but only one in ten had no educational qualifications at all. About one in five photographers had passed their baccalaureate. The majority of these (80 per cent) became craftsmen. The statistics here are detailed and extensive, but overall the study found that education was not the most significant factor in determining the nature of photographic practice.

Photography and Social Class

Photographers who did obtain professional qualifications were most often those whose scholastic careers were out of step with the norms of their originating social class: students at photography schools were characterized by their high rate of school failure, including those from the highest social classes with the lowest educational achievements. While in the population as a whole, almost all upper-class adolescents pass their baccalaureate, only half of the upper-class photographers had been successful at this level. Interestingly, a high proportion (57 per cent) of upper-class photographers without a baccalaureate claimed to have chosen the profession because of a vocation or artistic temperament. But these were not the people who practised photography intensely before entering the profession. As the study points out:

> asserting a spontaneous choice of a profession, and precisely this profession, enables one to negate one's failure in training for other professions… In yielding to the photographic vocation, adolescents from the upper classes are conforming to the norms of their class, according to which talent is the secret of scholastic success and the condition for one's choice of profession. (Bourdieu 1990a/1965: 158)

Photography recruits large numbers (46 per cent) from a middle-class background for whom this profession represents a status more or less the same as their originating class, but without the educational entry qualifications demanded by other professions. It is perhaps not surprising to find that social class is therefore the most significant factor in determining the views which photographers held about their profession.

Photographers most often defined themselves in relationship to the local photographer – the least valued practice and the most threatened by the increasing popularity of amateur photography. The likelihood of a photographer becoming a craftsman rather than an employee rises with social origin. As a consequence of all this, the title 'photographer' covers individuals with widely varying status. Promotion within the profession is not dependent on qualifications, and it is possible to significantly change activity and status without leaving the profession itself. Social mobility within the profession is high. Thus photography offers its practitioners, if not 'upclassing' itself, then at least practical strategies for realizing aspirations of 'upclassing'. A photographer's way of dressing and, less so, way of speaking, are organized into a clear hierarchy. Those who have inherited 'good taste' and 'good manners' from their families and social milieu are at a considerable advantage. Photographers of upper-class origins are able to transpose this sensitivity – taste – to fashion and its use in their actual photographs. Nonetheless, 'class' in bearing and manners are always available as one strategy for 'upclassing', since photographers with less prestigious social backgrounds can mimic 'taste'. Photographers saw their status as related to the status of their clientele: celebrity subjects equals prestigious photographer: A nice example here of the way in which social capital enhances symbolic capital, in this case, the photographer – extends the practical efficacy of habitus by 'borrowing' the cultural capital of clients.

Given the diversity of photographers and their practice, it is perhaps not surprising that there was little unanimity among them about who were the great photographers. Roughly a third of photographers cited produced magazine or book illustrations; a further third were photojournalists, for example, for *Life*, *Paris-Match*. Fashion photographers, those taking portraits, stage and publicity photographers were also cited, but none of the photographers considered great practised in scientific or industrial photography. As one interviewee puts it: 'The great photographers are the ones who photograph the stars' (p. 169). Ironically, photography is identified by its practitioners as a profession where the supreme consecration is marked by leaving the profession, but not the practice, since '...one abandons professional photography once one has reached the peak of one's career, to go on practising it only as an enlightened dilettante...' (p. 164).

So, what is it that marks photography as a distinct practice? These surveys from the early 1960s suggest that the diversity of the practice, amateur and professional, is such that there can be no one answer, but they do identify key characteristics of the functioning of the photographic field. 'Dissensus' is the term coined to describe the lack of agreement between and about the photographic profession. More than either economic or artistic aspiration, social class shapes the nature of an individual photographer's practice. A configuration of capital derived from membership of the highest social groups – that is, habitus which is high in inherited economic, social and cultural capital – greatly increases an individual's chances of economic success, of celebrated subjects and of prestigious practice. Cultural capital, in the form of either general or photographic qualifications, has least efficacy in the struggles for privileged positions within the field of photographic practice. In the photographic field, technology and technological developments have a more marked effect than in other cultural or aesthetic practices, but here, changing formats and sophisticated equipment have the effect of undermining previously valued craft processes. Technical expertise and interest is most closely associated with working-class amateur clubs and with those professional roles with least prestige – darkroom technicians and those requiring very specialized skills, such as in medical or scientific photography.

Although Bourdieu's investigation of photography as a cultural practice was based on data from the 1960s, it has a plausibility and explanatory power which leads to an altogether unscientific belief that it has general applicability across country and time. In the next part of this chapter, the limits of this applicability will be explored through a number of case examples – individual photographers and specific settings or times.

II

Photography and Photographers

Photography is a relatively young field that continues to evolve. Unusually, it is a cultural field whose beginnings can be clearly dated. This section will show how the extent and limits of the field of photography have changed over time in response to both innovations in science and technology and the demands of the wider sociocultural field. Accounts of the field of photography itself at particular times are juxtaposed against 'snapshots' of individual photographers discussed in terms of their habitus and field positions.

Bourdieu saw that the nature and range of the fields involved in the founding of any new field generated both the initial and subsequent structures of that field. While the agents and institutions that participate in the establishment of a field do not determine the nature and range of their successors, they do exert strong influence on them through the field positions which their actions make possible. Therefore, if we look at the founding of the photography field, we shall be able to identify the agents and other fields which are most likely to be implicated in its development over time.

The Founding of the Field of Photography

In the 1830s, scientific invention thrived and industry prospered in Europe – notable figures included Faraday, Humphry Davy, Stevenson and Wedgwood. The stylized conventions of romanticism in art were on the wane (see chapter 3). The empirical observation which informed realism was not yet ascendant, evidenced only by such examples as the scientifically precise observation of Constable's paintings of cirrus and stratocumulus clouds (e.g. Cloud Study 1822). There was an increasing interest and valuing of more realistic subjects such as landscape and portraits in painting, particularly as a response to the increasing middle-class market of newly rich industrialists. Artists who had wrestled with the problem of how to capture more and more lifelike images on their canvas were using light techniques like the camera lucida. Both scientists and artists searched for processes which would fix an image permanently. Thus, photography came from a meeting of these three fields – science, industry and art.

The diversity which Bourdieu noted (1990a/1965: 151) as characteristic of photography was there at its inception – different photographic processes were invented almost simultaneously in different places in the world: Daguerre in 1839, in France, Fox Talbot in 1834, in England, and Hercules Florence in 1832, in Brazil. These photographic processes were greeted with great general enthusiasm, and credit for the inventions was hotly contested. Photography was presented, discussed and recognized in the highest scientific and socio-political circles. Daguerre's process was presented to both the Academy of Science and the Academy of Fine Arts in Paris on 7 January 1939 by Arago, a scientist and member of the French government. This process was quickly copyrighted. Later in January 1839, Fox Talbot presented his ideas to the Royal Society in London and exhibited his photographic drawings as part of a Royal Institution lecture. Talbot's calotype process was also copyrighted, but not until 1841. Nonetheless, word spread quickly, crossing the Atlantic by April 1939, when the *New Yorker* carried an article about these processes, claiming them to be the future of art. Here, learned societies, government and media interacted with and through individuals to define a set of sociocultural positions and position takings which were later defined as the field of photography.

At this time, photographic equipment was cumbersome and the process complex and slow. The photographer and his subjects, therefore, required great commitment and patience to achieve a successful image. Nonetheless, the field of photographic production had now been established. Its rapid growth was possible only because the new processes fitted well with already existing patterns of cultural consumption and with the experimental spirit of the time, where the upper and middle classes at least were open to the new. There was already an audience with the pre-existing disposition necessary to interpret photographic images and their sociocultural usage. The transference of photography into the field of artistic consumption was made possible by renewed interest in the realistic portrayal of a subject. Portrait and landscape painting could easily be replaced by photographic images, since the habitus, capital and dispositions necessary for their consumption already existed in the upper and middle classes, who constituted the artistic market. In fact, although sitting for a photographic portrait required that the subject be stationary for minutes at a time, this must have seemed relatively rapid when compared to the hours, and possibly days, needed by a portrait painter. As Bourdieu points out: 'An act of deciphering unrecognized as such, immediate and adequate comprehension, is possible and effective only in the special case in which the cultural code which makes the act of deciphering possible, is immediately and completely mastered by the observer…' (Bourdieu 1993b: 215). In other words, it was the similarity between the photographic image and the painted portrait or landscape which rendered them comprehensible as art objects and open to interpretation and classification within the existing structures of the field of cultural consumption. Photographers also sought to reproduce recognized artworks – for example, an early photograph of Ingres' *Painting of Cherubini and Muse* (1841–42) – but reflected light presented a technical barrier to clear images and these earliest reproductions were not judged to be successful. In the case of photography, the disruption of the cultural field which was brought about by the invention of a new technological practice was minimized, since an audience already existed which possessed the ability to interpret and use the artistic products of a new medium. Painted images were simply replaced by photographic ones.

Photographic practice was legitimated early in its life by the degree and volume of consecrated cultural capital at play within the field – the prestige and power of its supporters and consumers – and through its high-status events, exhibitions and published books. In the Great Exhibition of 1851, Queen Victoria and Prince Albert instigated a display of British scientific and cultural achievements – telescopes, blast furnaces, printing presses – and included the first and largest international display of photographs, and a new variant of the photographic process, Fredrick Scott Archer's uncopyrighted collodion process. Royalty continued to support and encourage photography, so that when Queen Victoria commissioned Roger Fenton to take portraits of her family and of Windsor Castle, in 1855, the way was open for others to demonstrate (and accrue) their own cultural capital by following the same practice of cultural consumption as royalty. The upper classes commissioned family portraits and pictures of their stately homes. The middle classes, newly rich from the Industrial Revolution and previously purchasers of minor art works, could follow suit as both photographers themselves and consumers of photography. As commentators now put it: 'Photography seeped into every aspect of middle class life' (Marien 2002).

At a time when technological invention was greatly celebrated, photography – itself a product of the scientific field – became a means of recording evidence of other scientific findings. Subjects included sunspot photographs by Foucault and Fizeau in 1845, photographs of a microscopic section of clematis taken by Ettingshausen (1840) and a photographic record of an 'Early Operation with Ether' by Southworth and Hawes (1847). Photography also presented itself and its processes as a praiseworthy, and hence photographable, scientific invention. A good example of this reflexivity in photographic practice is the 1845 picture of Fox Talbot in his Reading 'laboratory', removing a lens cap from a camera.

Photography's relative position within the artistic and scientific fields had not stabilized as yet, but over a period of less than twenty years, photography had been established as a new cultural practice with a range of valued social and scientific uses. It had accrued sufficient scientific and consecrated social capital from its inventors, supporters and noble consumers, and from their dominant positions within the field of power, that it could occupy its own position within this broader social space, albeit a dominated one.

An Early Photographer: Roger Fenton

Roger Fenton was a 'second-generation' photographer whose active participation in the social and cultural fields of this time played a crucial role in developing the structures of the photographic field, in Britain at least. His short photographic career – from 1851 to 1862 – and his dramatic social trajectory – from mill owner's son to royal advisor and prominent barrister – serve to demonstrate how interactions between the artistic, scientific and larger socio-political fields shaped changes in the photographic field.

In 1819 Roger Fenton was born into a northern mill-owning family, newly rich from the Industrial Revolution. His grandfather established a successful bank and used the profits to build an equally profitable cotton mill and to purchase a number of manor houses. When his father became the local Member of Parliament, Fenton moved to London and, with his own income assured, studied law at University College for four years. This represented a sound field strategy, whereby his existing habitus, in which provincial, middle-class dispositions, combined with economic capital derived from the Industrial Revolution, would be reconfigured by the addition of the social, cultural and educational capital derived from the field of power through a socially legitimated profession like law. A good field move(!) – deferring further economic capital in expectation of later social and economic gain. However, Fenton abandoned law, discovering a new vocation as a painter. As others before him, he moved to Paris, where he acquired a quite different sort of educational capital by training in art composition in Paris with Paul Démarche and Drolling. Returning to London, he associated with artists including Ford Maddox Brown and helped establish an art school in North London, but when he duly exhibited at the Royal Academy, results were unspectacular. On the surface, he was an unrecognized artist like many others. Fenton's habitus included both artistic dispositions and a configuration of capital which was characteristic of a dominated position in the wider socio-political field. However, the cultural and social capital which he had inherited from his family combined with his own highly consecrated educational capital (law qualifications) to allow him to gain a more dominant field position. In 1851, now in his thirties and with a wife and family, he returned to law and was called to the Bar. Almost simultaneously, he saw and was greatly impressed by the photographs at the 1851 Great Exhibition and began to practise photography.

His first photographic expedition was at the invitation of a friend, Vignobles, who was designing and building a technologically advanced bridge for Czar Nicholas I. While in Russia, he also took photographs of the spectacular architecture in Moscow. When these photographs were shown in London, the exhibition, intended to last two weeks, was extended by popular appeal to several months. Fenton's reputation as a photographer was made and photography's place in popular London society was established. Having recognized the important role in cultural legitimation played by the French Académie and the *Prix de Rome* during his time in Paris, Fenton successfully led moves to establish a Photographic Society in England and was duly elected honorary secretary in 1853. Subsequently, he was chosen as guide and advisor for Queen Victoria and Prince Albert's visit to the Society. Their interest in photography and their purchase of Fenton's twenty-five Moscow photographs secured his artistic and social position. He later received commissions from Queen Victoria to photograph her family and Windsor Castle itself. In 1854, he undertook a technically challenging commission to photograph the collection of the British Museum, devising new illumination techniques to photograph sculptures and tablets to best effect, and reducing distortions by using five different cameras.

Fenton sought to distinguish his photographic practice from that of 'hack commercial portraitists', and took and exhibited pictures of the beauty spots of Wales and Yorkshire and of cathedrals and stately homes: the subject of a photograph determined its price – a clear hierarchy of subjects. Responding to royal concerns about the war, he visited the Crimea and photographed delicate and discreet war pictures: pleasing compositions of deserted battlefields and military leaders – Lord Raglan, Omar Pashe, but not injured soldiers or the battles themselves. Given his fine art training, Fenton was in a good position to imitate high art genres in his still-life pictures – opulent fruit displays and the more gruesome spoils of game hunting. His later work included a number of fine art photographs, composed to imitate the exotic orientalism of painting, including a reclining odalisque, reminiscent of Ingres.

All this in ten years! Then, in 1861, Fenton claimed that photography was all together too popular to provide an income. His decision to give up photography was as much a response to a dispute with a Royal Commission about the reproduction rights of his British Museum photographs, the collapse of the family cotton mill as a consequence of the American Civil War and family feuds, as it was a reflection of his struggle to keep up with rapid technological changes in photography. In the International Exhibition of 1861, photography was relegated from its earlier place within the fine art section to a place with other machinery, tools and instruments. This loss of field position coincided with Fenton's timely return to the law and his appointment in 1862 to the prestigious position of barrister for the courts of Manchester, Salford and York.

Given autonomy through his inherited economic capital, Fenton was able to gain consecrated educational capital from the fields of law and fine art, and used them successfully to switch between fields as economic necessity demanded. He was also able to accumulate highly consecrated social and cultural capital from commissions from royalty and public institutions, and artistic and scientific capital from learned societies, public lectures, published books of photographs and prestigious exhibitions.

He had learnt the effectiveness of the social capital derived from learned societies while in France and he successfully transferred this strategy when he led the establishment of the Royal Photographic Society. Like Manet and Hirst (discussed in chapter 5), Fenton also called on an extensive social (field) network. The rapid economic and social trajectories of his grandfather and father meant that Roger Fenton would not only have had social and cultural aspirations, but that he knowingly deployed effective strategies in seeking and creating powerful field positions.

Bourdieu (1990a/1965) found empirically that the diversity of photographic practice in 1960s France gave those who practised photography as a profession opportunities for social mobility, since the consecration of the subject photographed can be transferred to the photographer. Fenton's brief biography shows how his short photographic career offered him opportunities to photograph the most highly consecrated subjects – royalty, fine art objects, stately homes and international war. He was able to move from the nouveau riche, industrial middle classes to a highly consecrated dominant position in the field of power as a law maker. In nineteenth-century England, as in twentieth-century France, the ambiguity inherent in photographic practices provided fruitful opportunities for those with social aspirations.

Fenton's enduring acclaim derives from his photographic practice, not his social position. His photographs are now collected by major art museums, including

MOMA in New York, the Victoria and Albert museum in London and the National Gallery of Art, Washington, DC. His photographic work was also the subject of a solo exhibition in Tate Britain in 2005. In other words, Fenton's earlier avant-garde positioning – as neglected artist and pioneer of a new medium – over time has proved to be successful in terms of artistic and cultural legitimation. He might well be described as a master of the field.

Fenton's photographic career demonstrates important enduring characteristics of the field of photography itself: photography's changing relationship to fine art; the structural changes which result from frequent technological change; the continuing importance to the photographic field of popularization; and the homology between the habitus of the photographed subject and that of the photographer. As Bourdieu's French professional photographers showed, the way to become a celebrated photographer is to photograph prestigious subjects (Bourdieu 1990a/1965: 163) – and, at the time, there were few more prestigious than Queen Victoria.

Changing Times in Photography: 1880–1930

In the decades that followed Fenton, technological invention, global exploration and war were dominant features of the socio-economic field. Photography, as both a technology and a cultural practice, responded to these developments. The field of photographic production changed as its supporting technology improved. New cameras were developed – the first Kodak camera in 1888, Eastman's Brownie camera in 1900. When Leica's compact camera followed in 1924, only eighty-six years had elapsed between the first photograph and handheld compact cameras. Dry-plate processes appeared in 1881, together with photographic roll film and half-tone engraving suitable for newspaper printing in 1886. Only forty-seven years had passed from invention to multiple printing and mass distribution.

Maxwell's first scientific invention of a colour image in 1861 was followed by the Lumière brothers' autochrome process for colour in 1904, the flashbulb in 1924 and Technicolor's full-colour film in 1930. By the late 1920s, still photography could present a colour image. It could make use of artificial light and images could be wired across the Atlantic. Movies were becoming routine, for example, Eisenstein's *Battleship Potemkin* (1925). The first talkie, *The Jazz Singer*, coincided with the first demonstration of television in 1927 – all a far cry from the intangible camera obscura images of less than a century before.

Photography was by now so popular and technically sophisticated that it no longer demanded expert scientific skills. It became a discreet pastime for upper-class women and a practical paying profession for those prepared to cater for a mass market. By the 1890s, both family portraiture and photographic postcards were popular. Despite the rapid changes in technology, the patterns of consumption, as evidenced by notable photographs, settled down into several distinct patterns of usage: fine art images, war photography, anthropological usage and mass marketing of popular, often contrived images. With national expansionism, exploration and colonialism rampant, war proliferated, and with it, war photography. With less cumbersome equipment and simpler photographic techniques, the soldiers themselves now took the photographs, which were increasingly explicit about the horrors of war.

A taste for the exotic was shown in photographs of landscape and architecture from abroad, for example, O'Sullivan's 'Pyramid and Tufa Domes' (1878). With faster processes, images of people need no longer be blurred, so explorers could now make photographic records of countries and people previously unknown. This new use of photography to evidence findings of exploration led to a new discipline – anthropology. As discussed earlier, pictures were often used to offer confirmation of what was observed and to prove the anthropologist's theory, for example, Charnay's 'Mission to Madagascar' (1863) or 'Brinjara and Wife' (1868) by an unknown photographer. Some of these apparently ethnographic images were also exploited to appeal to a more popular Victorian audience, which could be described as receptive to the exotic, for example, images of attractive women – 'Arab Woman and Turkish Woman, Zangaki, Port Said' (1870–80) – who appeared demure but suggestive at the same time.

The strong but ambiguous relationship between 'high' art and photography persisted, and was disputed. 'Instant' photographic images ran side by side with Impressionism's snapshots and their paintings of light in the late 1870s, while photographs of movement in the 1880s provoked Italian Futurism at the turn of the century. Nudes were a common theme for artists and photographers, considered as beautiful images in themselves, or as more sexually ambiguous, for example, von Gloeden's 'Nude Sicilian Youths' (1885). However, both Baudelaire and Delacroix argued that photography was too unimaginative ever to be 'authentic art'. Artists themselves took photographs, for example, Degas' portraits of Renoir and Mallarmé in Berthe Morrisot's Salon in 1890, and, later, the painterly gum print of Steichen's 1902 'Self-portrait with Easel'. Like Fenton's appropriation of oriental images from the art of his time, photographers mimicked the style and composition of high art paintings; for example, James Craig Annan photographed Miss Janet Burnet in a composition closely resembling Whistler's painting of his mother. From the 1890s, the evocative and expressive photographs of 'pictorialism' moved away from the faithful depiction of an image and reflected the disillusion with industrial production which was also apparent in the arts and crafts movement. International camera clubs sprang into being in support of this avant-gardist photographic movement: Weiner Kamera Klub, Vienna Secession, Photo-Club de Paris, the British Linked Ring and the American Photo-Seccession launched by Stieglitz in 1902. These groups saw themselves as art photographers, opposing the conventional academic work of the older photographic societies in a way which mirrored the oppositional generations of the artistic avant-gardes of the period.

In contrast to this 'high art' field positioning of photographic practice, photography continued to supply a steady stream of popular and commercial images so that it also occupied a strong field position within the large-scale field of popular culture. As photography became more and more mobile and accessible, technological communication improved dramatically, so that by 1923 photographic images could be wired from one place to another. Newspapers' capacity to 'consume' images of current affairs and of famous people also gave rise to a new branch of photography – the documentary – and to a new profession – photojournalism.

Briefly, between the First and Second World Wars, the field position of photography within the field of culture and the broader social space had become significantly more complex and fragmented. Photography's role as a medium for recording scientific achievements was now taken for granted, while in the new fields of anthropology and journalism, and in the documentary recording of places and people, it could be seem to occupy a key positioning between the fields of culture and politics. Nonetheless, through the avant-gardist strategies of photographers like Steichen and Stieglitz, photography also occupied a field positioning within the restricted field of high art (see Bourdieu 1993b: 122). It was necessary to decipher both the aesthetic codes of high art and those of the history of photography in order to decode a pictorialist photograph. Thus, photography occupied a dominated position in the restricted field of art which is itself dominated by the field of power. Simultaneously, with the new ease in producing multiple reproductions of an image and transmitting images from place to place, photography clearly occupied a field position within the large-scale fields of popular culture and commercialism, where large-scale cultural production and consumption are mostly independent of prior education. These are the field structures within which several individual photographers' trajectories will now be discussed.

A French Photographer: Brassaï

In order to understand the sociocultural trajectory of any career, it is necessary to consider the habitus associated with the field positions which are successively occupied, as well as the capital accrued and its configuration. As Bourdieu emphasized, one must 'take into account not only capital volume and composition but also the historical evolution of these properties, i.e. the trajectory of the group as a whole and of the individual in question and his lineage, which are the basis of the subjective image of the position objectively occupied' (1984/1979: 453). Thus, Brassaï, whose father was a university professor who studied French literature at the Sorbonne and who had lived in France as a child, entered the sociocultural field with significant inherited educational capital and cultural capital derived from an international field. Born in 1899, his trajectory began in what Bourdieu (p. 452) had called the 'left wing dominated dominant' field position, as the child of a higher education teacher. As a young man, Brassaï served in the Austro-Hungarian cavalry and studied fine art in Budapest and Berlin. His companions included noted artists and musicians – Laszlo Moholy-Nagy,

Kandinsky, Kokoschka, Varese and Bartok. By 1924, when Brassaï moved to Paris, he had fine art training, was bilingual in German and Hungarian, and was studying French. In other words, he had accrued a significant volume of educational, cultural and social capital in his own right. Nonetheless, in keeping with his social origins, he chose to live on the Left Bank, earning his living by writing, and collecting and selling old photographs. He worked as a journalist for German and Hungarian magazines. He knew established photographers, Eugene Atget and André Kertész, but did not take his own photographs until 1929, when a friend lent him a camera. Shortly afterwards he bought a professional camera, a Voigtlander, and began taking the atmospheric photographs of Paris for which he became famous. During his nocturnal walks around Paris with Henry Miller, he took the photographs which established his reputation, which were published in 1932 as *Paris de nuit*. With a circle of artistic friends including Max Jacob, Fernand Léger and Le Corbusier, he was introduced to Picasso, who, liking his work, commissioned him to photograph his sculptures. Picasso – as the 'royalty' of the artistic avant-garde – through his patronage, offered a cultural consecration to Brassaï similar to that conferred on Fenton by Queen Victoria. When he was interviewed in 1974, Brassaï recalled his own skill as a painter and sculptor. He quoted Picasso, who, when he saw Brassaï's drawings in 1939, said, '"You're crazy, Brassaï. You have a gold mine and you spend your time exploiting a salt mine!" The salt mine was – naturally – photography' (Hill and Cooper 2005: 38). Nonetheless, Brassaï's career in photography, albeit a lesser art, was secure. His subjects included the studios of Picasso, Giacometti, Lipschitz, Astride Maillol and Matisse. He contributed to a number of editions of *Minotaure*, together with Man Ray and André Breton. Salvador Dali used some of his female heads in his collages. In other words, with highly consecrated social and cultural capital derived from the restricted artistic field of 1930s Paris, Brassaï now occupied a dominant field position within the dominated field of cultural production. Over the next three decades, Brassaï continued his successful photographic career, despite a short period during the war when he was banned from photography by the Germans. He became a regular contributor to Harper's *Bazaar* magazine, where he was permitted to choose his own subjects. His field position was further consecrated by prestigious international awards: a gold medal to mark Daguerre's centenary; a gold medal from the Venice Biennale; honorary membership of the American Society of Magazine Photographers; and, in 1978, the first Grand Prix National for photography – as successful a photographic career as is possible.

It was therefore rather surprising when, during the 1960s, he gave up photography and returned to fine art practice: sculpture, drawing and tapestries, and to writing and publishing. Brassaï himself explained: '…I have taken many photographs in my life and published relatively few books, so now I prefer to travel the universe of my photographs and make them better known' (ibid.). Brassaï's habitus, later in his life, showed a configuration of high-volume, highly consecrated social, cultural and educational capital derived from an international field, one which was dominated, since, as Picasso so graphically described, photography continued to be a 'salt mine'. Brassaï's social trajectory, although a steep and successful one, together with his family roots, were like his photographic subjects: always within the restricted cultural field.

American Photographers: Ansel Adams, Dorothea Lange and Margaret Bourke-White

On the other side of the Atlantic, photography also thrived. In 1937, the Museum of Modern Art (MOMA) in New York organized the first exhibition of photographic history. A group of art photographers, Ansel Adams and Edward Weston among them, established the group f64 to continue photographic developments in the spirit of the earlier Photo-Secession group. As the name f64 suggests, they were interested in achieving great depth of field and sharp detail in their photographs. Like Brassaï, Ansel Adams was a self-taught photographer. While still a child, Adams had used the family's Kodak Bullseye camera to take photographs in Yosemite National Park. In an interview in 1975 (Hill and Cooper 2005), Adams first claimed that there was no art background in his family, but later indicated that his father had been a painter and had taken him to see the Armory show in 1915. Hence, Adams' early habitus included significant inherited artistic capital, which was further strengthened by his early training as a pianist – cultural capital in the form of education. In 1918 he joined the conservation movement, photographing areas of natural beauty like Yosemite. Through his acquaintance with other photographers, Paul Strand, Dorothea Lange, Walker Evans, Edward Weston and Stieglitz, Adams established a career as a photographer. A teacher of photography, he founded the photographic society f64, and a department of photography at the California School of Fine Art, and was instrumental in the founding of the department of photography at MOMA. He took photographs for art exhibition catalogues and exhibited his work at Stieglitz's 291 Gallery and at MOMA. In the 1930s, he refused assignments from the Farm Security Administration (FSA), expressing a need to develop and print his own images, that is, to preserve his artistic autonomy.

Towards the end of the Second World War, his photographs and political support for Japanese Americans got him blacklisted by the FBI, but his work for Polaroid earned him support from Dr Land, the inventor of the Polaroid process; he was cleared after a year. In much of this trajectory, we see the action of social capital in enhancing the effectiveness of habitus within the field. Adams' later career was legitimated by the cultural capital he accrued through association with strongly consecrated regional and national institutions – art galleries, including MOMA; innovative commercial enterprises, such as Polaroid; and the conservation movement. By the end of his career, despite his apparent oppositional relation to government, his habitus was such that he could take them on and win, thus indicating a consecrated field position within the field of power.

Other contemporary American photographers, including Margaret Bourke-White and Dorothea Lange, used their photographs to make direct social and political statements.

With the secure habitus of a middle-class graduate, Dorothea Lange began work as an independent portrait photographer, but during the Great Depression she took photographs of the homeless. From 1935 she worked for the FSA, unflinchingly documenting the poverty of migrant workers. In the art world, she is now considered 'an icon of socially committed documentary' (Mibelbeck 2001). For us, her relatively unspectacular trajectory in the cultural field of photography belies the continuing power of her photographs in the socio-political field.

Margaret Bourke-White, a political and social-minded photojournalist, was a founder of *Life* magazine. In 1930, she attracted her first assignment from *Fortune* magazine to photograph industrial installations in the Soviet Union. She was a war correspondent in Germany and shocked the world with her photographs of liberated concentration camps. She visited India during its struggle for freedom, where she photographed Gandhi. She herself declared her photographs of black South African gold miners, glistening with sweat, to be her favourite images. Her interest in photography was commercial, since this is how she earned her living. Her habitus as a photojournalist would therefore demonstrate a configuration of economic and symbolic capital, including cultural capital from the large-scale field of popular culture. Nonetheless, the political content of her photographs and their widespread distribution endowed her with power from within the international field of politics.

A British Photographer: Lord Lichfield

With the coming of the 'swinging sixties' to London, established cultural practices were aggressively challenged by pop culture, a new sense of style and The Beatles. As we have seen, this was the time that Bourdieu's studies of photography and photographers were undertaken. The photographer Patrick Lichfield, born in 1939, was both a leading participant and chronicler of these times. As an upper-class professional photographer, his photographic career was a specific example of many of the principles which Bourdieu and his researchers uncovered. For example, as a member of the British and Danish aristocracy, Lord Lichfield was educated at Harrow and Sandhurst before going into the Grenadier Guards. As French upper-class photographers were found to do, he claimed a vocation for photography and joined the profession as a photographic assistant in opposition to his parents' wishes. But his decision to become a photographer in 1962 may have represented a desire to be an active participant in 'Swinging London' rather than a strategic field positioning to compensate for academic failure. He demonstrated what Bourdieu had called 'sensitivity to style' in his early decision to conform to a counter-culture, working-class stereotype, and used his father's name of Anson rather than his title. He gained his reputation by adapting to the new London style, photographing new celebrities, models and pop stars like Marsha Hunt, Jane Birkin and Michael Caine, and Bianca and Mick Jagger's wedding. Later, he made the most of his show-business friends and aristocratic connections (highly consecrated social capital) to build a photographic career taking beautiful pictures of beautiful people, for example, photographing the Duke and Duchess of Windsor, and Prince Charles and Lady Diana's wedding. Lichfield worked for *Life* and *Vogue*, for Unipart calendars, for the British Tourist Board and for Olympus cameras. While not an innovative photographer in style or composition, he was prepared to adapt his practice to match the structural changes in the photographic field, which occurred in response to technological change, and used both Polaroid and digital equipment. Since Lichfield's social origins were of the highest, his manners and connections gave him access to the most valorized subjects, and his photographic career prospered as a consequence; in this, he was able to exchange highly consecrated social capital for cultural capital. With typical upper-class understatement, what Bourdieu calls 'hypo-correction' he claimed: 'I sometimes think if I had devoted my life to photography, I might have done better, but I would not have enjoyed it as much' (Maitland 2005). Nonetheless, he entered the photographic field from a dominant position in the field of power – this remained unchanged throughout his life. When he left the game in 2005, he had accrued both consecrated artistic capital, through national photographic fellowships and a recent exhibition at the National Portrait Gallery, and high-volume, but low consecrated cultural capital from his position within the field of popular culture for what one might argue were essentially family photographs – of his royal relatives (highly consecrated social capital).

A Family Photograph Album: The Beatles

Family photographs of another celebrated group, The Beatles, have been published as a coffee-table book (The Beatles: 2000). Many of the early photographs were taken simply as the mementos of a working-class family, but these snapshots have accrued high-volume cultural capital as their subjects achieved consecrated and iconic status in the field of popular culture. Bourdieu writes of family photographs that: 'The taking and contemplation of family photographs presupposes the suspension of all aesthetic judgement, because the sacred character of the object and the sacrelizing relationship between the photographer and the picture are enough unconditionally to justify the existence of the picture…' (Bourdieu 1990a/1965: 90). In other words, these Beatles photographs, now loaded with both economic and symbolic capital, make no claim to aesthetics, but reflect the quasi-religious status of their valorized subjects, their photographers forgotten.

Transgressive Photographers: Mapplethorpe and Serrano

A distinctly aesthetic, but controversial field trajectory is offered by the career of Robert Mapplethorpe. His social origin was conventionally middle class. He was born in 1946, the third of six children in a Roman Catholic family living in suburban America, Long Island. He graduated in fine art from Brooklyn, producing mixed media art works. Following in the established footsteps of Picasso, Braque and Duchamp, he used commercially produced materials and pre-existing photographic images in his collages. His first celebrity portrait made use of a torn photograph of Warhol, whom he claimed as his role model. The effect of the wider social group, in this case, of artists and musicians like Bruce Nauman, Joseph Kosuth, Warhol and his Factory friends, can be read in his position taking within the artistic field. Thus, his early habitus was typical of many fine art graduates in the 1960s – inherited middle-class social and cultural capital combined with more 'alternative' artistic capital in the form of educational qualifications and artistic practice.

In the early 1970s, when Mapplethorpe began to take his own photographs, he followed the practice of Andy Warhol and David Hockney, and chose a Polaroid. The pictures he then assembled included a self-portrait of overlapping photographs, framed by a purple paper bag, images of transvestite star Cindy Darling and of his friend Patti Smith. Mapplethorpe's enduring interests in the 'photograph as an object' and in male nudity and sadomasochistic imagery can be seen even in these early art works. Mapplethorpe highlighted what he considered the most shocking area of his pictures – often genitalia, or the mouths in his 'Kissing Boys' (1972). Courting controversy brought him to notice and helped him secure a left-wing field positioning within the New York artistic avant-garde. In the mid-1970s he acquired a large-format press camera and photographed his wide circle of friends and acquaintances, including visits to underground sex clubs. This 'field move' shows a direct and probably knowing deployment of social capital in a strategic position taking within the cultural field. Mapplethorpe's later pictures in the 1980s developed a more elegant and gentler beauty. He became an expensive and sought-after portraitist. He also produced still-life photographs of delicate flowers, with shimmering light and classical symmetrical beauty – a symmetry which he blamed on his Catholic childhood. Mapplethorpe's work became highly consecrated through many national and international exhibitions. Prestigious art galleries also purchased his photographs – the Smithsonian Institute in Washington, DC, and San Francisco's Museum of Modern Art, for example – but many of his photographs are owned by private collectors, perhaps perceived as affordable luxury goods.

When it became known that Mapplethorpe had Aids, the price of a single one of his photographs rocketed to $500,000 by December 1988. After reluctantly coming to terms with his illness, Mapplethorpe, as ever aware of his position in the artistic field, took care in disposing of his now valuable archive of photographs by establishing the not-for-profit Mapplethorpe Foundation. The Foundation's dual purposes are to promote photography as a fine art of equal worth as painting and sculpture, and to support medical research to fight HIV and Aids. Mapplethorpe died in March 1989, ten months after the creation of his Foundation.

In the same year, a major scandal broke about National Endowment for the Arts (NEA) funding, which had financed Andreas Serrano's photographs of works using semen and blood, and 'Piss Christ', a crucifix seen through a urine haze of tiny bubbles. As Hans Haacke explained in an interview with Bourdieu: 'The alarm signal from Richmond triggered a flood of letters to members of Congress, charging that public funds had been used to subsidize a sacrilege' (Bourdieu 1995a/1994: 3). In the year before federal elections, right-wing fundamentalists mounted a strident campaign, led by Senator Jessie Helms from North Carolina, against obscenity and sacrilege in art, a campaign which threatened public funding to artists.

An exhibition of Mapplethorpe photographs, organized by the Contemporary Arts Centre in Cincinnati in 1989, and also funded by NEA, included sadomasochistic images and was caught up in the so-called Serrano Scandal. Jessie Helms accused Mapplethorpe of pornography and the gallery director, Dennis Barrie, of pandering to obscenity. After a much publicized trial, Barrie and the gallery were acquitted. By then, Haacke claims (ibid.: 4), Helms had used political pressure with the threat of adverse publicity to ensure that few colleagues would vote against an amendment in Congress to prohibit the spending of public funds on obscene materials. The chairman of NEA now had power of veto, which he used. Although the law was ruled to be unconstitutional when challenged in the Federal District Court of Los Angeles, Haacke reports that 'artists and institutions applying for public funds are now driven to exercise self-censorship. It is well known that self-censorship is often more effective than open censorship. And it doesn't leave a dirty trail' (ibid.: 6). In this, art and photography, in particular, are seen to be active constituents in the field of power. As Bourdieu points out: 'Museums need cultural respectability to be able to influence sponsors... There is a whole series of dependencies ... museums need to be recognised by public authorities in order to have sponsors. And all this creates a set of dependencies which, even if there is resistance, continue to exist' (ibid.: 10). One can see here that, although the scandal surrounding both artists – Serrano and Mapplethorpe – has now abated, its effects have irrevocably altered what constitutes effective position taking within the cultural field, with the need for new caution by museum sponsors and artists. Bourdieu himself expresses concern for the artistic autonomy necessary in support of avant-garde field positioning: 'One of the antinomies of cultural policy, no matter what the area, has to do with the fact that the most autonomous productions do not have a market and cannot survive without public funding...' (ibid.: 13). Since Serrano's photographs were, in just this sense, autonomous and dependent on public funds, his field position might have been seriously undermined. However, this is to underestimate the complicit role of patronage and the media. Charles Saatchi, for example, recognizing the attractiveness to the media of artistic controversy, exhibited Andreas Serrano's work in the Saatchi

Gallery in 1993. Much to Saatchi's taste, Serrano, famous for his infamy and sacrilege, could trade political scandal with Saatchi for the economic and artistic capital of his private patronage. Needless to say, the price of Serrano's work soared. Some time later, Damien Hirst, ever a master of the field, returned to drawing – religious or sacrilegious images!

A Working-class Photographer

Controversy has been a field strategy of choice for many recent art photographers. Richard Billingham, an art student from northern working-class roots (low economic and cultural capital), studied painting in Sunderland. His college's external examiner recognized potential in the photographs he was using as sketches for his painting and suggested that he work directly with these photographic images of his family. Only a few years later, but now with Saatchi's patronage, Billingham presented huge, unsettling colour photographs of his dysfunctional family in the unlikely consecrated artistic settings of the Royal Academy's 'Sensation' exhibition and, subsequently, in the Tate, as a contender for the Turner Prize. This cultural trajectory – working-class boy makes good through transgressive art – matches that of other young British artists. For Billingham, it may yet prove to be an example of the social mobility or 'upclassing' (Bourdieu 1990a/1965: 161), which Bourdieu identified as a characteristic of the photographic professional's struggles for legitimated field position. Here, consecrated cultural capital, which is derived by a photographer from within the photographic field through the prestige – cultural capital – of the photographic subject, is opened to deployment in the wider social field, where class itself is at stake.

III

Photography: Field and Sub-fields

The structures of the field of photographic production are established through the differential and increasingly fragmented patterns of photographic practice: artistic, scientific, social, anthropological, glamour, journalistic and reflexive. These were identified earlier as present at the turn of the nineteenth century, and in Bourdieu's studies in 1960s France were still recognizable as sub-fields of cultural production. By the turn of this century, however, these photographic sub-fields have substantially blurred into one another, increasingly dependent on an audience's knowledge of a photographer's purpose, medium and context to distinguish between them. One example of the softening of these field boundaries is the photographer Cindy Sherman. She constructs photographic images of herself to create visual charades which challenge gender stereotyping, for example, in her B-movies series, *Untitled Film Still 1978*. She has also constructed repulsive and chaotic images such as *Untitled No 180*, apparently a picture of herself as a newly dead corpse, which provokes the viewer into awareness of the photographer's intention – nausea and disgust – all while undermining the apparent 'reality' of the photographic image. However, all this is dependent on prior knowledge of the reflexive nature of Sherman's photographic practice and familiarity with the cultural images, albeit popular, to which her work refers. Thus, the cultural capital – probably artistic, and certainly educational – needed to 'read' these images in full, positions these photographs as high art within the 'restricted' field, that is, the avant-garde artistic field.

Similarly, Yinka Shonibare, an Anglo-Nigerian artist photographer, addresses racial stereotypes through his staged photographs of drawing-room scenes, reminiscent of eighteenth-century painting – Hogarth, for example – but he interposes his own image as an admired, socially prominent, but black party-goer in a challenge to his audience's social presuppositions. Without familiarity with eighteenth-century painting, an understanding of the British slave trade and some knowledge of Shonibare's own personal history and intentions, these photographs have only superficial meaning. Thus, without the means to decode the image, Shonibare's appropriation of high art cultural capital from Hogarth's consecrated position within the artistic field and his historically based commentary on the racial structures of the broader social space are rendered invisible.

Even more disturbing is the apparent merging of photojournalism, documentary form and artistic composition to be found in Luis Camnitzer's photographs from 'Documenta 11' (2001). Here, the globally aware photographer, born in Germany, living in New York, but a citizen of Uruguay, confronts the viewer with four captioned photographs of mutilated hands from his 'Uruguayan Torture Series, 1983–84'. In one of these photographs, electric wire cuts into the flesh of a finger and is entitled 'Her fragrance lingers on'. Should the images, beautifully composed as they are, be read as art? Are they in fact real – potential documentary evidence in a political trial? Barthes suggested that a personal choice was needed about photography, 'to subject its spectacle to the civilized code of perfect illusions, or to confront in it the awakening of intractable reality' (Barthes 1982/1980: 119). Bourdieu asks that the viewer sees photography as, simultaneously and inextricably, structuring and structured by the struggles of society and politics in the field of power, and by the position taking of artistic agents in the cultural field. In this, as in the photographic examples above, one sees the interpenetration of the artistic and socio-political fields and the transferability of symbolic capital from one field to another – what Bourdieu calls meta-capital (see Bourdieu 1992a: 114).

Each of the photographers considered in this chapter has a distinct habitus with a unique configuration of symbolic and economic capital, and hence differentiated field positions. In Figure 6.2 these photographers are included in a level 1 analysis, which shows the interrelations between the fields of art and culture, the field of science, technology and education and the field of power. Lichfield is perhaps the most difficult to position since he could be seen as occupying a dominant position

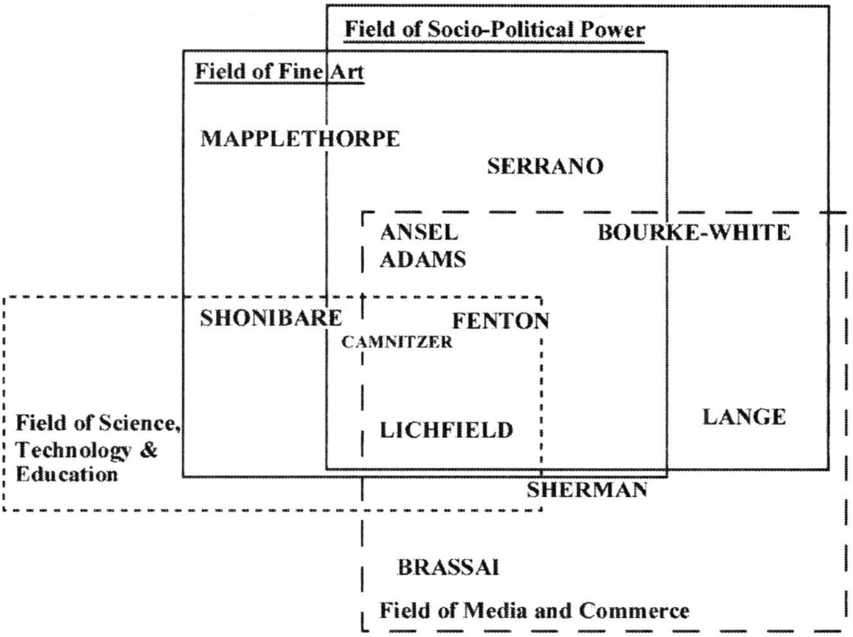

Figure 6.2 Photographers. Level 1 analysis: fields in relation to the field of power.

in the field of power through his social ranking, or a position within the field of media as a photographer.

Photography: The Digital Age

Today, the ubiquity of digital photography and mobile phones, with instant transmission of images, are reconfiguring the photographic field and the photographic object itself. Walter Benjamin's concern for the authenticity of an artwork in the 1930s (Benjamin 1969) now fades into a much starker concern for the lack of object-hood or substantive materiality in the ephemeral and infinitely modifiable digital message, which is all that now remains of a photograph. If, as Benjamin claimed, 'Mechanical reproduction of art changes the reaction of the masses towards art' (Benjamin 1969), what are the implications of digital technology for the field of photographic consumption and its positioning in relation to high art and popular culture?

In popular culture, images – some computer-generated but most still dependent on photography – are in use everywhere. Many go completely unobserved. Although the population is now habituated to a wide range of photographic images in advertising, in newspapers and magazines and on television, individuals are not necessarily any more able to decode the social, political or art historical meanings of what they see. Like the Béarnais peasants who did not recognize the photograph as an object in itself, the necessarily insubstantial digital image is not acknowledged, but is solely a means to share an accurate representation of 'everyday experiences'. Thus, the practices of photographic consumption which Bourdieu found in the Béarn, are even today reproduced when the professional photographer is called in to capture the 'family' at weddings, Christmas and birthdays. The photographic products remain unchanged, stored as ever in the family photo album, but now accompanied by a video of the event. The medium may have diversified, but the practice remains intact. For the middle-brow collector who has been able to afford photographs but not more valorized art works, the transience and reproducibility of a digital photograph may represent a significant loss of value, that is, cultural and economic capital.

The effect of the digital camera on the field of photographic production is complex. For a professional society photographer like Lichfield, with extensive technical support, the transition to digital technology was apparently seamless. For the amateur, choosing and capturing an image is possibly easier than ever, and composition unproblematic, since unwanted images can be rejected instantly. Producing a concrete photographic print can now be done at home without a darkroom, but still demands considerable technical expertise, this time in software, printers and paper.

Barthes wrote: 'The noeme of photography is simple, banal, no depth: "that has been"' (Barthes 1982/1980: 115). In an age of digital reproduction, this may simply be an outdated view. For an art photographer, and even more so for the artist using photography, images are now a plastic medium in themselves. Jeff Wall, for example, has used computer imaging in his photographic collages for some decades. In other words, it is consecrated cultural capital associated with high-brow art which is most affected by computer imaging and digitization. Galleries like the Tate now exhibit digital art, made specifically for electronic display on a website: images which are, technically at least, endlessly reproducible simulacra of themselves. All this is to say that, as in the past, new technologies have restructured the field of photographic production, this time by digitization. Dramatic changes in the field of consumption have followed; not simply in the ease and speed of communicating images, but in a new commodity – reproduction rights.

It has been reported (Levi Strauss 2003: 189) that one of the largest collections of historical photographs, the Bettman and United Press International archive – 17 million images – purchased by Bill Gates in 1995, is being digitized so that the originals can be buried and preserved in a sub-zero, low-humidity storage vault. Gates, at present, owns the rights to show about 65 million images, including two other photo agencies and the digital reproduction rights of works in some art museums. Since he has already achieved the most consecrated and dominant position within the field of information technology, these purchases anticipate, and perhaps hasten, an irrevocable change in the market for photographic images. The shift from photograph as commodity to copyright as commodity shows not a homology, but a future identification between the field of photographic consumption and the field of information technology. There is also room for disquiet about the consequences of such a position taking within the wider socio-political field of power. Has Bill Gates just bought our visual history?

Concluding Remarks

To return to the more gentle landscape of French photographers, Bourdieu found that, 'Photographic aesthetes are clearly aware of the social situation of their art' (1990a/1965:149). This has indeed been demonstrated in the photographic work of artists like Roger Fenton, Brassaï, Ansel Adams and, most particularly, Luis Camnitzer. Bourdieu also argues that 'Individual aesthetes can therefore only be completely understood if one takes into account the relationship that the photographers have with the groups that define the meaning which they find scattered in things' (p. 145). Thus, photography exists as a high-brow art if an artistic group defines it as such and continues to use it as one of the media in which an artist may choose to work, that is, the group grants its products consecration. At the same time, within the family, photography still provides legitimation to the events and relationships it offers to the camera's lens, be it digital or not. Photography, then, is a fragmented field and photographic practice is necessarily diverse. Nonetheless, in the apparently ever changing field of photography, there still appear to be stable structuring principles. This is a field where, over time, differentiated sub-fields emerge and then coalesce with other sub-fields in response to changes in both the technological and socio-political fields.

In photography, education – particularly professional education – plays little role in determining success, unlike social class which does. For the individual photographer, photography is a medium which does not of itself provide legitimation within the wider social space; it is almost essential to enter the field from the middle or upper classes in order to have access to the appropriately valorized subjects (cultural capital) and social circles (social capital). The cultural capital of the photographed subject is shared by the photographer, so that a successful photographer is one who takes photographs of people or objects associated with dominant field positions: nobility and celebrity. Richard Billingham's use of his own working-class background as his subject is a high-risk field positioning, perhaps rescued by the high volume of consecrated capital accrued from his patron, Saatchi.

Does photography continue to be a middle-brow art? As 'Documenta 11' and other exhibitions show, photography is a medium of choice of many living artists and can therefore be argued to have achieved 'fine art' status, but with a dominated field position within the field of power. The left-wing, Left-Bank stance to society and politics which Bourdieu has associated with the field positioning of an artistic avant-garde is confirmed in the many politically powerful, but oppositional images produced by artist photographers. In sharp contrast, technological advances, specifically digital photography, have accelerated the popularization of photography as an art. Today, anyone can be a photographer and, increasingly, it is assumed that everyone is! There is in this little evidence that 'middle-brow' is an adequate description of the dislocation of practice between everyday and fine art usage which occurs in this fragmented field.

Part III

Visual Arts in the Twenty-first Century

–7–

Back to the Future

Introduction

In this chapter we revisit the approach that Bourdieu is offering us to consider the visual arts. Modern aesthetics has been a preoccupation of writers, artists and philosophers for well over 200 years, since Kant gave it contemporary relevance by defining it as a unique part of human consciousness. Aesthetics, in a sense, is inextricably entwined with culture in all its manifestations in the modern world, and has been since the birth of post-Enlightenment societies. Yet, in many ways, it is still not entirely clear how it can best be seen. We begin by reconsidering the philosophy of aesthetics and the 'problem' it poses. We shall then examine a range of the responses which have been made to this 'problem' in order to highlight the space in which we feel Bourdieu is most useful. In the last three chapters we examined Bourdieu's own work on museums, photography and painting, applying similar approaches and perspectives of his work to other examples at specific times and places. Here, we set out explicitly what Bourdieu intends by a 'science of the history of art' and its component parts. We consider a range of issues connected with his theory and the implications they have for all those in transit through the 'art field'. Finally, we discuss the consequences such an approach has for visual arts in general.

Theory of Aesthetics or Economy of Aesthetic Practice?

In chapter 3 we began to address the question: what is aesthetics? For some, it is the formulation and application of certain value concepts used in the appreciation of art. For others, aesthetics is related to issues of form, representation and meaning. For others still, it is concerned with a theory of art perception per se. In each of these, there are formalist and idealist aspects to aesthetics, as well as the personal, individual and social. Aesthetic judgements are present in all matters of the visual arts and are applied to both the artistic product and its consumption and critique. In chapter 3 we referred to the way that the word 'aesthetics' was, in fact, of Greek derivation and was used to describe beauty and to communicate knowledge and truth. In a way, these issues still hold contemporary relevance. In effect, we might see the whole of Bourdieu's approach to art and aesthetics as an engagement with what we mean by truth and how we can articulate it ('In truth, what is at stake is truth itself', Bourdieu states at one point). However, we have also seen that in pursuit of such truth, Bourdieu's critique is in direct opposition to Kant and the Kantian traditions which have dominated, one way or another, contemporary treatments of beauty and truth – aesthetics.

Bourdieu always encourages us to consider the historical conditions of social phenomena. We can say, then, that it is not by chance that Kant wrote when he did and said what he did. As we saw earlier, the birth of modernity, through the Age of Enlightenment and industrialization, had uncoupled man from the tight matrix which fused individual life experiences within the communities in which they were set and which bound them to the laws of Church and the Crown. The social exodus that resulted in Europe, which moved many from rural to urban environments and ruptured the long-established ties within this matrix, served to release men and women from the feudal structures which had held them previously. A freedom of sorts was won. Obviously, it is easy to oversimplify this move. We must be aware that this was more or less the case, but with considerable regional and national variations. Although there were also countervailing trends, the general direction of change was one-way.

We already know enough about Bourdieu's theory of knowledge to understand that such social structural changes cannot occur without a corresponding change in thinking, without which the one would be unjustifiably privileged over the other. The basis of Bourdieu's 'ontological complicity' of modern man is that his very being is formed in the crucible which places field and habitus side by side: if the field changes, so does the habitus, and vice versa. If the world of religion and the king was being replaced, it follows that, structurally, something was needed to replace them. Not only must that 'something' fill their place, but the very function of the new form must also be changed. Just as urban man now lived in semi-autonomous spheres – home, work, leisure, the community, family – his thinking itself became divided up, compartmentalized, and linked only by formal connections.

There is a structural simile between the ideas of the philosopher Kant and those of the German sociologist Max Weber (see Joughin and Malpas 2003: 9f.). Weber argued that the modern experience had been separated into three distinct and autonomous spheres: scientific truth, normative rightness and beauty. These can be seen as corresponding to the philosophical disciplines of epistemology, ethics and beauty, themselves giving rise to self-sufficient forms of social practice: the sciences of technology, the law and morality, and modern art and culture. These disciplines, in turn, provide the basis of economic capitalism, bureaucracy and individual self-identification. As semi-autonomous spheres – cutting across Bourdieu's fields, if you like – they each operate according to their own internal laws – or their own distinct logics of practice. They also affect one another. For example, advances in knowledge and technology will require new forms of legislation (administration), which in turn lead to new forms of cultural practice. Quoting from Habermas, Joughin and Malpas argue that the very nature of rationality had changed in the nineteenth century: in place of the 'substantive rationality' of a religious world view, there had emerged a 'procedural rationality'. It is with this procedural rationality, and, in particular, by the means that it gives for internal differentiation, that we interpret the world. They further argue that a similar conflictual relationship between the spheres can be seen between the faculties of pure reason, practical reason and judgement in Kant's three critiques of the same name:

> In the first two critiques, of pure reason (epistemology) and practical reason (ethics), a chasm between truth and justice is opened. Between epistemology and ethics, Kant draws a division that cannot be crossed. By arguing that knowledge is bound by the 'limits of experience' which cannot be exceeded without falling prey to antinomy, he makes room for a separate ethical realm in which human freedom rests upon a 'categorical imperative' that is not reducible to knowledge because it is not generated by experience. (Joughin and Malpas 2003: 10)

It is in the third, *The Critique of Judgement* that Kant sets out to form a bridge between ethics and epistemology in order to make a coherent account of individuals in the world. However, it is accepted that this third critique, in effect, fails to reconcile epistemology, ethics and aesthetics and therefore creates a space for the separation of the sphere of values from knowledge, and from morality. Truth and goodness are separated from art. Art is therefore in a realm of its own – this is the space that is opened up and which postmodernist philosophers would eventually occupy.

Returning to the birth of the modernist world, we now see that Kant was the perfect philosopher to define a way of thinking which mirrored the socio-structural changes of his age. We might interpret the above in terms of the changing socio-political world which accompanied the development of capitalist economies at that particular time. With advances in technology and science came industrialization. With the advent of the technological age, greater law and bureaucracy were required. The fact that Kant expressed the philosophical issues at stake in terms of 'pure' and 'practical' reason can be seen as evidence that he recognized that 'thought' itself was changing. This was indeed 'the age of reason', of cognition prioritized over lived experience and the normative rightness which this implied. This age announced the birth of modern personal subjectivities, individual rights and freedoms. With hindsight, we see Kant as the grandfather of a contemporary metaphysics which has given us such philosophies as phenomenology and hermeneutics and other philosophies of experience. This opening up of the 'individual' sphere could also be seen in the socio-political sphere, with the Declaration of Human Rights and modernist universals such as equality, freedom and progress.

Within all three of these – the philosophical sphere, the political world and the everyday world of men and women – the nature of thought itself was changing. In a sense, as the lifeworld became more compartmentalized, experience increasingly was a series of fragmented events and experiences, with no single unifying logic.

The cost of the uncoupling of human cognition from transcendent values, which had emanated from the Church and the king, was a world of multiple realities and fragmented psyches, and a normlessness which was personified so graphically in the Marxist concept of alienation and in Durkheimian anomie. In a sense, the separation of knowledge and value was endemic to this process. As a consequence, science lost the 'moral' basis it had in pre-industrial alchemy, while art and aesthetics occupied a world of their own. One question here is whether this separation was unavoidable with the arrival and advance of modernism. Another question is what the consequences of this separation were for human thought and for practice. In particular, we now begin to see the results of this modern world for art and aesthetics. If the modern world brought us contemporary science and secular morality, it also brought us disenchantment, confusion and rootlessness. Curiously, if Kant failed philosophically to reconcile knowledge, morality and art, Bourdieu seeks to bring them together in a single theory of practice through a critical, reflexive account of all three. In doing so, he is defining the ground for rationality itself. It is in this sense that 'the truth is that truth itself is at stake'.

Art, Manet and the Modern World

Faced with the social, economic and philosophical changes considered in the last section, it is possibly all the more understandable that the art world itself had to change. We saw in chapter 5 how Bourdieu used Manet as an exemplar of an artist of his time and what this signified. It is worth pausing for a moment to reconsider Manet, his significance and why Bourdieu focused on him in particular.

In fact, Foucault had already considered the case of Manet as early as 1967 (see Foucault 2004). However, two subsequent events prompted a response from Bourdieu. First, the publication in 1983 of a pamphlet from a fellow professor from the Collège de France, Jacques Thuiller, in which he defended the heritage of the Ecole des Beaux-Arts against charges of elitism and political subordination – a view with which Bourdieu disagreed. Second, the opening in 1986 of the Musée d'Orsay in a former railway station, in which Manet was exhibited alongside the very artists he had opposed – 'academic' artists such as Bouguereau. Bourdieu wanted to draw attention to Manet's revolutionary achievement in establishing an art that was genuinely autonomous, and by which the 'academic' eye was forever destroyed, and with it, the values to which it subscribed. We saw how Manet defined an art-for-art's-sake approach, which was to shape all that came after it. In this sense, the artist had reclaimed ownership of his art, most noticeably of his craft – technique – which henceforth became the prerogative of the individual, not of the Church, king or aristocratic patron.

We might argue how this principled change in the degree of conquered artistic independence resonates with Kantian aesthetics and the notion of 'pure aesthetics'. It represents a new world: a transcendent realm of a priori categories which are not dependent on experience itself, but, by implication, are in the lap of the gods (or in this case, of individual muses!). The paradox, however, is that according to Bourdieu's socio-structural analysis, this realm itself has a logic of practice, the principles of which lay in the ascendancy of the middle classes and their search for social legitimation and consecration. In other words, such individualism also resonated with the belief in 'self-worth' which was so apparent in the emerging middle classes of the day.

Of course, it is necessary not to oversimplify the many and intricate changes and developments that had to take place, both within and between fields. For example, in reality, the 'academic eye' did not die overnight, as it were, and the significance of Manet and the Impressionists was not fully acknowledged by the French art establishment until well into the twentieth century. Nevertheless, from a twenty-first century viewpoint, we see that, over the past 150 years, artists have increasingly asserted their ownership of technique and, more generally, their autonomy. However, in this there are ironies, since artists, by definition, need both an audience and a market.

In chapter 4 we saw how museums themselves have come to represent art and artistic practice for certain dominant groups in society. This conclusion on the sociocultural place of museums formed part of Bourdieu's analysis of cultural capital, the way in which certain groups in society use culture as a medium for their legitimation and ultimate reproduction. Here, culture is not a democratizing force, and individual artistic expression is condemned to play a part in the field of artistic production in terms of buyers, sellers and critics. In chapter 6 we considered photography and the way it has offered an 'art for everyman'. In this sense, photography *is* a democratic art form in the way that everyone engages in it. In this context, art moves outside of the realm of the gifted – the artist – and becomes an activity in which all can be involved. The paradox is that, just as Bourdieu saw in his analyses of the field in terms of the forces of autonomy and heteronomy, individual artistic freedom can never really be independent of the context in which it is expressed. In chapter 6 we saw how American abstract expressionists, given a high degree of autonomy through government support from the Federal Arts Project and its like, followed the pattern of an assertion of content over form, in this case, artists insisting on the primacy of subject matter – albeit mythic or emotional – which transcended form, but which was expressed through their insistence on a monopoly of control over form. Similarly, the yBas of the 1990s often characterized themselves by their assertion of independence from, and of an oppositional stance to, technical skill as it had been recognized by earlier fine art practice – a form of what Bourdieu would call hypo-correction; in other words, the artist asserts control over technique by transgressing its conventional forms.

In our times, however, we seem to be confronted with a situation where artists themselves have seized control over both what they produce and how they offer it to the world – their products and the means of their communication and distribution. This is especially true in an age of digitization and the Internet. Indeed, the worldwide web is part of a general 'democracy of choice' in which people are themselves free to choose what they want, when they want it and what they want to do with it. Society at large appears to have recognized a new universal – individual choice. In these cases, we might conclude that a universal process of democratization has taken place for both producer and consumer. For Bourdieu, our present times could hardly be described as 'heroic' in the same way as Manet's. In fact, Bourdieu expressed increasing concerns about role of the media and their insatiable demand for novelty, the dramatic and the controversial.

We have seen that, for Bourdieu, art performs a function in society which is akin to that of religion in earlier times. This is why he calls art a 'collective act of magic'. Art offers a view of the 'absolute', the world beyond everyday experience. And yet it is rooted in the secular world. At the same time, the art field makes the artist. This latter view is quite contrary to a picture of the charismatic artist as visionary seer who is beyond the everyday world. In this, an art museum is a kind of church in the way that only those who 'believe' come to worship. However, Bourdieu is aware of the revolutionary potential of artists. In his conversation with Hans Haacke (1995a/1994: 20f.), he praises the latter for the way he has used his work as a 'symbolic weapon' against the ruling bureaucratic and political elite. He clearly sees that in a world which is increasingly symbolic, and through which debates and battles are carried out in symbolic forms, art itself can exert a powerful political force in the world; indeed, may even have more potential power than traditional forms of political action. We have seen this, for example, in the case of artist photographer Luis Camnitzer's work from 'Documenta 11'. Bourdieu states that 'Intellectuals – but also unions and political parties – are truly unarmed; they are three or four symbolic wars behind'. Artist action, on the other hand, can force journalists, 'to speak against the symbolic action exerted by corporations, particularly through patronage and sponsorship' (ibid.). Yet, in discussing art with a group of art students in Nîmes in 2001, he also talks about there being a 'crisis of belief' in contemporary art. What is the nature of this crisis?

Bourdieu describes an artistic world which is increasingly inward-looking in some respects (2001d: 34). Its autonomous principle, fought for and won during the nineteenth century, has created a situation where there is a symbiotic interdependence between artists, critics, collectors, and so on. As a result, modern art has cut itself off from the world at large and from the average citizen. In other words, in order to maintain symbolic capital and preserve its capital value, artists have increasingly intensified their own technical control. Bourdieu makes the point that no one 'likes' modern art, produced as it often is for a select cognoscenti. Certainly, faced with modern art, it is necessary to have in one's head the entire history of artistic categories in order to appreciate it – to decode its meanings. The average person does not have this artistic habitus, this *libido artistica*, producing the necessary intellectual and aesthetic impulse to be able to understand the art which confronts them. In this respect, modern art is exclusive, it heightens the inequality of the cultural capital available to different individuals in society, as it would in this time of greater competition for distinction. Bourdieu notes that what we have here is a 'theodicy of privilege'. In fact, it takes the right education and training to understand modern art these days: 'the Museum of Modern Art in Paris has a more "cultured" audience than the Louvre' (ibid.). The established masters and the consecrated forms of art no longer offer the same possibilities for distinction; they have become popularized. In this respect, the irony of modern art is that despite its often unorthodox and controversial forms, it still performs the important function of social differentiation. And it is in this way that the nature of artists as both dominant and dominated is most clearly expressed as 'dominated members of the dominant class'.

Art, Commerce and Politics

If Manet, along with other artists and writers, struggled for autonomy from state patronage, the logic of that independence calls into question extreme and intensive expressions of art for art's sake, so much so that the social function of art as a challenge to orthodoxy is threatened by the way it might now be seen as existing in a world of its own. We no longer live in heroic times; indeed, we have questioned the idealism of the avant-garde and asked whether much of what goes on in the name of art is more self-serving than challenging, simply a consequence of the struggle for the most desirable field positions. It is clear from what Bourdieu writes that he sees much modern art as a sort of game in which opportunism and gesture are the order of the day: those who appeal to a popular aestheticism by asserting conservative values in art – William Bouguereau; those who are able to be subversive while being supported by state aid – Andreas Serrano; those who calculate what it looks like to be avant-garde while remaining politically conservative – Roger Fenton or Damien Hirst. For Bourdieu, there is a kind of 'conformism of transgression' (2001d: 40), where artists are subversive by fashion: 'some politically progressive works (according to their content and intention) can be aesthetically conservative while some politically neutral art (formalist) can be aesthetically progressive'. Of course, this blurring of categorization is the stuff of modern art. With the yBas, we saw the principles which characterized their work: appropriation, site specificity, impermanence, accumulation and hybridization. In these cases, the implicit question often asked is, what is art? Such a position was a logical extension of modernism and began in the 1950s and 1960s, with such movements as pop art, performance art and conceptual art. What are we to make of a glass of water next to the title 'Oak Tree' (Michael Craig-Martin, 1973)?

Autonomy is a key issue for artists. However, Bourdieu sees a situation where the line between autonomy (jealously guarded) and the ivory tower (cut off from social involvement) is a chronic choice for artists. He also sees the relationship between artists and their market as particularly delicately poised in our modern times. If artists are prone to existing in an ivory tower, Bourdieu, as we suggested above, is also fearful of the present invasion of commercialism, which threatens artists' autonomy:

> *The threats to autonomy* result from the increasingly greater interpenetration between the world of art and the world of money. I am thinking of new forms of sponsorship, of new alliances being established between certain economic enterprises (often the most modernizing, as in Germany, with Daimler-Benz and the banks) and cultural producers... But the grip or empire of the economy over artistic or scientific research is also exercised inside the *field* itself, through the control of the means of cultural production and distribution, and even of instances of *consecration*. Producers attached to major cultural bureaucracies (newspapers, radio, television) are increasingly forced to accept and adopt norms and constraints linked to the requirements of the market. (Bourdieu 1996a/1992: 344f.)

Bourdieu reasons that, since the nineteenth century, there have existed two markets: on the one hand, the small market of 'producers for producers', which guaranteed the exclusivity of art; and on the other, the mass production market of commerce. However, in our postmodern age, with direct access to information and art from modern communication systems, this division had been blown apart. Access for all, at base a seemingly legitimizing principle, can be a disguise for rampant commercialism, as merely another way to expand markets, as has been demonstrated in art museums' increasing role in tourism. In this sense, the logic of commercial production tends more and more to assert itself over avant-garde production:

> It would be necessary to analyse the new forms of stranglehold and dependence, like the ones introduced by sponsorship, and against which the 'beneficiaries' have not yet developed appropriate systems of defence since they are not fully aware of all the constraints imposed by state sponsorship – even though it seems to escape the direct pressures of the market – whether through the recognition it grants spontaneously to those who recognize it because they need it in order to obtain a form of recognition which they cannot get by their work alone, or whether, more subtly, through the mechanism of commissions and committees – places of negative co-optation which often result in a thorough standardization of the avant-garde, either scientific or artistic. (ibid.)

Of course, art – museums, photography, and painting – is part of the field of cultural production, which is a large field, including the media (television, radio, newspapers), the entertainment industry (music, theatre, books) and culture generally (fashion, lifestyle). Bourdieu launched a major critique of the way the field has been invaded by international commercialism, in particular, through the doctrine of liberal economics exported from America to an apparently receptive audience in Europe. In publications in the last decade of his life (*Contre-feux* and *Contre-feux 2*), Bourdieu mounted so-called 'acts of resistance' against globalization and its pernicious effects (1998a). He also targeted the media (*Sur la Télévision* 1998b/1996) for its complicity in providing the cultural conditions for neoliberal invasion. It is not possible to detail his main concerns here. Briefly, these include: the social construction of taste implicit in media commercialism;

the way public opinion is created and manipulated; the audiences sought; the editorial policy of newspapers; the increasing monopolization of the media as more of it is owned by larger and larger conglomerates; the political influence of commerce in the public media through mechanisms of inclusion and exclusion (recognition and misrecognition) and direct patronage.

Bourdieu exemplifies the power of the invasiveness of neoliberal commercialism through the case of housing. For example, he shows how (2000b) the French policy of providing public housing had been transformed into a civic responsibility, where, increasingly, people were obliged to purchase a house or apartment for accommodation. In order to meet the increased demand for housing, commercial companies have constructed 'production-line-houses', sold as possessing the style and character of traditional homes. The reality is often crippling loans, lack of local services and long commuting journeys, as the new houses are built on land away from places of work. Moreover, the 'new' house is sold along with an entire lifestyle package, including all the appliances and accoutrements of modern living. These possessions are themselves sold through the media, completing the loop of fabricated consumer demand and supply which is so much more effective when, as in the case of TF1 (France's number one TV channel) and Maison Bouygues, the media and housing companies are owned by the same family individual!

This is the world of which art now forms a part.

Postmodern Art

In this book we have sought to ground 'art rules' in changes in the society and culture of the eighteenth and nineteenth centuries – the birth of modernism. We have argued that transformations in society and the economy had an impact on the way men and women lived. However, more than simply changes in lifestyle, what was transformed was thought and experience itself. Social reality became fragmented as individuals divided their lives between different spheres of activity. Human cognition also changed with the separation of Church and Crown and a new-found sense of individual freedom and destiny. We have seen that, essentially, Kant was *the* philosopher to announce the Modern Age. With Kant, we saw how his philosophical taxonomy separated out lived experience from aesthetics so that the latter now existed as an 'a priori pre-given'. After Kant, aesthetics is no longer concerned simply with the question of the 'objectivity of taste' – for example, what constitutes it and is it legitimate? – but with 'a critique of critique' (cf. Joughin and Malpas 2003). Aesthetics thereafter offered an a priori realm of values which allowed for (and continues to allow) the possibility of such a critique. What Bourdieu has done is to challenge the a priori nature of 'taste' in sociological terms. Earlier, we explored the way Kant had 'failed' to integrate his critiques of pure and practical reason with judgement, and, in so doing, created an 'autonomous' realm in which aesthetics could exist, almost apart from life experience. What Bourdieu did, in effect, was to reconnect the realms of epistemology and morality, practical life experience itself and values through his own theory of practice, based on social philosophy. While he was not the first to see beyond the modernist project, his approach has proved to be both robust and enduring.

We have argued that art and aesthetics in the nineteenth century developed in a way which can be seen as resonating with the principles of the modernist age apparent in both the economy and the socio-political system, and in systems of thought such as that of Kant. The principles of modernism include rationality, truth, humanism, freedom, progress, individual rights (equality, liberty, fraternity) and emancipation. It is possible to see these principles reflected in some way in all aspects of modern culture. In terms of art per se, what is asserted first is the independence of the artists themselves and their freedom of artistic expression. However, this artistic and aesthetic freedom also implies an artistic value system against which such activity can be judged by artist, audience or market. If the value of art is to be judged according to values of creative originality, talent and technique, what is presupposed is an ultimate (a priori) aesthetic of a Kantian sort. Such artistic styles and trends as social realism, expressionism, cubism and Impressionism are a logical extension of artistic freedom expressing modernist values, more or less – whether it is asserting the 'truth' of the line Klee drew, individual artistic vision as in Picasso, or social commentary as in Richard Billingham.

In modern art, it sometimes seems as if it is the mission of the artist, indeed their *raison d'être*, is to act as a medium of the muse in a secular world, whatever that expression may lead to. We have seen that Bourdieu questioned the 'truth' of this view of the artist, and drew attention to other social factors which determine what is potential, possible and feasible in art, according to the field conditions it resides in at any one time – culture, education or commerce. But Bourdieu was not the first to see that modernist art was far from representing some humanist aesthetic purity, but was actually imbued with issues of class, gender, race and politics. In short, such analyses reject the idea that there ever was an ultimate universal value system – aesthetics – against which art can be judged, and that art might better be understood in terms of a particular and particularized moral idealism (even ideology – although Bourdieu rarely used this concept, possibly because of its Marxist connotations). We can see these approaches in a wide range of philosophies throughout the twentieth century, for example, the critical theorists of the German Frankfurt School and feminist aesthetics (see Neill and Ridley 2001: 272–318). If this (essentially modernist) argument led to the uncoupling of art from its transcendent humanist aesthetic values, and its linking with a range of political imperatives, this (essentially twentieth-century) development moved beyond its original modernist realization, and in this sense became known, as a consequence, as 'postmodernist'. However, the second crucial ingredient to this uncoupling arose from philosophy itself.

The founding grandfather of postmodernism can rightly be considered to be Ferdinand de Saussure, the French linguist. In a series of lecture notes, Saussure sought to establish the fundamentals of a philosophy of language. Central to his thinking was the notion that words needed to be understood in terms of 'signifier' and 'signified': the word (signifier) represented a thing or concept (signified). However, he also realized that, in fact, the signifier was an arbitrary; in other words, any commonly agreed word could do the job. This realization can be understood as being akin to a computer virus: it got into human philosophy and set about reshaping it, if not destroying it; so much so that, eventually, the 'philosophy of man' in the twentieth century became a 'philosophy of language'.

If words are arbitrary, then such concepts as truth, beauty and freedom must also be arbitrary in that we cannot know that we all mean the same thing by them – there is no ultimate representation. The fact that such modernist principles could be seen to be saturated with political issues, and, finally, were also highly relative and subjective, led to the collapse of a viable subscription to them as a modernist project. From this point, caught in a kind of spiral vortex of philosophical logic, everything is relative, everything is subjective. It ultimately follows, therefore, that nothing really exists. These are harsh words, but it is difficult to overestimate the nihilistic nature of postmodernism. For art, postmodernism provoked and supported a crisis in representation. Neither reality nor human values could be directly represented – hence, everything was seen as an act of abstraction or as abstract in itself. However, the postmodernist deconstruction of representation does not end there. Indeed, finally, painting itself collapses, as does criticism of it. In this world, all is narrative, and thus fiction – there is no truth or higher aesthetic. In the end, even art itself is questioned: can art exist?

We have seen in some of the artists presented in this book that this question is very much to the fore in their work. Indeed, their engagement with the art field *is* the art. There is irony in content, technique and presentation. Ruse is used as a way of challenging the spectator – simultaneously pointing *away* from and *towards* what is represented.

Of course, there is a paradox at the core of postmodernism, in that even the word itself includes 'modernism'. In other words, the irony is that it is not so much, in substance at least, an 'anti-modernism', but rather a logical extension of modernism: a kind of 'hyper-modernism'; even though its form seems to destroy many of the tenets of modernism per se. This paradox is at the heart of Bourdieu's work, since it poses a dilemma for him. He is against any philosophy which does not recognize the relativity of its own socio-historical contexts; for example, he criticizes aesthetics for offering a scheme of classificatory thought that turns a particular way of seeing the world into an 'essential universal'. He declares that 'beauty is nothing but a fiction' (1996a/1992: 274): belief in 'the beautiful as eternal essence' is nothing but 'pure fetishism' by which the creator (and presumably consumer) 'bows down before the projection of an illusory transcendence'. He quotes Mallarmé (who had defended Manet) approvingly in a passage which might be seen as a precursor to postmodernism:

> We know, captives of an absolute formula that, indeed, there is only that which is. Forthwith to dismiss the cheat, however, on a pretext, would indict our inconsequence, denying the very pleasure we want to take: for that *beyond* is its agent, and even its engine... I venerate how, by a trick, we project to some forbidden – and thunderous! – height the conscious lack in us of what is bursting up there. Why should we do this? It is a game. (ibid.)

Bourdieu himself questions what makes a piece of art, and concludes that it is only in its acceptance within the 'institution' of art that it can be consecrated as such. It is therefore an illusion – *illusio* – to attribute any value to it other than as a social construction. For Bourdieu, the 'pure aesthetic' itself was nothing other than the invention of a new social personality. Quoting Flaubert: 'The only way to live in peace is to place yourself in one leap above all humanity, and to have nothing to do with it but an ocular relation' (ibid.: 110). Here, Bourdieu writes that, when taken to its logical end, aestheticism leads to a 'moral neutralism' and an 'ethical nihilism'. Ironically, this was as true for the eighteenth-century bourgeoisie as it is for the twenty-first-century postmodernist transgressor of orthodoxy. This point lies at the heart of Bourdieu's position on these issues. While aesthetics and the modernist project must be understood in their social context, as a social construction, an extreme version of such a deconstruction leads to a destruction of ethical and moral values, and norms. To put it succinctly: we throw out the baby with the bath water. In one sense, this loss was always implied in the Kantian failure to reintegrate aesthetics with life experience, knowledge and ethics. Bourdieu pulls back from the postmodernist abyss, but still wants to ground his scientific vision in Enlightenment principles of truth and universality – albeit in a highly 'sociologicalized' way. Indeed, postmodernism is dangerous for Bourdieu, precisely because it leads to the destruction of human values and principles hard won in the process of modernization. For Bourdieu, therefore, it is not just that the modernist project was misguided, it was simply a bourgeois means to an end. Although this must be considered 'true', it is nevertheless equally true that, in the course of its inception and development, certain liberties were achieved only with difficulty. The risk of postmodernism is that these liberties (for example, artistic autonomy) may be destroyed. If such modernist concepts of truth, freedom and individual expression are exposed as being merely relative – riddled with ideology – then a vacuum is created where values should be. Here, the risk – and Bourdieu obviously believed that this is exactly what did happen – is that old reactionary values move in to take their place. Postmodernism, therefore, is seen as having brought about a 'conservative revolution': 'the restoration of the past presents itself as a progressive revolution or reform, a regression, or a step back which gives the appearance of progress, a leap ahead and makes itself seen as such' (2001d: 32). With this in mind, we might think again of modern art and its cult of transgression as rendering art impossible, thus robbing it of its social function to challenge. Bourdieu's support of Hans Haacke is important here, as he was one artist who continued to use art as a way of challenging the socio-political status quo. It is perhaps unsurprising if marginalization or commercialization take over elsewhere; in either case, art's critical potential is neutralized. Of course, we must take care not to overestimate the power of art on its own to challenge orthodoxy. However, if we can say, and we think we can, that postmodernism touches every aspect of culture, society and the economy, we might see that what is in danger of occurring is a loss of faith with the modernist project and a return to the reactionary values and systems of the past.

Postmodernism ruled the day for much of the second half of the twentieth century, when the postmodernist mood could be sensed in all aspects of living. In philosophy, writers such as Foucault, Lyotard, Barthes and Lacan were all working on some aspect of it, to a greater or lesser extent. However, it was with fellow Frenchman and former ENS pupil, Jacques Derrida, that Bourdieu took most exception. In *La Distinction*, Bourdieu details his objection to Derrida's position. Derrida (1987/1978) had written his own commentary on Kant's *The Critique of Judgement*. Derrida can be seen very much as *the* postmodernist philosopher. His work focuses not simply on philosophical issues, but on the language of the discourse itself. The signifier and signified, which we referred to earlier, are forever separated in Derrida's own view of philosophy; his intention is to bring them together. However, in order to do this, Derrida has to play close attention to the form of his writing, which no longer conforms to conventional narrative structures. So, play, irony and ruse are all employed as means of generating effects which open up the philosophical terrain. For Bourdieu, Derrida's attempt to break free from philosophical discourse – in this case, with his critique of Kant – only ends by accomplishing the very opposite of what it sets out to do; its means actually assert the end itself in Kantian terms rather than breaking from it.

Bourdieu (1984/1979: 494) begins his critique of Derrida by acknowledging that his reading of *The Critique of Judgement* does indeed show up the opposition between 'pleasure' and 'enjoyment': 'agreeable arts which seduce by the "charm" of their sensuous content and the Fine Arts which offer pleasure but not enjoyment'. Enjoyment, simple 'sensations of the senses', are therefore contrasted with 'pure taste'. Disgust with sensual pleasure is seen as rooted in 'pure' taste in that the latter separates one from attachment and provides the disinterestedness of existence or non-existence of an object. Desire 'ensnares' and, therefore, has to be kept at a distance. Similarly, there is a distinction between 'free art', involving 'free will' and 'mercenary' or 'commercial' art. Bourdieu argues that, although these issues are present in Derrida's text, they are not explicit and connections are left unmade. Bourdieu's point is that the approach and style that Derrida adopts mean that he is in fact reperforming the separation he is criticizing Kant for making. In other words, Derrida is constructing a philosophical text whose only *raison d'être* is as a piece of philosophy, and he does so by leaving out the socio-historical conditions both of its production and of the text it is addressing:

> To summarize a discourse which, as is shown by the attention Derrida devotes to the writing and typography, is the product of the intention of putting content into form, and which rejects in advance any summary aiming to separate content from form, to reduce the text to its simplest expression, is in fact to deny the most fundamental intention of the work and, by a sort of transcendental reduction which no critique has any thought of carrying out, to perform the *époche* of everything by which the philosophical text affirms its existence as a philosophical text, i.e. its 'disinterestedness', its freedom, and hence its elevation, its distinction, its distance from all 'vulgar' discourse. (ibid.: 495)

In other words, what Derrida is doing is re-enacting Kant's own *prise de distance*: the masses from the bourgeoisie, the popular from the elite, the vulgar from the refined – ultimately, the sociological from the philosophical. For Bourdieu, this amounts to an intellectual game:

> It is an exemplary form of denigration – you tell (yourself) the truth but in such a way that you don't tell it – which defines the objective truth of the philosophical text in its social use...
>
> Because he never withdraws from the philosophical game, whose conventions he respects, even in the ritual transgressions at which only traditionalists could be shocked, he can only tell the truth about the philosophical text and its reading, which (apart from the silence of orthodoxy) is the best way of not telling it, and he cannot truly tell the truth about Kantian philosophy of art and, more generally, about philosophy itself, which his own discourse has helped to produce. Just as the pictorial rhetoric which continues to foist itself on every artist produces an inevitable aestheticization, so the philosophical way of talking about philosophy de-realizes everything that can be said about philosophy. (ibid.)

Bourdieu argues that this game allows the perpetrator to exist both within and outside the field: an intellectual space where 'one can combine the profits of transgression with the profits of membership'. The postmodern condition affects both philosopher and artist: 'Like the religious nihilism of some mystic heresies, philosophical nihilism too can find an ultimate path of salvation in the rituals of liberatory transgression' (p. 496). It is the same logic of practice applied in different fields. Needless to say, Bourdieu has in mind 'the countless acts of derision and desacralization which modern art has perpetuated', which, although some of them can hardly be considered to be artistic acts as such, 'always lead to the glory of art and the artist'. Similarly, he argues that postmodernist philosophy is itself a response to and avoidance of the destruction of philosophy, 'when the very hope of radical reconstruction has evaporated'. In this, of course, Bourdieu means a philosophy which has been reconstructed according to his own epistemological principles.

The Science of the History of Art

This is perhaps a long way to get to the point of saying that for Bourdieu what is at stake is really consciousness and knowledge, and, by implication, 'truth' (as we have previously said) represented in them. He is against philosophical aesthetics since they universalize the cognitive consequence of one particular point in time, namely, the mid-nineteenth century. There is an ambiguity in that he agrees and sees that art can indeed have a revolutionary function in challenging the status quo – the *nomos* – of everyday life, which ultimately reflects the power of the state, in this case, represented in the media and culture. There is in this the possibility of winning independence: 'free will' can be won! Yet he clearly sees that the modernist project of the nineteenth century has gone (or been led) astray, through an inward gaze, individual excesses and commercialization. Perhaps his most caustic argument is that even the most explicit acts of artistic transgression can be seen as a strategy of self-ascendancy in the art world, and thus of capital gain (see the cases of Mapplethorpe or Serrano, for example, in chapter 6). Bourdieu made the point that, 'to be a revolutionary, you need *capital*' – social, cultural and economic. The implication is that in procuring sufficient capital, art is compromised and eventually lost all together, given over to the mercy of gallery owners, museum curators, the media and press, and critics.

Furthermore, for Bourdieu, postmodernism, that logical practical extension of modernism, suffers from the same self-serving logic. He interprets its very form of expression as simply another way of asserting philosophical text over sociological thinking – a kind of transcendence and thus a claim to privilege. Bourdieu makes the point that it only does this because it needs to preserve a philosophical discourse and, by implication, exclude a sociological one. However, he is particularly critical of postmodernist philosophy, since, by doing this, in effect, it destroys many of the values and principles gained in post-Enlightenment society. The cost of philosophy protecting itself is therefore, in these terms, the destruction of values fought for and hard won, and the re-emergence of reactionary forces. The fact that Bourdieu sees this everywhere expressed in culture, society and the economy only means that what is happening in art is simply a reflection and symptom of what is occurring elsewhere.

Bourdieu is also against what he calls the *skholè* of art and philosophy. By *skholè*, he means the studious leisure time available to those who can make art, or consume art, or think and write about art, for that matter. *Skholè* implies a time surplus once the imperatives of life have been taken care of, so that a reader, for example, who assumes *skholè*, has socially instituted, studious leisure time where one may play seriously. Reflecting on the 'pure gaze' of nineteenth-century aesthetics in terms of literature, Bourdieu writes on 'pure reading' as a sort of dehistoricized activity where the reader assumes that books are decoded through the logic of the field. This logic only increases with the autonomy of the field (1996a/1992: 305). As a result, the 'pure reader' excludes any reductive reference to the social history of production and of producers. Bourdieu argues that the ultimate logic of the intention of 'pure literature' is to exclude everything except that inscribed in the very form of the work itself. However, this logic itself is 'misrecognized': 'It follows that the scholastic view...is never so invisible as when scholars of all countries, shut within the perfect circle unknowingly outlined by their aesthetic theories, plunge...the pure gaze of dehistoricizing reading into the mirror of a pure and perfectly dehistoricized work' (ibid.).

Truth is a modernist concept. We have referred to Bourdieu's assertion that 'the truth of the matter is that truth itself is at stake'. But what is the order of this truth? Bourdieu seems suspicious of artistic vision; he argues against philosophical aesthetics; yet he also criticizes postmodernist deconstructions of aesthetics – to this extent, he is anti-intellectual as well. It follows that simple narratives which overestimate the significance of artistic techniques and movements are not enough for him. Neither are the quasi-Marxist accounts – for example, Hauser and T J Clark – that attempt to relate particular art works to socio-economic conditions and changes. Postmodernism is simply not sufficiently inclusive in its scope because it excludes the socio-historical in its philosophical treatment of art.

Feminist critiques fall within Bourdieu's general criticism of gender politics. In *Masculine Domination* (2001a/1998), Bourdieu meets the latter issue head-on. He accepts that the feminist critique of androcentric dominance in the world is correct, but he goes on to argue that it is still mainly derived from, and thus the product of, the very field structures produced by masculine domination. Feminist aesthetics such as Pollock's (see also the discussion of Ziarek in Joughin and Malpas 2003: 51–67) therefore simply do not go far enough. Seeking to uncover the field positions and the struggles for positions of the minority of women who are active participants in the artistic field may give a more balanced view of the functioning of the artistic field, but, of itself, it cannot dismantle the already existing field structures which have been produced by a largely masculine dominant field of power. As our analyses of the yBas have shown, with time, more women are able to occupy more favourable field positions, but, as in the field transformations considered earlier, both the broader social space itself and its ideational structure (our ways of thinking) must change before gender-neutral field structures will be the result of interactions *in* the artistic field. Nonetheless, since all artists, through their need for audiences and markets, can occupy only dominated positions within the field of power, women, like men, will continue to be subject to the socio-economic field conditions of their times. Change in the broader social space may bring release for all genders.

In the preceding section there are many refusals and criticisms on Bourdieu's part, and the reader may be excused for thinking that we are caught in a trap of sociological deconstruction. What is Bourdieu offering as an alternative? The answer to this question is, basically, his theory of practice as we have set it out and applied it earlier in this book. Put briefly, this amounts to a procedural rationality. First, for Bourdieu, the science of the history of art is:

> an act of decoding – [with] the goal of reconstructing the artistic code, understood as a historically constituted system of classification (or of principles of division) which is crystallized in an ensemble of words permitting us to name and perceive differences; that is to say more precisely, the goal of writing these codes, instruments of perception which vary in time and space, notably as a transformation in the material and symbolic instruments of production. (1996a/1992: 313)

We have seen that, for Bourdieu, the way to do this was to analyse the artistic field in terms of the homology between the social space of the position takings and the space of the positions occupied in the field. And by 'position', we mean both physical and ideational. Such an analysis proceeds mainly in terms of habitus and field, and the configurations of capital which act as a medium through which they interrelate. Central to this analysis, first, is the precise nature and expression of the logic of practice which acts as a currency base for differentiation (valuing) within the field – one must reconstruct the code, then, 'to understand historically the historical situation in which what it labours to understand was formed' (ibid.: 310). Second, we must not only analyse and understand the field in our own terms, but part of that understanding must involve grasping the artistic field and object as they were understood at the time *in their own terms*. Again, such an analysis will proceed through Bourdieu's thinking tools: habitus, field, and so on. What matters here are the structures of the field as they are used as guiding principles by those who actively participate in them at any one particular time.

However, should such an analysis lead to a 'sociological reification', Bourdieu applies a third stage in which the researcher's own position is brought into the picture. We noted above that Bourdieu was suspicious of 'scholastic reason'; this was one of his major objections to postmodernism, that it was the product of a certain 'detached' disposition. And yet the nature of knowledge and understanding is also at stake for Bourdieu. We need to 'understand understanding' itself in all its cognitive, philosophical and sociological aspects. Only then can we escape from a historically created understanding. 'To escape from history', Bourdieu writes, 'understanding itself must know itself as historical and to give itself the means to understand itself historically' (ibid.: 310). Such a historically constructed understanding is based on four presuppositions:

> There are those associated with occupation of a *position* in social space, and the particular trajectory that has led to it, and with gender (which can affect the relationship to the object in many ways, in as much as the sexual division of labour is inscribed in social structures and in cognitive structures, orientating for example the choice of object of study). Then there are those that are constitutive of the doxa specific to each of the different fields (religious, artistic, philosophical, sociological, etc.) and, more precisely, those that each particular thinker owes to his position in a field. Finally, there are the presuppositions constituting the doxa generically associated with the *skholè*. (2000a/1997: 10)

In order to escape from being misled into simply insisting on the historical genesis of the art field and its objects, while maintaining the detachment that scholastic reason gives when researchers forget their own historical genesis (in epistemological terms), it is necessary to apply the same theory of practice to the researcher and the researched. Bourdieu terms this 'objectivation of the subject of objectification'.

So, to sum up, in order to understand a work of art, first, we need to do a field analysis in terms of habitus, field, and so on; second, as a part of this, we must analyse the initial perception of the art as a practice at the time; third, we must apply the same principles of analysis to ourselves as researchers in 'objectifying the knowing subject'; and, fourth, in order to fully comprehend art, we must do all these things simultaneously! Anything else is partial and does not capture the potential dynamic of understanding involved.

In this way, if art is the subject of a double 'dehistoricization' – *at* the time and *of* the time – we must approach any analysis of it through a double 'historicization' – *of* the time and of *our* time (and space). These are the principles which underlie the discussion and analyses offered in this book.

Implications

We have seen that the modern version of aesthetics, with its notion of the 'pure gaze', has been subject to critique, almost by the very philosophy that gave rise to it. Postmodernism eventually challenged aesthetic essentialism, as well as the dichotomies and hierarchies on which such philosophy was based. Theory itself is a form of textual expression and therefore subject to a philosophy of language which sees all human articulations as a form of discourse. In a way, both art and the language to speak about art are 'texts' and must be viewed in terms of their material conditions. Bourdieu's argument against postmodernist philosophers, however, is that they do not explicitly address the socio-historical conditions, either of art production, the way art was perceived at the time, or our own way of viewing it today. What is at stake is ultimately 'freedom of thought'; what is being contested are the 'schemes of perception' used to understand the world. The fact that painters such as Manet and the Impressionists were able to establish an autonomous space counted as a freedom gained. However, subsequently, Bourdieu suggests, artistic thinking and practice have been 'recaptured' by modern commercial markets; so much so that our very schemes of thinking about art have been privatized and now largely express commercial values.

One can be caught in the 'aesthetic illusion' from many different sides. Clearly, straight narrative accounts of art in terms of biography and technical progress do not go far enough for Bourdieu because, in effect, they play the game of the field. 'One cannot found a genuine science of the work of art', Bourdieu writes, 'without tearing oneself out of the illusion and suspending the relationship of complicity and connivance which ties every cultivated person to the cultivated game'

(1996a/1992: 230). For Bourdieu, neo-Marxist accounts of art in terms of social class simply do not go far enough in uncovering the systems by which art rules; neither do postmodernist or feminist accounts, since they are often trapped within their own ahistorical discourses and/or employ language derived from the illusion itself. Bourdieu argues that the virtue of his approach is that it escapes these errors. As we have seen above, the approach involves analyses in terms of habitus, field, capital, and so on, together with a process of participant objectivation 'that consists in objectifying the subject of objectification. I mean by that, the one that dispossesses the knowing subject of the privilege it normally grants itself…to bring to light the presuppositions it owes to its inclusion in the order of knowledge' (2000a/1998: 10). The way to do this is again to turn the tools of analysis on oneself *as part of* the analysis itself. This necessity goes to the heart of Bourdieu's approach. We noted earlier the way he constantly used his own social milieu to provide insider accounts of the systems which surrounded him. As such, he used insider and privileged information. Yet his 'method', his 'theory of practice', is also used on the observer himself, in such a way that the angle of refraction is exposed as part of establishing a deeper truth. In books such as *The Rules of Art* and *Pascalian Meditations*, Bourdieu was arguing for this aspect of socio-philosophical study as a way of escaping the 'presuppositions' of the intellectualist stance. Indeed, the centrality of this theme became even clearer in his reflections of his professional activity and its relationship to his biography in *Esquisse pour une auto-analyse* (2004a).

His treatment of art and aesthetics might seem quite an intellectual approach to something which is essentially 'beyond' intellect. We have seen that if Bourdieu was against aesthetics, he was equally opposed to intellectualism and intellectuals, in particular. This position raises questions about the role of the intellectual in the field of artistic production. In Manet's time, certain intellectuals had participated in the revolution in the way of thinking about art which, indeed, could not have occurred without them. Mallarmé, we have noted, was a strong defender of Manet. This case is itself part of a process which was leading to the invention of a new social role for intellectuals to match the new ways of thinking. As we noted in chapter 2, up until the eighteenth century, writers were credited in society with a subordinated diversionary function, separated from the worlds of politics and theology. For Bourdieu, it was only in the nineteenth century that the modern 'intellectual' was born; that is, one who intervenes in the socio-political realm in the name of autonomy and the specific values of the field (1996a/1992: 129). This process culminated in the case of Zola, when he published *J'accuse* in 1898, and the subsequent Dreyfus affair. Here, again, this social function to speak out in the name of freedom had gone astray. On the one hand, the twentieth century gave rise to the 'total intellectual', who spoke in universal terms; Sartre was a good example of someone who was an 'intellectual of universality'. On the other hand were the *doxosophes* (see Bourdieu 1972), engaged in the production of the dominant discourse, namely, those trained by the state to serve the state, both for the production and the legitimation of its political policies. And there is a third type of intellectual still, whom Bourdieu called the 'journalist philosophers', who were characterized by their media presence and influence – those who presented themselves as specialists while offering only what the media could cope with. The French media intellectual star, Bernard Henri-Lévy – whom Bourdieu referred to as his 'favourite whipping boy' (see Bourdieu 1998b/1996; Halami 1997) – is a good example of the latter type.

Bourdieu opposes each of these types of intellectual, while at the same time wishing to take salient elements from each of them. For him, intellectuals were not the spokesmen of the universal for the people. Nevertheless, they did have an 'interest in the universal' (1985: 94). What Bourdieu had in mind as an alternative is a sort of 'collective individual', 'who might be capable of making a discourse of freedom heard, a discourse that recognizes no other limit than the constraints and controls which each artist, each writer and each scholar, armed with all the acquisitions of his or her predecessors, enjoin themselves and all others' (1996a/1992: 340). What Bourdieu is pointing towards is a 'collective intellectual action'. His own call for an 'International of Intellectuals' (1992b) was partly met with the formation of an International Parliament of Writers in 1993, a group of which he was a member and which met to define new forms of militant protests. As Bourdieu claims, this type of action:

> Should lead them to assert themselves as an international power of criticism and watchfulness, or even of proposal, in the face of the technocrats, or…to get involved in rational action to defend the economic and social conditions of autonomy of these privileged universes in which the material and intellectual instruments of what we call Reason are produced and reproduced. This *Realpolitik of reason* will undoubtedly be suspected of corporatism. But, it will be part of its task to prove, by the ends to which it puts the sorely won means of its autonomy, that it is a corporatism of the universal. (1996a/1992: 348)

However, obviously the first job of such a corporatism is to 'master the various kinds of historical consciousness separating us', which, for Bourdieu, can be done by employing his own theory of practice in order to objectify 'the specific histories of intellectual universes which have produced our categories of perception and thought' (p. 344). In other words, for Bourdieu, we escape both from the illusions of art and the illusions of intellectualism by replacing the language of *illusio* with language derived from his theory of practice, because that language itself has built within it an emancipatory function.

Above, we asked whether Bourdieu's project was not really quite an intellectualist one, even though he was essentially against intellectualism. Certainly, he argued the practical usefulness of his theory of practice in complex and sophisticated philosophical terms. However, clearly he did not believe that this project was exclusive – quite the contrary. In the last ten years of his life, Bourdieu became much more the public intellectual, intervening in a number of fields on political matters. These 'acts of resistance' (1998a) were attempts to bring the logic of his analysis to a wider field and to influence practical outcomes. Moreover, his magnum opus account of social suffering in France – *La Misère du monde* (1999/1993) – can be read as an effort, in a way similar to Manet's visual project, to bring the representation of the poverty of experience to a wider public, purged of sociological jargon. Bourdieu later claimed (2000c) that this approach, and, indeed, his brand of sociology, could act in a therapeutic way, as if the act of individuals objectifying themselves and the social forces which created their social malaise held the potential for liberation (or at least distance) from them.

It is perhaps unsurprising, therefore, if we find Bourdieu recommending his own conceptual thinking tools to art students in Nîmes (2001d). Here, he recognizes that the 'crisis in belief' as he sees it in the world of modern art can lead to disillusionment, and that his sociological vision risks disenchantment. 'It is not sociology which is sad', he states, 'it is the social world' (p. 44). He also acknowledges that, unsurprisingly, behind the young artists' anxiety about what he has to tell them is the wish for there to be something 'which is not reducible to social categorisations' (p. 43). Only this a priori 'sensitive eye' can justify and legitimate artists' claim to talent, individual voice and aesthetic function. Clearly, the answer to this anxiety is long and complex. Bourdieu is against the 'mystery' of creation, which he describes as being in the transcendental tradition of Höderlin and Heidegger. Yet, despite his doubts about both modern art and the commercialization of aesthetics, Bourdieu does hold on to a vision of the social function of artists. This is evident in his discussions with Hans Haacke (1995a/1994), where he talks about artistic acts as examples of 'exemplary prophecy' (p. 83) and that artists and intellectuals, by working with it, can begin to reform the state (p. 72). However, constant vigilance is needed on the part of artists to maintain a precarious balance between seeking aid and selling out. For Bourdieu, his thinking tools can help to do this. Moreover, they shift understanding of the artistic impulse away from belief in the uniqueness of the artist and their creativity, and embed it in an understanding of art as something that is collective and historical. Indeed, art is not 'historically necessary', but is 'historically necessitated' (1993b: 239).

In effect, Bourdieu is arguing for a sociological intervention into the thinking about art – whether as producer or consumer – which frees it from social determinants and develops a *libido artistica* in place of the illusion of the ruling *nomos*. We have seen in the course of this book how *nomos* and *illusio* function in the field of art: painting, photography and museums. Bourdieu's theory of practice is as applicable to the reader as to the writer, the photographer and their subject, the artist and the viewer. In every case, Bourdieu is looking for a theory of practice which will lead to a new way of acting and seeing the world. It is a reflexive aesthetics leading to a changed sense of perception: 'a *conversion of one's* gaze…a *metanoia*, a mental revolution, a transformation of one's whole vision of the social world' (1992a: 251). We might call such vision a *post-postmodern humanism*, since it does not break with the humanist project of the Enlightenment to seek the 'truth' in things, nor does it fall into the postmodernist abyss of hyper-reflexivity and subjective referentiality. More significantly, perhaps, we might make a distinction here between 'social art' and 'reflexive art'. The first is the world of artistic illusion as described above, but it is a world we can 'sociologicalize'. However, undertaking such an operation opens the door to a new form of aesthetics and artistic action, which we might term 'reflexive' because it is constructed in the full light of a socio-historical reflection on its means and ends. Such activity also allows us to move away from art as a private, subjective impulse and allows for the possibility of a truly 'objective art'.

–8–

Conclusion

In this book we have offered the case for a Bourdieusian perspective on art and aesthetics. This approach has involved a presentation of a particular theory of practice and the application of it to a series of case examples. In the opening chapter we asked the questions: Why do it? And what happens when one does? In this final chapter we offer some reflections of what has gone before and pull together some concluding remarks in response to these questions.

In Part I, we gave an account of Bourdieu and his intellectual trajectory. This consideration of the life of Bourdieu was not simply a way of providing background to the work and ideas we employed subsequently. Rather, we set out to establish two things: first, the way Bourdieu's work needs to be understood as of its time, in terms of both the socio-historical context and the intellectual climate which surrounded him; and second, to establish the position of his work on art and culture in his entire output. We made the point that art and culture were central to his thinking in terms of what they provide for men and women in society. In this respect, they offered one side of a coin which has education on the other. Education, art and culture – these themes run throughout Bourdieu's work. However, this preoccupation was not simply a biographical detail of Bourdieu's work. The same themes have dominated, and continue to dominate, our contemporary world. In a world of mass communication, the media and the Internet, we are all subject to art and culture – both high and low – in one form or another.

Part I therefore examined Bourdieu's theory of practice, and what using it 'opened up' in terms of taste, culture, art and aesthetics. It was necessary to delve into philosophy in order to consider the foundations of modern aesthetics in the work of Immanuel Kant. This philosophical perspective was contrasted with Bourdieu's own sociological account – an account which itself needs to be understood in terms of the epistemology, the philosophy which underpins it. We presented Bourdieu's 'thinking tools' and showed how they are employed. We also made a distinction between art production and art consumption.

Part II then took these 'thinking tools', this theory of practice, to three contemporary case examples. Our project was to apply a Bourdieusian perspective to cases other than those offered by Bourdieu himself. Chapter 4 examined three major world-class museums/galleries: MOMA, the Tate and the Musée d'Orsay. We discussed their operations in terms of their position in the field of cultural consumption and connected Bourdieu's own findings with what we can see in different social spaces. We then took the example of painting, in particular, the cases of Manet (whose work Bourdieu himself studied in depth), the young British artists of the 1990s and American abstract expressionism. Here, we studied individual artists' habitus and artistic trajectories in terms of the cultural fields through which they passed. Finally, we considered photography – Bourdieu was an enthusiastic practitioner. We addressed the issue of photography as a 'middle-brow art' and showed its ever-changing position in the overall field of cultural production and consumption.

In the course of our text, it has sometimes been necessary to be deeply philosophical. At other times, we have employed a range of diagrams to illustrate the analyses we are making in order to justify the conclusions we have drawn. We have taken an approach, which we intended to be highly theoretical and highly practical in equal measure, the grounding principle for the necessity of which is the final legacy of Bourdieu's work. Behind much of our discussion have been two implicit questions: first, is art possible? And second, what is the nature of an aesthetic response? On more than one occasion we have evoked the image of the 'aesthetic gaze' present as someone stands before an art work as a reminder that, for Bourdieu, and for us, an artistic experience is indeed a personal, individual and essentially embodied one.

In chapter 7 we came back to these questions quite explicitly and addressed them in terms of our previous philosophical discussion and in the light of the practical examples we have included. We referred to Kant's three spheres: beauty, ethics and knowledge. Our own analyses have returned consistently to three key interrelating areas: namely, the field of art and culture; the field of power; and the fields of education and technology. With a slight adjustment to language, we can express a relationship between Kant's spheres and these fields:

- Art and Culture – Beauty
- Power – Ethics
- Science, Education, Technology – Knowledge

We argued that there are distinct similarities between the concerns of Kant and Bourdieu. However, while Kant saw his categories as a priori and transcendent, for Bourdieu, these differentiated areas (fields) had arisen from analysis of empirical data grounded in human experience and the practice of everyday people. We have made the point strongly that underlying the 'aesthetic response' for Bourdieu lies a social attitude and mechanism based on distinction and privilege, which, in turn, has to be justified conceptually by a philosophical position, itself constituted from the same social structural shift in the development of modern society. The fact that this is misrecognized is the contemporary tragedy of art and aesthetics.

Chapter 7 also went some way to suggesting what Bourdieu saw as an alternative. In effect, this amounted to internalizing his own epistemology and consequent 'thinking tools'. When this is done, we have suggested, a 'reflexive' stance is opened up; what is, in effect, 'social art' – in other words, art which is the reflection of socio-economic forces in society at large – can be replaced by a more 'objective art' – one that is more fully cognizant of the social, economic and political forces which have been active in its own production. Thus, art itself is not undermined, but more fully understood. Art becomes both product, physical and ideational, and social practice, together with the dynamic interrelationships of these two.

Bourdieu's own relationship to art – both personal and professional – is clearly ambiguous, and, as is true for many of us, there is a kind of unresolved tension between the countervailing positions articulated in our two fundamental questions. On the one hand, we have the possibility of seeing art and aesthetic responses as nothing more than 'social constructions', fabrications, a kind of collusion between who we are and the market for cultural consumption. On the other hand, we can see them as possessing genuine potential to develop and change, not only individual personalities, but society at large. In a sense, answers to both questions are continually deferred.

If we are seeking an 'authentic' aesthetic response, it might be best not to search in the social world. One cannot judge the quality of a personal aesthetic response through its manifestations in the social space, in other words, by its social, political and economic consequences for artist or audience. If, instead, we are interested in why artists produce what they do, or why some art works are seen as more desirable than others, our understanding may well be extended by an analysis of the social space of a particular time and setting. That social space, of course, is increasingly complex in a so-called postmodernist world. In the world of the Internet, e-learning and virtual realities, we also have 'virtual fields', where triggers and responses are short-lived. Aesthetic response in this realm can evaporate almost instantly; there can be few claims to lasting legitimation and consecration. The logic of practice here is something other than artistic distinction. Both the human experience and the art product itself are 'digitized'; what is valuable is copyright rather than object; what is experienced is individual and private rather than public.

As part of this modern reality, the field of the media has also taken on a position and role which transcends its traditional place in a wider field of communications. The power of journalists to control 'what is art' has grown, but in a field where they themselves have increasingly come under the influence of media markets, journalists are also becoming a public front for government and multinational business. What has resulted, in effect, is the commercialization of art. That these features go misrecognized results, for Bourdieu, in a major threat to art's role (in both its production and its consumption) to challenge and create alternative views about the world. In a sense, we might conclude that what is needed is an 'education' on such misrecognitions. Education has and continues to play a crucial role in the production of art. Chapter 5 showed the determining influence of education on particular groups of artists and their practice – yBas and Goldsmiths College, for example, or Black Mountain College and abstract expressionists. We saw, in chapter 4, that in 1960s France, the consumption of art – museum visiting – was determined by level of education, and, for some, enhanced by an early informal art knowledge acquired from parents and family, themselves at ease with art and culture. It is therefore depressing to find that, despite active widening participation policies, which promote access nationally and internationally, cultural consumption, and museum visiting in particular, continues to be a mark of 'education' and privilege. Education, at least as far as schools, colleges and universities are concerned, does not provide the necessary knowledge to develop a more socially accessible, but nonetheless authentic view of art. What would such a view amount to?

In a sense, Bourdieu is wishing to replace the 'pure gaze' of Kant with a 'sociological gaze'. Once this is accomplished, he seems to suggest, art and aesthetics might reclaim their 'heroic' role in society. Yet, in the course of establishing this gaze, a number of cherished illusions have to be dispelled. Such a process is hardly likely to be popular or welcomed, in particular, by those with most to lose, when, as we quoted earlier, the sociologist 'puts the love of art under the scalpel' (Bourdieu 1996a/1992: xvi). It is not simply individual aesthetic sensation which is challenged, but the economic interests of all concerned in the cultural market. We might anticipate, therefore, cries of protest and outrage. Bourdieu justifies this undertaking for a variety of reasons. The approach first attempts to 'construct systems of intelligible relations capable of making sense of sentient data' (ibid.). In other words, the intention is to escape from pure sensation constructed within the cultural field for profit. By doing so, the social space is recreated in terms of the forces which gave rise to it, those involved in it and the reasons why they acted in such a way – from what immanent necessity. This action is consequently understandable in terms of the socio-historical logic of the field. In this way, our appreciation of art might even be enhanced, as we are able to understand what we are engaging with, what produced it and preceded it as it is, and, indeed, the source of our own responses to it. For Bourdieu, such a perspective seems 'to be more reassuring, more humane, than belief in the miraculous virtues of pure interest in pure form' (1993c: 188).

In giving the title *Art Rules* to our book, we were aware of the double sense of the phrase. We wanted to assert our own belief in the importance of art and the way it pervades every aspect of our lives and society. However, we also wanted to disclose something of the underlying 'rules' of art in a way similar to Bourdieu in *The Rules of Art*. Of course, this play on words was present for Bourdieu as well. In fact, he was always insistent that 'rules' as such do not exist, and it is rather 'strategies' which guide behaviour in the maximization of positive outcomes for those involved. Our conviction is that to view art and aesthetics from a perspective derived from Bourdieu's theory of practice does indeed provide insights in a way which is not available in other approaches. Our discussion here has sought to show operational rules across different areas within the field of art and culture, and therefore to extend Bourdieu's own empirical work by applying a similar practical theoretical perspective; to demonstrate that art rules in the way that it does because of the *art rules* which govern its practice. But, there is an alternative...

Bibliography

The bibliography gives details of all the references cited in the book. In order to aid an English-speaking reader, we have used English translations of Bourdieu's works wherever possible. These are cited and listed below with two dates: the first refers to the English publication; the second to the French publication. Occasionally, the French publication is a reprint of an earlier work. In these cases, we have given the original publication as a third date. Bourdieu always argued that his work should be read in terms of its 'socio-genesis', namely, the context in which it appeared. Therefore we feel it is important to make as explicit as possible the details of time of publication. Where the reference is cited in French only, the translation in the text is our own.

Accardo, A and Corcuff, P (1986) *La Sociologie de Bourdieu: Textes Choisis et Commentés*. Paris: Le Mascaret.

Alexander, E P (1997) *The Museum in America*. Walnut Creek, CA: AltaMira Press with Sage Publications.

Anderson, N (1923) *The Hobo: The Sociology of the Homeless Man*. Chicago: University of Chicago Press.

Archive of Association of Museum History (2004) Email correspondence between Andrew McClellan and other art historians in American Universities, October/November.

Arendt, H (ed.) (1969) *Illuminations*. New York: Stocken.

Bajac, Q (2002) *The Invention of Photography: the First Fifty Years*. London: Thames and Hudson.

Baldwin, G et al. (2004) *All the Mighty World: The Photographs of Roger Fenton 1852–1860*. New Haven, CT: Yale University Press.

Barker, E (ed.) (1999) *Contemporary Cultures of Display*. London: Yale University Press with The Open University.

Barnes, R et al. (1999) *The 20th Century Art Book*. London: Phaidon.

Barthes, R (1982/1980) *Camera Lucida: Reflections on Photography* (trans. Farrar, Straus and Giroux). London: Fontana Paperbacks [*La Chambre clair*. Paris: Editions du Seuil].

Bateson, G and Meade, M (1942) *Balinese Character: A Photographic Analysis*. New York: Academy of Sciences.

Becker, H (1974) *Photography and Sociology, Studies in Anthropology of Visual*

Communication, 1, 1: 3–26.
—— (1995) 'Visual sociology, documentary photography, and photojournalism', *Visual Sociology*, 10, 1–2: 5–14.
Benjamin, W (1969) 'The work of art in the age of mechanical reproduction', in H Arendt, *Illuminations* (trans. H Zohn). New York: Stocken (first published in 1936 in *Zeitschrift für Sozialforschung*, V, 1).
Berger, J and Mohr, J (1975) *A Seventh Man*. New York: Viking.
Berger, P L and Luckmann, T (1971) *The Social Construction of Reality*. Harmondsworth, Middlesex: Penguin.
Bocola, S (1999) *The Art of Modernism*. Munich and London: Prestel Verlag.
Bolloch, J (2004) *War Photography*. Paris: Musée d'Orsay.
Bourdieu, P (1958) *Sociologie de l'Algérie* (new revised and corrected edition, 1961). Paris: Que Sais-je.
—— (1961) 'Révolution dans la révolution', *Esprit*, January: 27–40.
—— (with Darbel, A, Rivet, J P and Seibel, C) (1963) *Travail et travailleurs en Algérie*. Paris and The Hague: Mouton.
—— (with Sayad, A) (1964a) *Le Déracinement, la crise de l'agriculture traditionelle en Algérie*. Paris: Les Editions de Minuit.
—— (with Passeron, J-C) (1964b) *Les Etudiants et leurs études*. Paris and The Hague, Mouton: Cahiers du Centre de Sociologie Européenne.
—— (1968) 'Structuralism and theory of sociological knowledge', *Social Research*, 35, 4: 681–706.
—— (1971a/1967) 'Systems of education and systems of thought', in M F D Young (ed.), *Knowledge and Control: New Directions for the Sociology of Education*. London: Macmillan ['Systèmes d'enseignement et systèmes de pensée', *Revue Internationale des Sciences Sociales*, XIX, 3: 338–88].
—— (1971b) 'The Thinkable and the Unthinkable', *Times Literary Supplement*, 15 October: 1255–6.
—— (1972) 'Les Doxosophes', *Minuit*, 1: 26–45.
—— (with Passeron, J-C) (1977a/1970) *Reproduction in Education, Society and Culture* (trans. R Nice). London: Sage Publications [*La Reproduction. Eléments pour une théorie du système d'enseignement*. Paris: Les Editions de Minuit].
—— (1977b/1972) *Outline of a Theory of Practice* (trans. R Nice). Cambridge: Cambridge University Press [*Esquisse d'une théorie de la pratique. Précédé de trois études d'ethnologie kabyle*. Geneva: Droz].
—— (with Passeron, J-C) (1979/1964) *The Inheritors, French Students and their Relation to Culture* (trans. R Nice). Chicago: University of Chicago Press [*Les Héritiers, les étudiants et la culture*. Paris: Les Editions de Minuit].
—— (1980) 'Le capital social', *Actes de la Recherche en Sciences Sociales*, 31: 2–3.
—— (1982) *Leçon sur une leçon*. Paris: Les Editions de Minuit.
—— (1984/1979) *Distinction* (trans. R Nice). Oxford: Polity Press [*La Distinction. Critique sociale du jugement*. Paris: Editions de Minuit].
—— (1985) 'Les intellectuels et les pouvoirs. Retour sur notre soutien à

Solidarnośc', in *Michel Foucault, une histoire de la vérité*. Paris: Syros.
—— (1988/1984) *Homo Academicus* (trans. P Collier). Oxford: Polity Press [*Homo Academicus*. Paris: Les Editions de Minuit].
—— (1989a) 'Social space and symbolic power', *Sociological Theory*, 7: 14–25.
—— (with Wacquant, L) (1989b) 'Towards a reflexive sociology: a workshop with Pierre Bourdieu', *Sociological Theory*, 7, 1: 26–63.
—— (with Boltanski, L, Castel, R and Chamboredon, J C) (1990a/1965) *Photography: A Middle-brow Art* (trans. S Whiteside). Oxford: Polity Press [*Un Art moyen, essai sur les usages sociaux de la photographie*. Paris: Les Editions de Minuit].
—— (1990b/1980) *The Logic of Practice* (trans. R Nice). Oxford: Polity Press [*Le Sens pratique*. Paris: Les Editions de Minuit].
—— (1990c/1987) *In Other Words: Essays Towards a Reflexive Sociology* (trans. M Adamson). Oxford: Polity Press [*Choses dites*. Paris: Les Editions de Minuit].
—— (1991a/1982) *Language and Symbolic Power* (trans. G Raymond and M Adamson). Oxford: Polity Press [*Ce que parler veut dire*. Paris: Fayard].
—— (with Chamboredon, J-C and Passeron, J-C) (1991b/1968) *The Craft of Sociology* (trans. R Nice). New York: Walter de Gruyter [*Le Métier de sociologue*. Paris: Mouton-Bordas].
—— (1991c/1988) *The Political Ontology of Martin Heidegger* (trans. P Collier). Oxford: Polity Press [*L'Ontologie politique de Martin Heidegger*. Paris: Les Editions de Minuit].
—— (with Darbel, A and Schnapper, D) (1991d/1969/1966) *The Love of Art. European Art Museums and their Public* (trans. C Beattie and N Merriman). Oxford: Polity Press [*L'Amour de l'art, les musées d'art européens et leur public*. Paris: Les Editions de Minuit].
—— (with Wacquant, L) (1992a) *An Invitation to Reflexive Sociology* (trans. L Wacquant). Oxford: Polity Press [*Réponses. Pour une anthropologie réflexive*. Paris: Editions du Seuil].
—— (1992b) 'Pour une Internationale des intellectuels', *Politis*, 1: 9–15.
—— (1993a/1980) *Sociology in Question* (trans. R Nice). London: Sage Publications [*Questions de sociologie*. Paris: Les Editions de Minuit].
—— (1993b) *The Field of Cultural Production: Essays on Art and Literature*. Oxford: Polity Press.
—— (1993c) 'Principles of a sociology of cultural works', in S Kemal and I Gaskell (eds), *Explanation and Value in the Arts*. Cambridge: Cambridge University Press.
—— (1993d/1987) 'Manet and the Institutionalization of Anomie' (trans. Juliette Parnell), in P Bourdieu, *The Field of Cultural Reproduction: Essays on Art and Literature*. Oxford: Polity Press ['L'Institutionalisation de l'anomie', *Les Cahiers du Musée d'art moderne*, 19–20 June: 6–19].
—— (1993e/1968) 'Outline of a Sociological Theory of Art Perception', in P

Bourdieu, *The Field of Cultural Production: Essays on Art and Literature*. Oxford: Polity Press ['Eléments d'une théorie sociologique de la perception artistique', *Revue internationale des sciences socials*, 20, 4: 5–14].

—— (1993f/1985/1971) 'The Market of Symbolic Goods' (trans. R Swyer), in P Bourdieu, *The Field of Cultural Production: Essays on Art and Literature*. Oxford: Polity Press. Also in *Poetics* (1985), 14, 1–2: 13–44 ['Le Marché des biens symboliques', *L'Année Sociologique*, 22: 49–126].

—— (with Haacke, H) (1995a/1994) *Free Exchange* (trans. I Utz and H Haacke). Oxford: Polity Press [*Libre-échange*. Paris: Editions du Seuil].

—— (with Grenfell, M) (1995b) *Entretiens*. CLE Papers 37, University of Southampton.

—— (1996a/1992) *The Rules of Art* (trans. S Emanuel). Oxford: Polity Press [*Les Règles de l'art. Genèse et structure du champ littéraire*. Paris: Editions du Seuil].

—— (1996b/1989) *The State Nobility. Elite Schools in the Field of Power* (trans. L C Clough). Oxford: Polity Press [*La Noblesse d'état. Grandes écoles et esprit de corps*. Paris: Les Editions de Minuit].

—— (1998a/1998) *Acts of Resistance. Against the New Myths of our Time* (trans. R Nice). Oxford: Polity Press [*Contre-feux*. Paris: Raisons d'Agir].

—— (1998b/1996) *On Television and Journalism*. London: Pluto Press [*Sur la Télévision, suivi de l'emprise du journalisme*. Paris: Raisons d'Agir].

—— (1998c/1994) *Practical Reason* (trans. P Parkhurst Ferguson). Oxford: Polity Press [*Raisons pratiques. Sur la théorie de l'action*. Paris: Editions du Seuil].

—— (1999/1993) *The Weight of the World. Social Suffering in Contemporary Society* (trans. P Parkhurst Ferguson, S Emanuel, J Johnson and S T Waryn). Oxford: Polity Press [*La Misère du monde*. Paris: Editions du Seuil].

—— (2000a/1997) *Pascalian Meditations* (trans. R Nice). Oxford: Polity Press [*Méditations pascaliennes*. Paris: Editions du Seuil].

—— (2000b) *Les Structures sociales de l'économie*. Paris: Editions du Seuil.

—— (with Swain, H) (2000c) 'Move over, shrinks', *Times Higher Education Supplement*, 14 April: 19.

—— (2000d) 'Participant Objectivation', *Mimeograph* (address given in receipt of the Aldous Huxley Medal for Anthropology, University of London, 12 November) (trans. R Nice).

—— (2001a/1998) *Masculine Domination* (trans. R Nice). Oxford: Polity Press [*La Domination masculine*. Paris: Editions du Seuil].

—— (2001b) *Contre-feux 2. Pour un mouvement social européen*. Paris: Raisons d'Agir.

—— (2001c) *Science de la science et réflexivité*. Paris: Raisons d'Agir.

—— (2001d) 'Penser l'Art à l'Ecole', *Actes Sud/Ecole Supérieure des Beaux-Arts de Nîmes*, June: 13–55.

—— (2002a) 'Pierre par Bourdieu', *Le Nouvel Observateur*, 31 January 2002: 30–1.

—— (2002b) *Le Bal des célibataires. Crise de la société en Béarn*. Paris: Editions du Seuil.

—— (ed. T Discepolo and F Poupeau) (2002c) *Interventions (1961–2001)*. Marseilles: Agone.

—— (2003) *Images d'Algérie*. Paris: Actes Sud.

—— (2004a) *Esquisse pour une auto-analyse*. Paris: Raisons d'Agir.

—— and Bourdieu, M C (2004b) 'The Peasant and Photography', *Ethnography*, 5, 4: 601–16.

Boyer, M (1972) *Le Tourisme*. Paris: Editions du Seuil.

Buck, L (1998) *Moving Targets: A User's Guide to British Art Now*. London: Tate Publishing.

—— (2000) *Moving Targets 2: A User's Guide to British Art Now*. London: Tate Publishing.

Burnett, C (2005) *Jeff Wall*. London: Tate Publishing.

Calhoun, C, LiPuma, E and Postone, M (eds) (1993) *Bourdieu: Critical Perspectives*. Oxford: Polity Press.

Casey, B et al. (1996) *Culture as Commodity*. London: Policy Studies Institute.

Clark, T J (1984) *The Painting of Modern Life: Paris in the Art of Manet and his Followers*. London: Thames and Hudson.

Collier, J Jnr (1967) *Visual Anthropology: Photography as a Research Method*. New York: Holt, Reinhardt and Winston.

Cotton, C (2004) *The Photograph as Contemporary Art*. London: Thames and Hudson.

Crawford, W (1979) 'Photographic Syntax', in *The Keepers of Light*. New York: Morgan and Morgan.

Davidson, B (1970) *East 100th Street*. Cambridge, MA: Harvard University Press.

Davies, S (2005) 'Still Popular: Museums and their Visitors 1994–2004', *Cultural Trends*, 14, 1 (March): 67–105.

Derrida, J (1987/1978) *The Truth in Painting* (trans. G Bennington and I McLeod). Chicago and London: University of Chicago Press [*La Verité en Peinture*. Paris: Flammarion].

Didion, J (1989) *Some Women: Robert Mapplethorpe*. London: Secker and Warburg.

DiMaggio P et al. (1979) *Audience Studies of the Performing Arts and Museums: A Critical Review*. Washington, DC: National Endowment for the Arts, Research Division, Report 9.

Documenta und Museum Fridericianum (ed.) (2002) Documenta 11: Platform 5: Exhibition. Ostifildern-Ruit, Germany: Hatje Cantz Publishers.

Dreyfus, H and Rabinow, P (1993) 'Can there be a science of existential structure and social meaning?', in C Calhoun, E LiPuma and M Postone (eds), *Bourdieu: Critical Perspectives*. Oxford: Polity Press, 35–44.

Durkheim, E (1952/1897) *Suicide: A Study in Sociology*. London: Routledge and Kegan Paul.

—— (1964/1933) *The Division of Labour in Society*. London: Macmillan.

Edwards, S (ed.) (1991) *Art and its Histories: A Reader*. New Haven, CT: Yale University Press with The Open University.

Fisher, J A (2001) 'High art versus low art', in B Gaut and D McIlver Lopes (eds), *Aesthetics*. London: Routledge, 527–40.

Foster, H (ed.) (1985) *Postmodern Culture*. London: Pluto Press.

Foucault, M (2004) *La Peinture de Manet*. Paris: Editions du Seuil.

Gaut, B and McIver Lopes, D (eds) (2001) *Aesthetics*. London: Routledge.

Genet Delacroix, M-C (1986) 'Vie d'artistes: Art academique, art official et art libre en France à la fin du XIX siècle', *Revue d'Histoire Moderne et Contemporaine*, 33 (January–March).

Greenberg, C (1939) 'The Beggar's Opera – After Marx: Review of *A Penny for the Poor* by Bertolt Brecht', *Partisan Review*, Fall, reprinted in J O'Brian (ed.) (1986), *Clement Greenberg: The Collected Essays and Criticism, Vol. 1*. Chicago: University of Chicago Press.

—— (1940) 'Towards a newer Laocoön', *Partisan Review*, 6, 5: 296–310.

—— (1945) 'Kandinsky, Mondrian and Pollock', *The Nation*, 7 April.

—— (1955) 'American-type Painting', *Partisan Review*, Spring, reprinted in J O'Brian (ed.) (1993), *Clement Greenberg: The Collected Essays and Criticism, Vol. 4*. Chicago: University of Chicago Press.

Grenfell, M (1998) 'Language and the Classroom', in M Grenfell and D James, *Bourdieu and Education: Acts of Practical Theory*. London: Falmer.

—— (2004) *Pierre Bourdieu: Agent Provocateur*. London: Continuum.

—— and Hardy, C (2003) 'Field manoeuvres: Bourdieu and the Young British Artists', *Space and Culture*, 6, 1: 19–34.

Halami, S (1997) *Les nouveaux chiens de garde*. Paris: Raisons d'Agir.

Harper, D (2003) 'Framing photographic ethnography', *Ethnography*, 4, 2: 241–66.

Harrington, M and Adleman, B (1981) *The Next America: The Decline and Rise of the United States*. New York: Holt, Reinhardt and Winston.

Harrison, C (1970) 'Abstract Expressionism', in N Stangos (ed.) (1994), *Concepts of Modern Art*. London: Thames and Hudson.

Hauser, A (1951) *The Social History of Art*. London: Routledge.

Haxthausen, C W (2002) *The Two Art Histories: the Museum and the University*. New Haven, CT: Yale University Press.

Heidegger, M (1962) *Being and Time* (first published 1927). Oxford: Blackwell Publishing.

Hill, P and Cooper, T (2005) *Dialogue with Photography*. Stockport, UK: Dewi Lewis Publishing.

Hooper-Greenhill, E (1988) 'Counting visitors, or visitors who count', in R Lumley, *The Museum Time Machine*. London: Routledge.

Hooper-Greenhill, E (2000) *Museums and the Interpretation of Visual Culture*. London: Routledge.

Hudson, K (1975) *The Social History of Museums: What Visitors Thought*. London: Macmillan Press.
Hughes, R (1980) *The Shock of the New*. London: BBC Books.
—— (1990) *Nothing if not Critical*. London: Harvill Press.
—— (1997) *American Visions: The Epic History of Art in America*. London: Harvill Press.
Jeffrey, I (1981) *Photography: A Concise History*. London: Thames and Hudson.
—— (ed.) (1997) *The Photo Book*. London: Phaidon Press.
Joughin, J and Malpas, S (2003) *The New Aestheticism*. Manchester: Manchester University Press.
Kant, I (1956) *Critique of Practical Reason* (first published 1788). New York: Liberal Arts Press.
—— (1961) *Critique of Pure Reason* (first published 1781). London: Macmillan.
—— (1987) *The Critique of Judgement* (first published 1790). Cambridge: Hacket.
Kent, S A (1994) *Shark Infested Waters*. London: Zwemmer.
Kirili, A (1988) 'Self hatred or castration at Orsay', *Art in America*, January: 95–6.
Krauss, R E (1997) *The Originality of the Avant-Garde and other Modernist Myths*. Cambridge, MA: MIT Press.
Kudielka, R (2002) *Paul Klee: the Nature of Creation*. London: Hayward Gallery.
Kuhn, T S (1962) *The Structure of Scientific Revolutions*. Chicago: University of Chicago Press.
Le Lay, P (2005) 'Jean Baudrillard: L'Evidence du oui a fabriqué le non', *Le Monde*, 28 May.
Lévi-Strauss, C (1995) *Saudades do Brasil: A Photographic Memoir*. Seattle: University of Washington Press.
Levi Strauss, D (2003) *Between the Eyes: Essays on Photography and Politics*. New York: Aperture Foundation.
Lord, B et al. (1983) *Planning our Museums*. Ottawa: National Museum of Canada.
Lucie-Smith, E (1996) *Visual Arts in the Twentieth Century*. London: Laurence King Publishing.
—— (1999) *Lives of the Great 20th-century Artists*. London: Thames and Hudson
—— (2001) *Movements in Art since 1945*. London: Thames and Hudson.
Maitland, A (2005) 'Lichfield', *Digital Photography*, 40: 27–30.
Marien, M W (2002) *Photography: A Cultural History*. London: Laurence King Publishing.
Marshall, R (1988) *Robert Mapplethorpe*. London: Secker and Warburg.
Mathieu, C (1992) *Guide to the Musée d'Orsay*. Paris: Réunion des Musées Nationaux.
McClellan, A (ed.) (2003) *Art and its Publics*. Oxford: Blackwell Publishing.
Merriman, N (1989) 'Museum Visiting as a Cultural Phenomenon, in P Vergo (ed.), *The New Museology*. London: Reaktion Books.

Meyer P G (ed.) (2001) *Brushes with History: Writing on Art from the Nation 1865–2001*. New York: Thunder's Mouth Press.

Mibelbeck, R (ed.) (2001) *20th Century Photography Museum Ludwig Cologne* (trans. R Fricke and P Riefler-Bonham). Cologne: Taschen.

Monad, J-C (1995) 'Les deux mains de l'Etat', *Esprit*, 214: 156–71.

Myerscough, J (1988) *The Economic Importance of the Arts in Britain*. London: Policy Studies Institute.

National Endowment for the Arts (1997) *Demographic Characteristics of Arts Attendance*. Washington, DC: National Endowment for the Arts, Research Division, Report 71.

Neill, A and Ridley, A (2001) *Arguing about Art: Philosophical Debates*. London: Routledge.

Nochlin, L (1971) *Realism*. London: Penguin.

Nochlin, S (1988) 'The Musée d'Orsay: a Symposium', *Art in America*, January: 85–7.

O'Brian, J (ed.) (1986) *Clement Greenberg: The Collected Essays and Criticism, Vol. 1*. Chicago: University of Chicago Press.

—— (ed.) (1993) *Clement Greenberg: The Collected Essays and Criticism, Vol. 4*. Chicago: University of Chicago Press.

Oldenburg, R E (1984) *The Museum of Modern Art New York*. London: Thames and Hudson.

Owens, B (1973) *Suburbia*. San Francisco, CA: Straight Arrow Books.

Parsons, T (1949) *The Structure of Social Action*. Glencoe, NY: Free Press.

—— (1951) *The Social System*. London: Routledge and Kegan Paul.

Pearce, S (ed.) (1994) *Museums and the Appropriation of Culture*. London: Athlone Press.

—— (ed.) (1995) *Art in Museums*. London: Athlone Press.

Peuple et Culture (1945) *Un Peuple: Une Culture*. Paris: Peuple et Culture.

Pollock, G (1988) *Vision and Difference: Femininity, Feminism and the Histories of Art*. London: Routledge.

Preziosi, D and Farago, C (2004) *Grasping the World: The Idea of the Museum*. Aldershot: Ashgate Publishing.

Prince, D (1983) 'Behavioural consistency and visitor attraction', *Journal of Museum Management and Curatorship*, 2, 3: 235–47.

—— and Higgins-McHoughlin, B (1987) *Museums UK: The Findings of the Museums Database Project*. London: Museums Association.

Prior, N (2002) *Museums and Modernity*. Oxford: Berg.

—— (2003) 'Having one's Tate and eating it', in A McClellan (ed.), *Art and its Publics*. Oxford: Blackwell Publishing.

Rewald, J (1980) *The History of Impressionism*. London: Secker and Warburg.

Rice, D (1987) 'On the ethics of museum education', *Museum News*, June: 13–19.

Rosenberg, P (1995) *Louvre: French Painting: The Visitors' Guide*. Paris: Réunion des Musées Nationaux.

Rothenstein, J (1963) *The Tate Gallery, London*. New York: Harry N Abrams Inc.

Rosenthal, N (1997) *Sensation*. London: Royal Academy of Art.

Sandell, R (ed.) (2002) *Museums, Society, Inequality*. London: Routledge.

Sartre, J-P (1969) *Being and Nothingness* (first published 1943). London: Methuen.

Sayad, A and Lionel-Marie, A (eds) (2000) *Brassai: No Ordinary Eyes* (trans. J Brenton and R Mason). London: Thames and Hudson in association with the Hayward Gallery.

Schoenholz, B H and Heliczer, C (eds) (2004) *MOMA Highlights*. New York: Museum of Modern Art.

Schubert, K (2000) *The Curator's Egg*. London: One-Off Press.

Schuster, J Mark Davidson (1985) *The Audience for American Art Museums*. Washington, DC: National Endowment for the Arts, Research Division, Report 23.

Sears, H (1983) 'Visitors' characteristics and behaviour', in B Lord et al., *Planning our Museums*. Ottawa: National Museum of Canada.

Simon, P and Mungo, R (1972) *Moving On, Standing Still*. New York: Grossman.

Smith, C (1998) *Creative Britain*. London: Faber and Faber.

Stangos, N (ed.) (1994) *Concepts of Modern Art*. London: Thames and Hudson.

Staniszewski, M A (2001) *The Power of Display*. Cambridge: MIT Press.

Stich, S (2000) *Britain and Ireland: Contemporary Art and Architecture Handbook*. San Francisco, CA: art-SITES Press.

Tagg, J (1988) 'Evidence, Truth and Order', in *The Burden of Representation*. Basingstoke: Macmillan Education, Chapter 2.

Taylor, J (1994) 'Kodak and the English Market between the Wars', *Journal of Design History*, 7, 1: 29–41.

The Beatles, (2000) *The Beatles Anthology*. London: Cassell & Co.

Thrasher, F (1927) *The Gang: A Study of 1313 Gangs in Chicago*. Chicago: University of Chicago Press.

Unknown author (1892) *Society*, 20 February.

Urry, J (1990) *The Tourist Gaze*. London: Sage Publications.

Varnedoe, K and Karmel, P (1999) *Jackson Pollock*. London: Tate Gallery Publishing.

Vergo, P (ed.) (1989) *The New Museology*. London: Reaktion Books.

Weill, N (2001) 'Pierre Bourdieu, sujet du dernier cours de Pierre Bourdieu', *Le Monde Interactif*, 29 March.

Weiss, J (1994) *The Popular Culture of Modern Art*. New Haven, CT and London: Yale University Press.

Wells, L (ed.) (2003) *The Photography Reader*. London: Routledge.

West, S (1995) *The Devaluation of 'Cultural Capital'*, in S Pearce (ed.), *Art in Museums*. London: Athlone Press.

Wright, P (1989) 'The Quality of Visitors' Experiences in Art Museums', in P Vergo (ed.), *The New Museology*. London: Reaktion Books.

Index